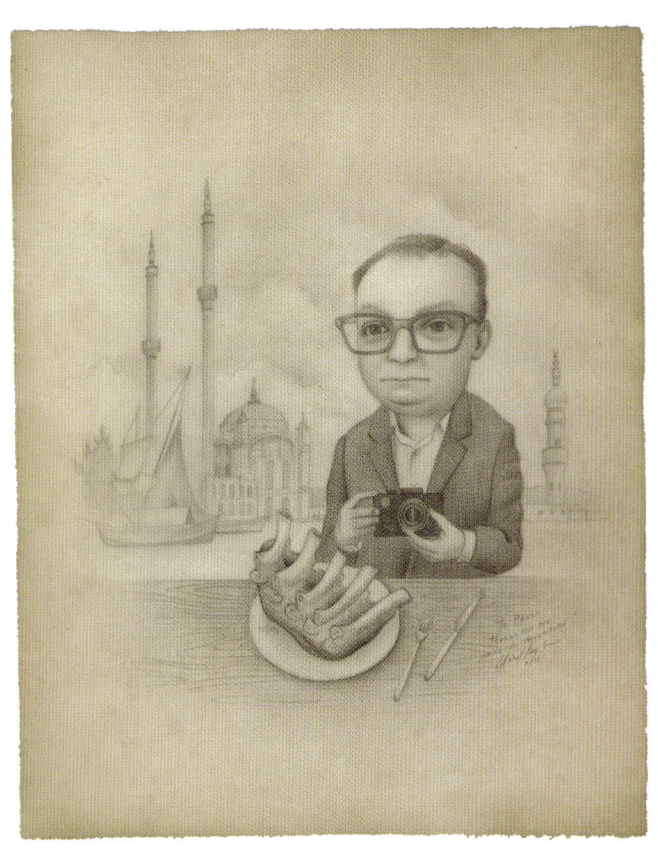

Dedicated to Paul Kasmin (1960–2020)

MARK RYDEN

ANIMA ANIMALS

PERROTIN

KASMIN

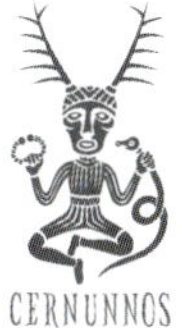

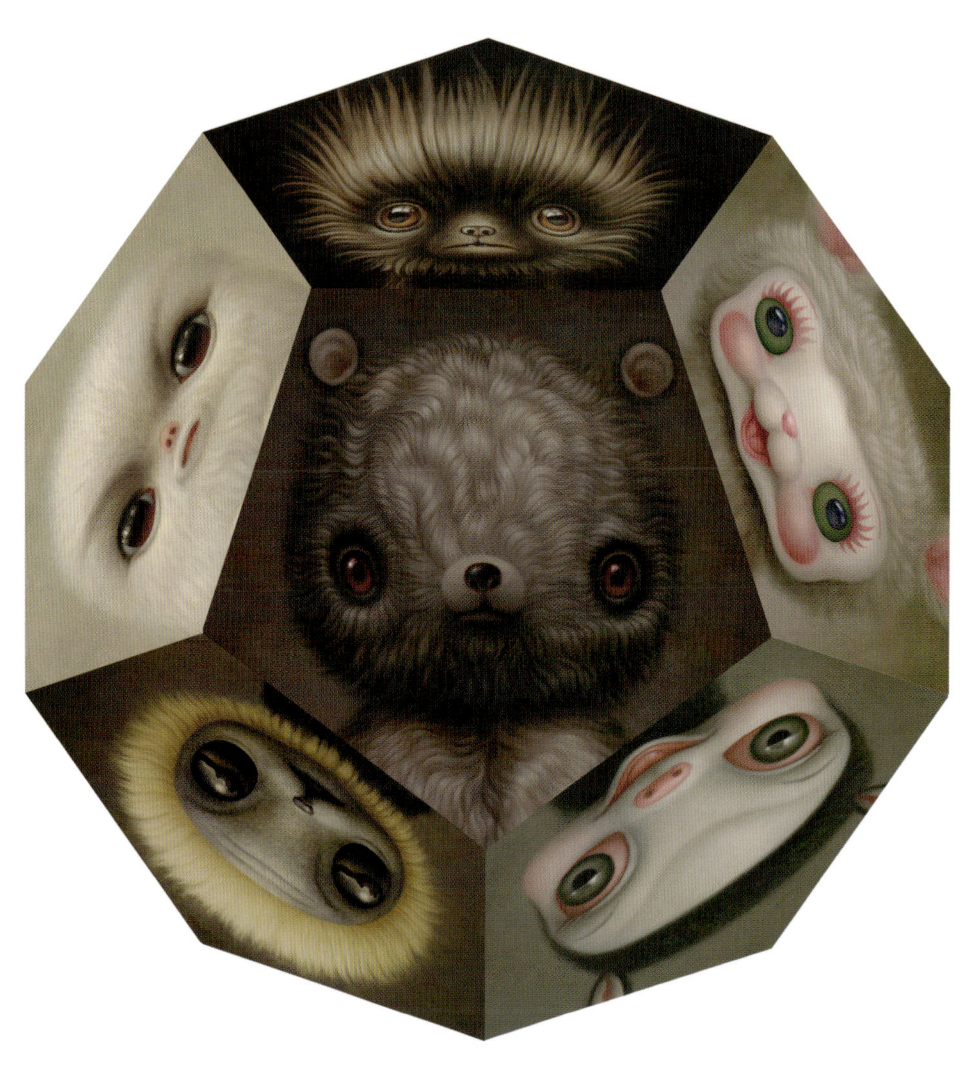

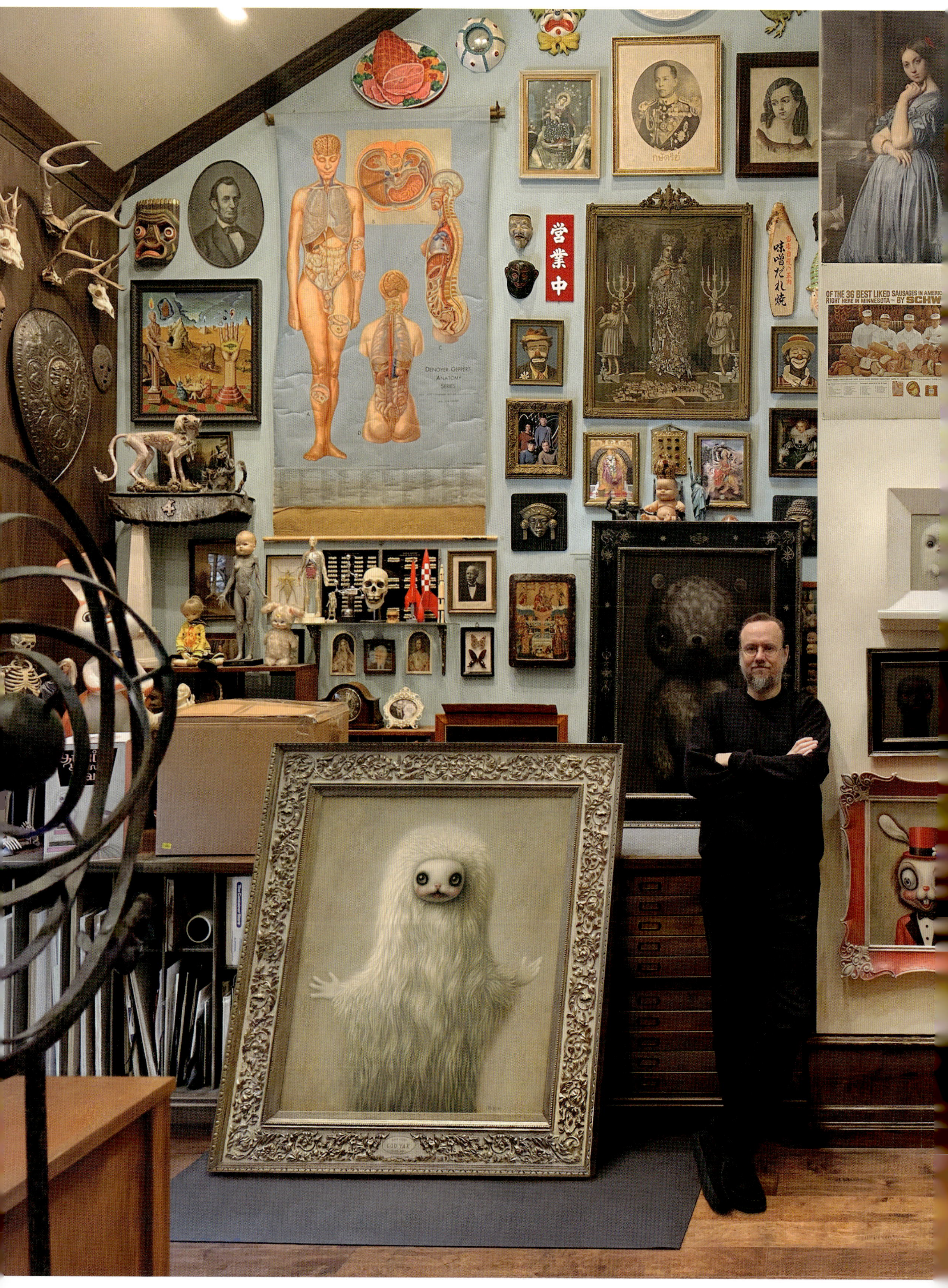
営業中
味噌だれ焼
OF THE 36 BEST LIKED SAUSAGES IN AMERIC
RIGHT HERE IN MINNESOTA — BY SCHW
DENOYER GEPPERT
ANATOMY
SERIES

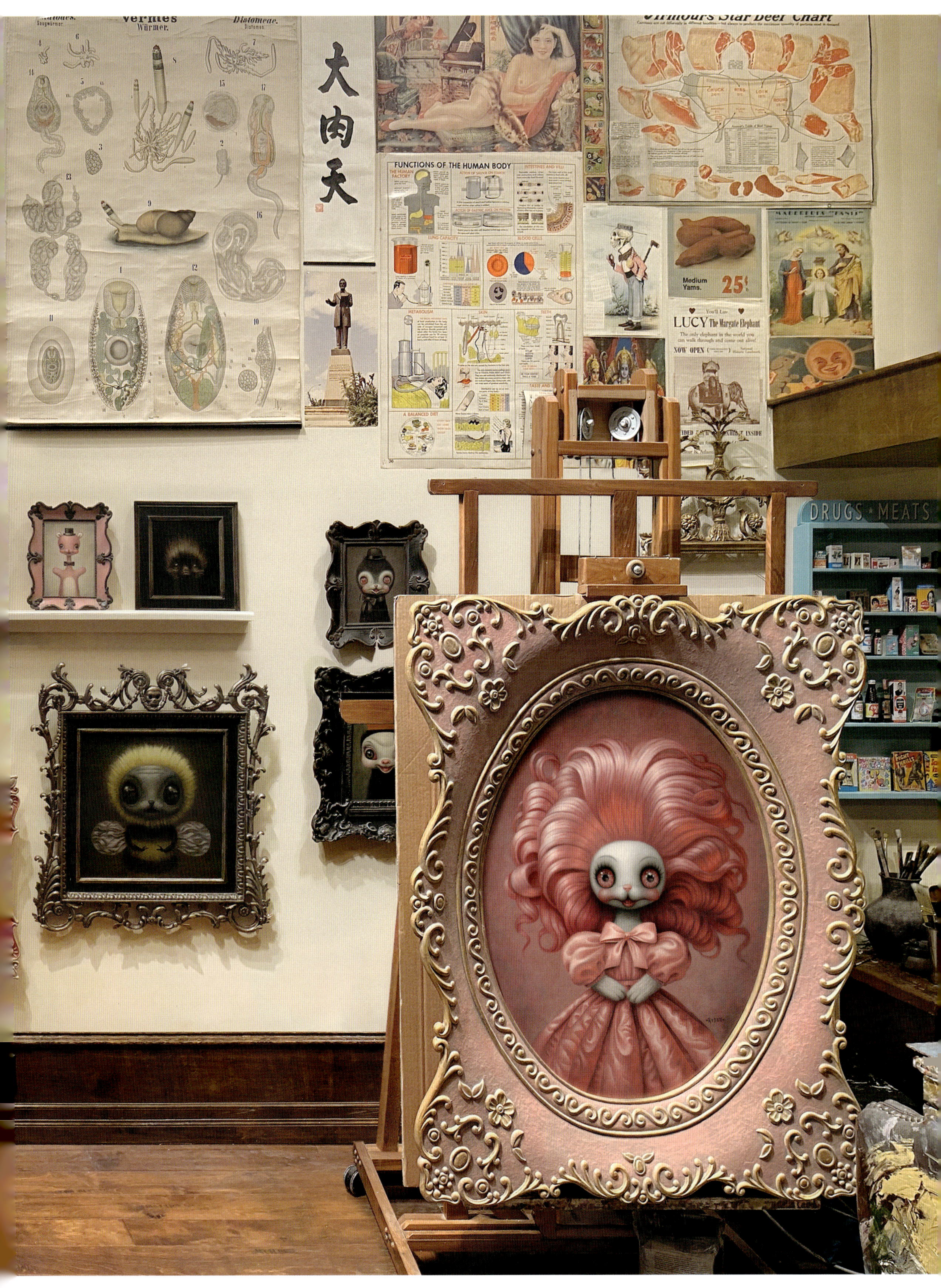

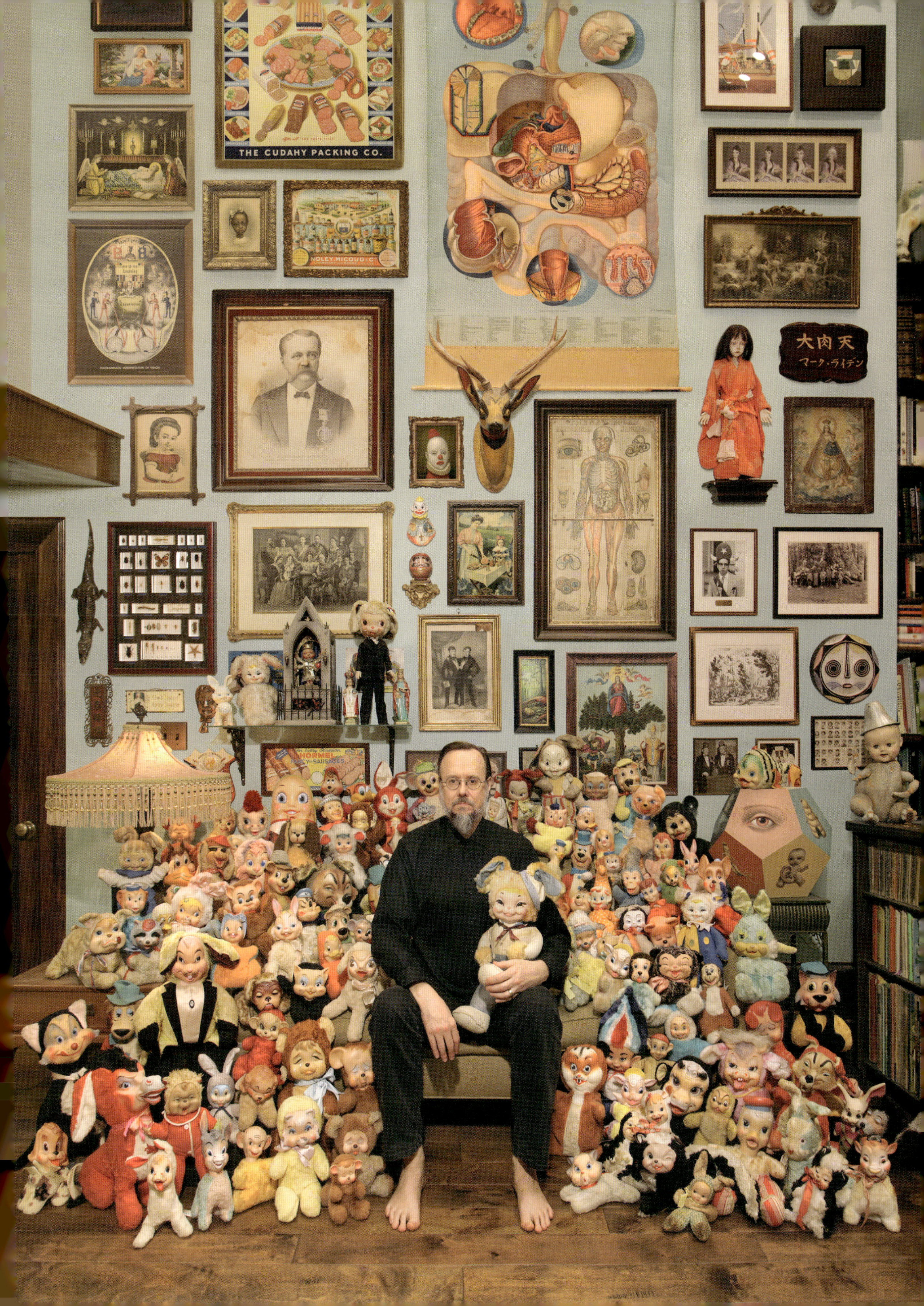

THE CUDAHY PACKING CO.
NOLEY MICOUD
大肉天
マーク・ライデン

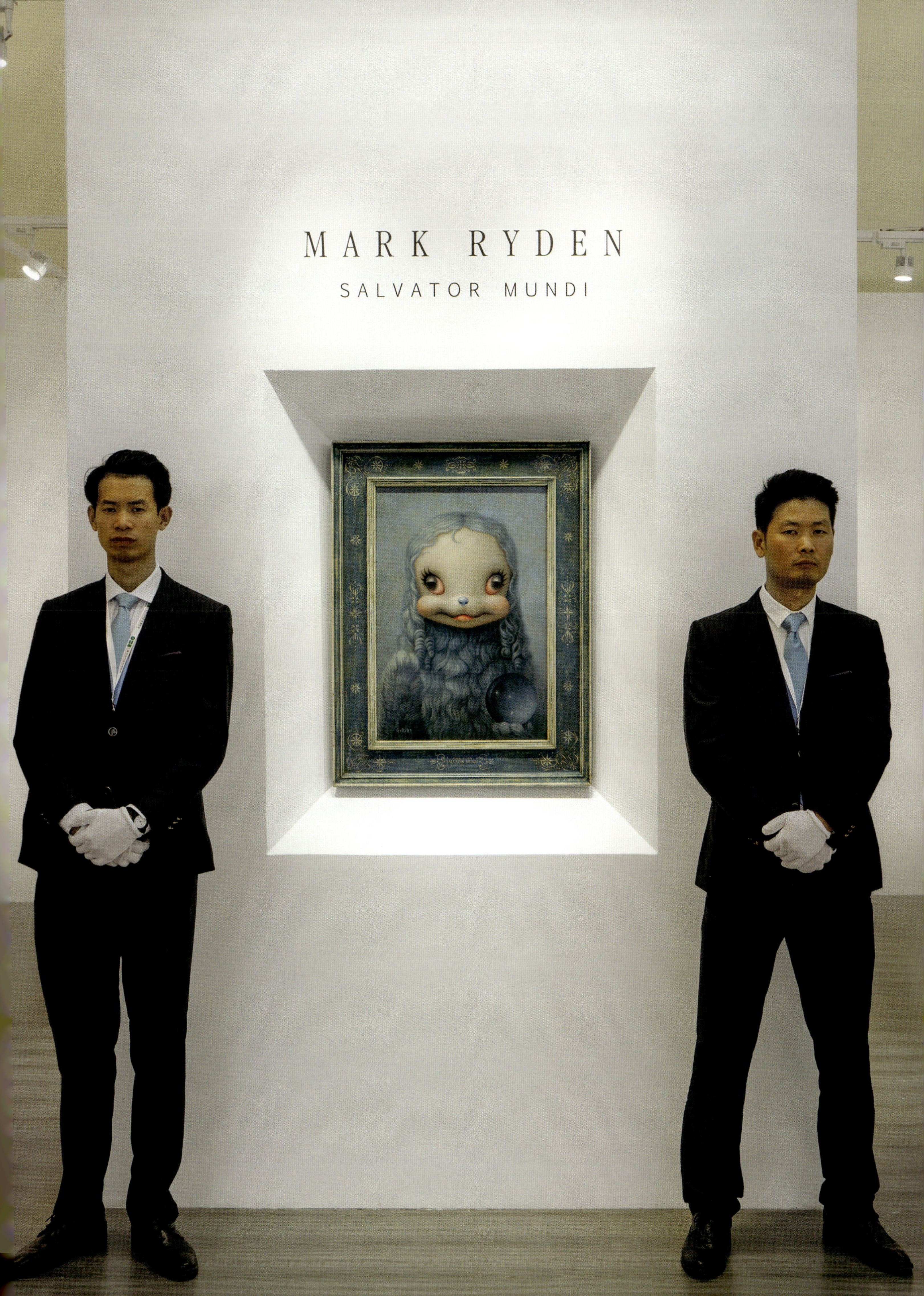
MARK RYDEN
SALVATOR MUNDI

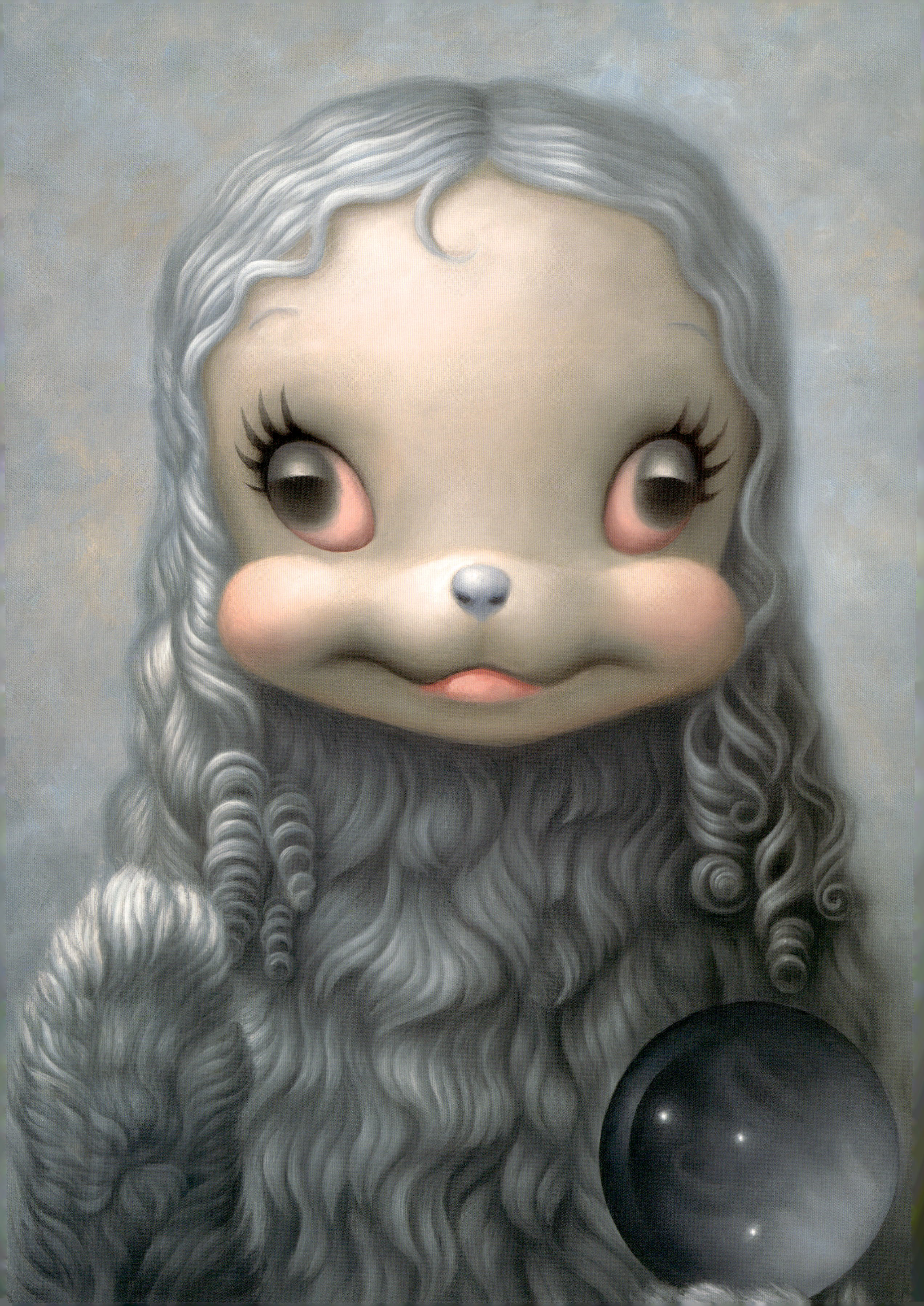

The origins of this series goes all the way back to a painting I did about twenty years ago, the central piece of my first solo exhibition, *The Meat Show*. The painting, *Snow White*, included an important figure, a special divine messenger who visits a reclining feminine subject. Manifesting this messenger was a considerable struggle for me. The decision of what form he would take was not an arbitrary one, not a simple matter of a surreal juxtaposition to other elements in the composition; it was an important and subtle choice of character. This isn't the kind of decision an artist can make by "thinking" their way to the answer. That kind of literal thinking is limited to a consciousness that exists at a lower level than inspiration's mysterious unknowable creative source. The messenger figure went though many different variations in the sketches and comps. Several times I took it to an almost finished stage in the painting, but then changed it, painted it out, and replaced it with an entirely new figure. The answer finally came to me while browsing a flea market, a place where I find much of my inspiration. When my eyes fell upon a scruffy old stuffed rabbit with a rubber face, I knew with complete certainty that it was the divine being I was searching for. Ever since, variations of this character have been showing up in my paintings, and I have also amassed a large collection of these vintage rubber-faced plushies.

At the time I couldn't explain why this old stuffed animal was the "correct" entity for my painting, I just knew on an instinctive level that he was. Explanations with mere words are not adequate. Language is linear; paintings are multidimensional; they show what can't be said. Nevertheless, I will attempt to explain why this unassuming toy fulfilled such an elevated place in my art. There is a special "presence" about this mass-produced toy, this scruffy old stuffed animal, an intriguing quality about his strange face and his well-worn coat of fur that goes beyond the simple physical materials he is made of. In some ways, he has what can only be described as a "soul" : a spiritual presence that permeates the physical materials he is made from. Most of my work deals with this relationship between the physical world and the spiritual world.

The first work I created for this series is called *Salvator Mundi*. My painting is a response to a piece attributed to Leonardo da Vinci, which was recently part of a sensational auction. I find it absolutely fascinating that a relatively humble object, a piece of wood simply painted with an image by an artist, would be valued at almost half a billion dollars. How could that object hold such unfathomable value? It was the creation of an individual taking wood and paint and making something that transcends those simple physical materials, something that shines with the sacred and eternal.

The subject of da Vinci's painting is Jesus, "Savior of the World." In Jesus, the celestial divine God was said to become material, a transformation of the cosmos known as the "Incarnation." I painted my *Salvator Mundi* with the same reverence I imagine went into the original painting five hundred years ago, taking care to make my version the exact same size, with a frame that emulates the original's. I meticulously worked every brushstroke with the devotion and state of consciousness I imagine a devout Christian would have felt while painting the face of his Lord, but I painted the face of the divine as quite a different subject than that of Jesus. If your eyes are open, you can see the face of the divine wherever you look. I found the face of the divine in a tattered stuffed animal radiating the inner light of kitsch.

The spiritual power of animals was vividly revealed to me on a recent trip to the Maasai Mara National Reserve in Kenya, Africa. Friends who had taken similar trips tried to prepare me for what I would encounter. "It is a life-changing experience," I was told so many times that I felt a cynical disbelief. But life-changing it was. The experience of witnessing a majestic elephant or a magnificent lion freely roaming in their natural domain is nothing less than awe-inspiring. I kept asking myself why the experience felt so profoundly different from looking at the same species of animals in a zoo back home. The spiritual energy radiating from those free beasts can be felt on a deep level. It is simply breathtaking.

We each travel life's journey with a spiritual guide. It can appear in different forms, such as an angel, mythical creature, or an animal. It can appear in different places, perhaps a meditation or in a vivid dream, or even a flea market. These spirits can give us guidance and provide meaningful insight in our lives. They give us strength and comfort as they share their wisdom and illuminate the path. If you ask, your spiritual animal guide will come to you. Close your eyes, look inward, and ask your Anima Animal to come, then keep your eyes open for a visitation.

—Mark Ryden

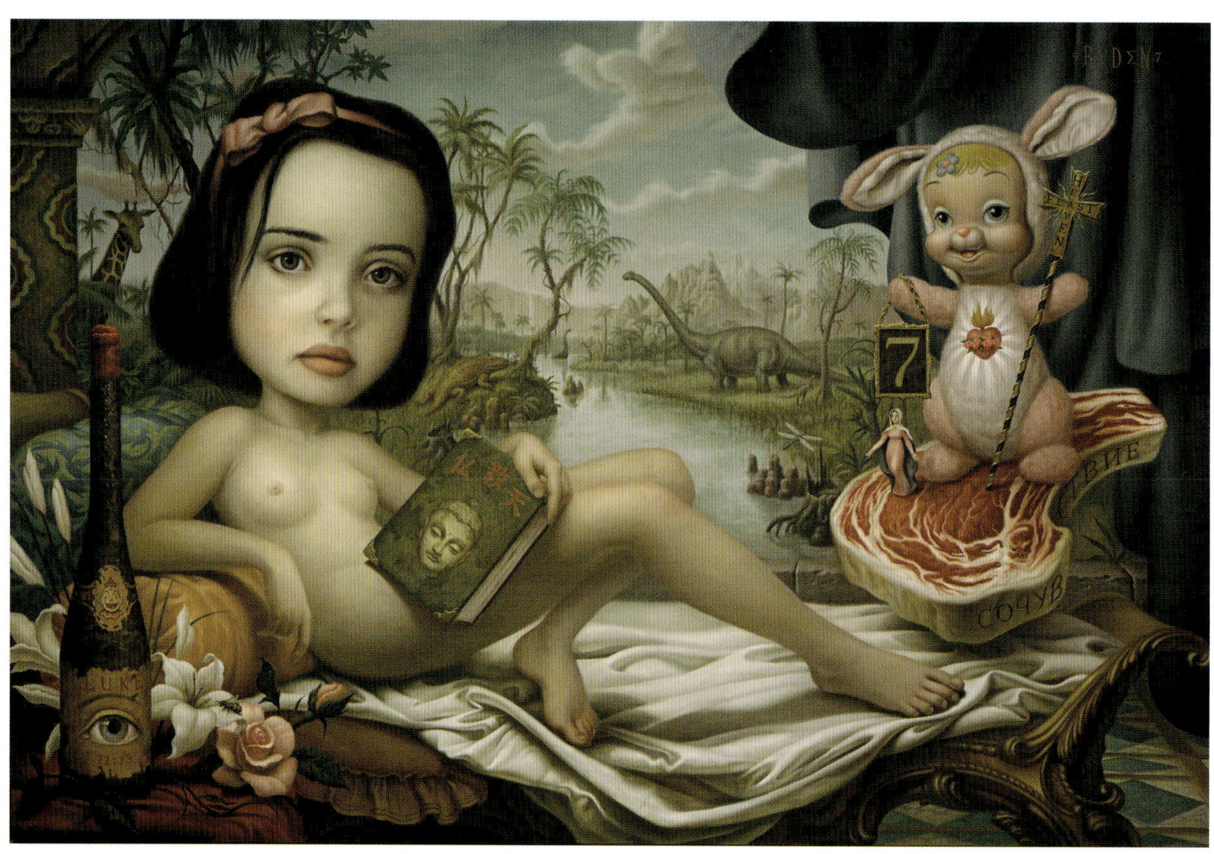

"Snow White" No. 7, oil on canvas, 48 x 72 inches, 1997

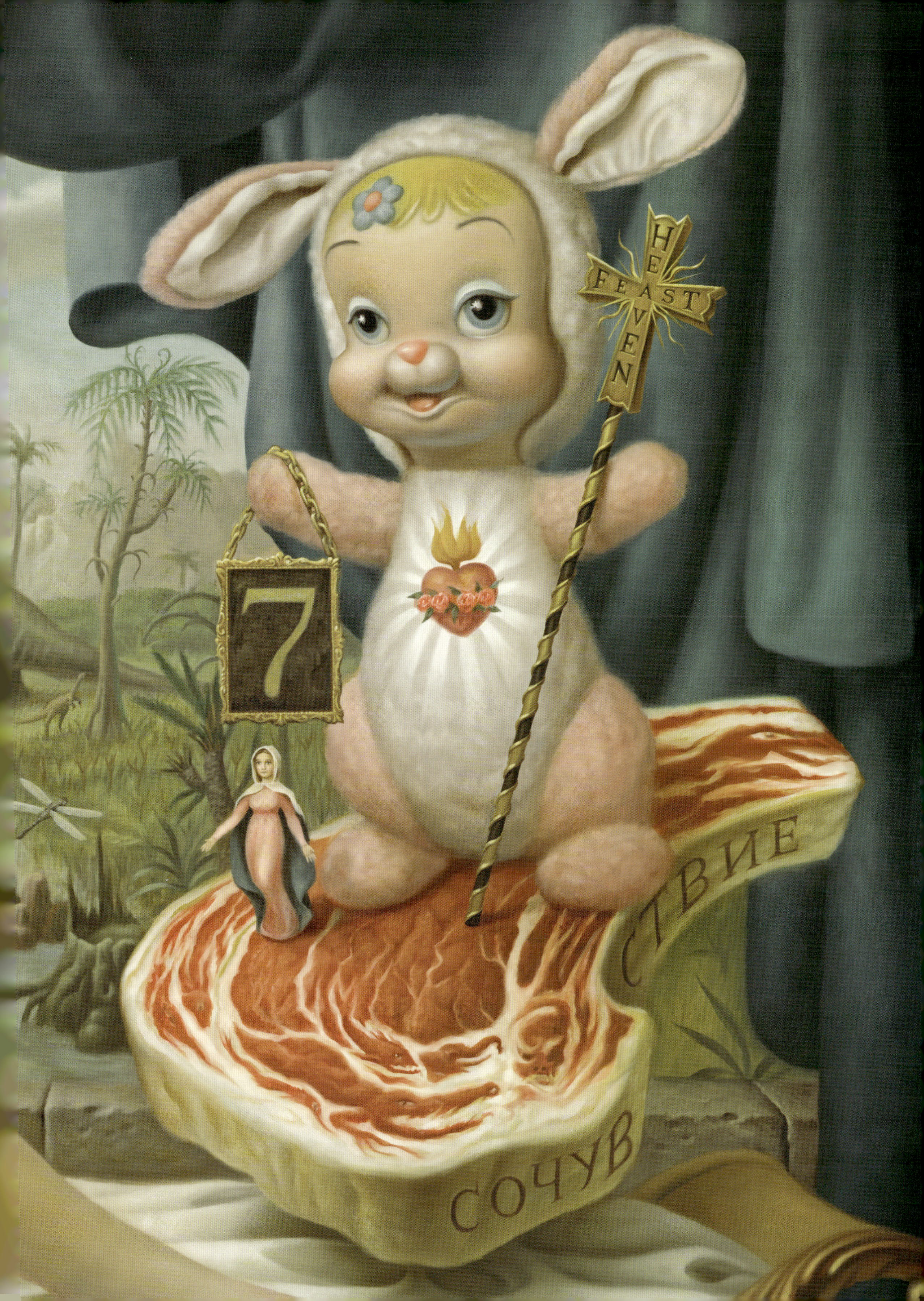

HEAVEN
FEAST
7
СТВИЕ
СОЧУВ

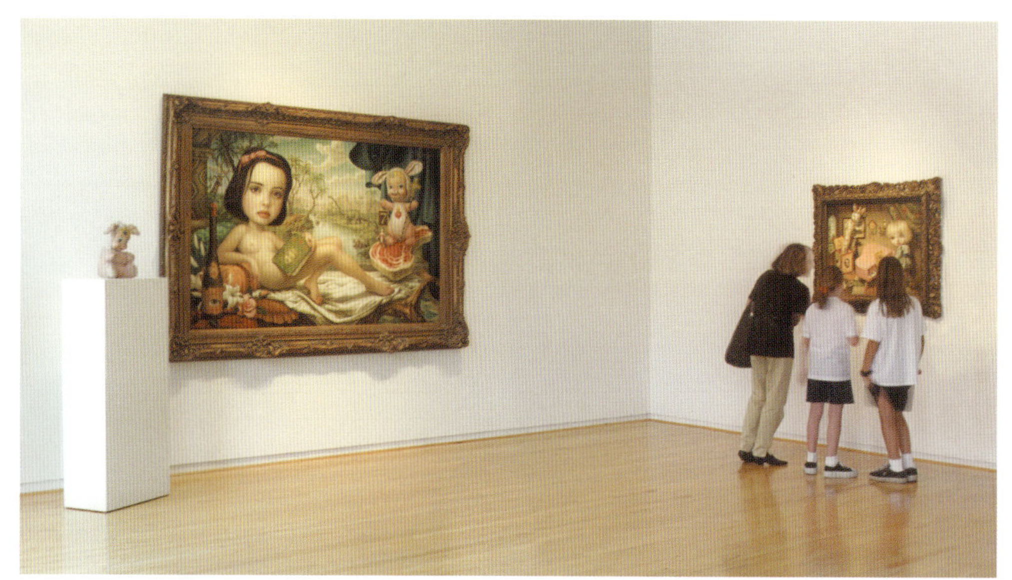

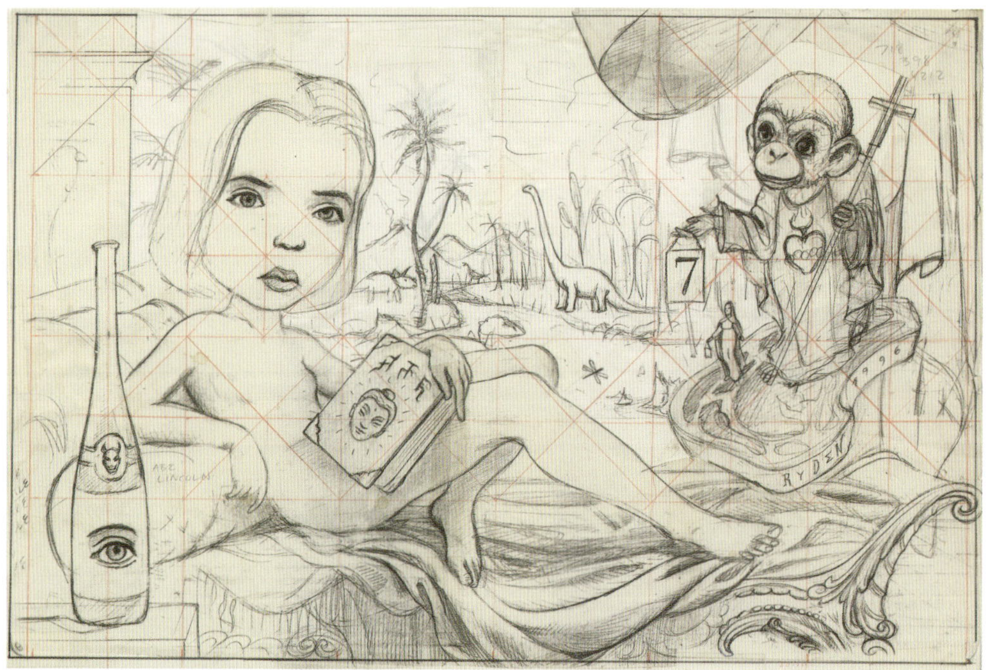

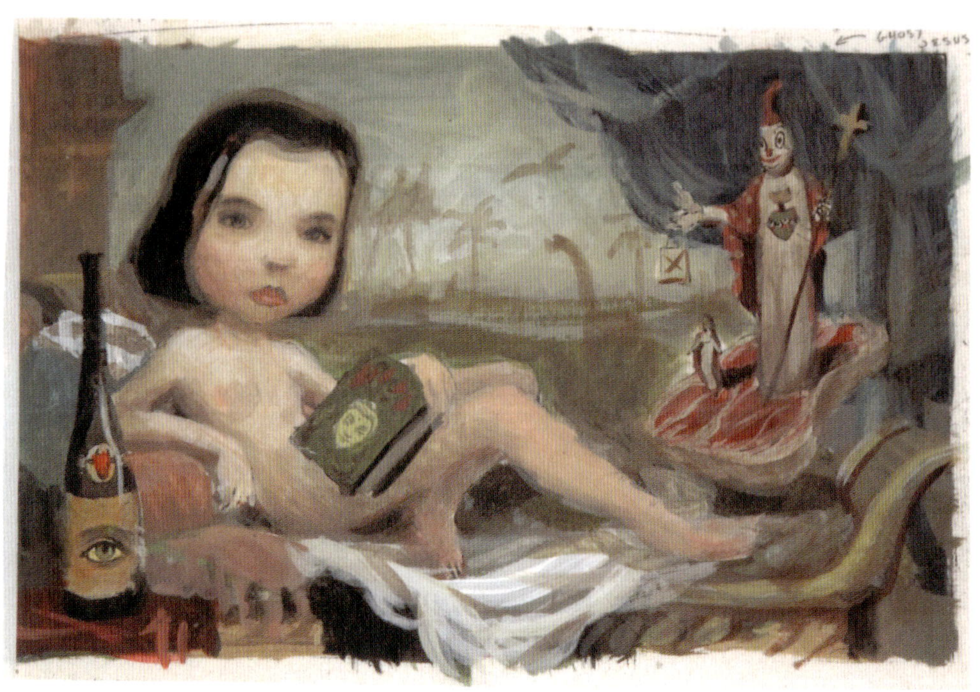

LEFT PAGE

Installation image from "The Meat Show," 1998

"Snow White," working drawing, 1996

"Snow White," color comp, 1996

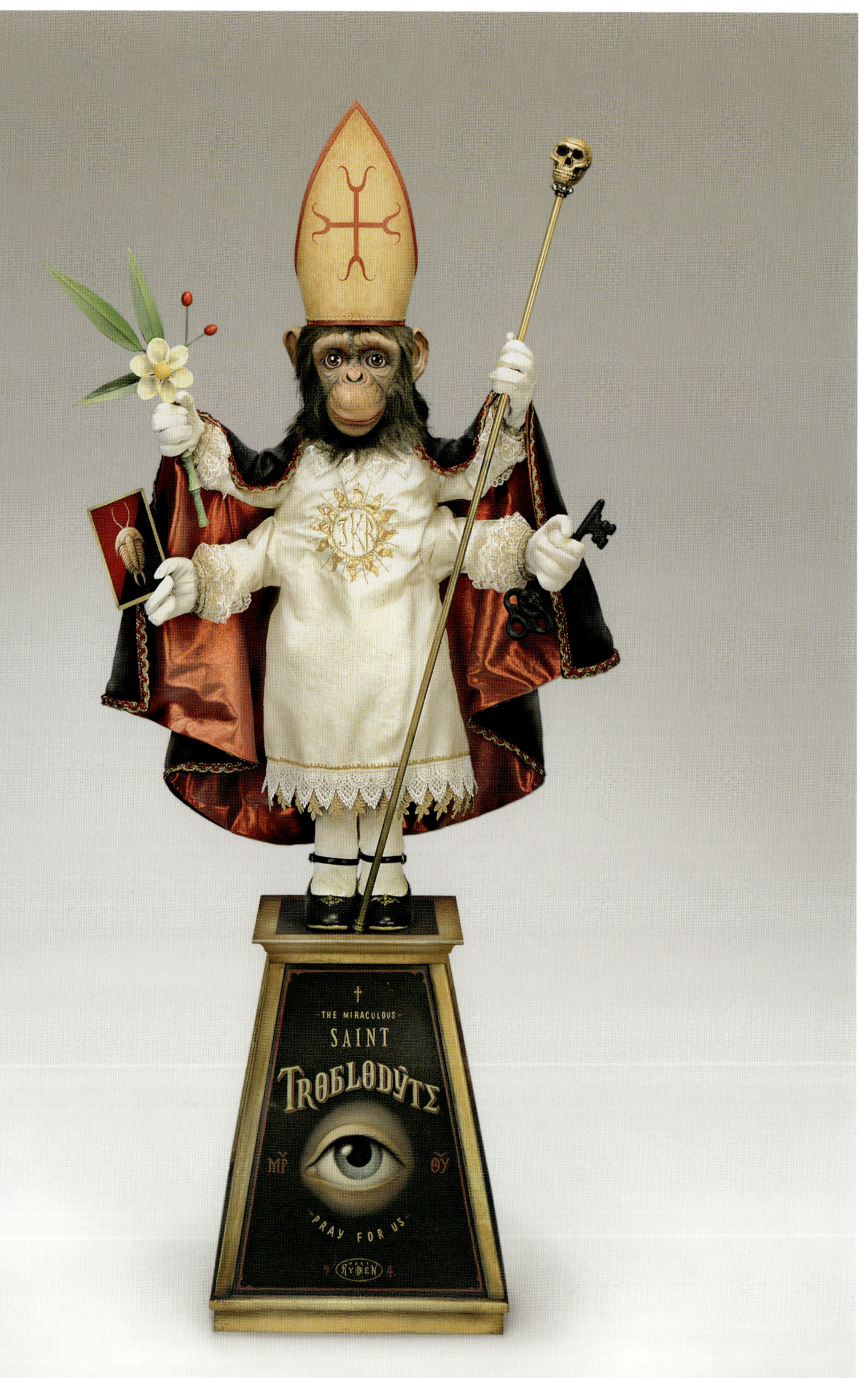
THE MIRACULOUS
SAINT
TROGLODYTE
MP   OY
PRAY FOR US
9 RYDEN 4

All of my originality consists in bringing fantastic beings to life by making them plausible, and, as much as possible,
in putting the logic of the visible at the service of the invisible.
Odilon Redon, 1909

How could one possibly conjure an image—a painting—that would bring comfort to someone condemned to death? As incomprehensible as this sounds, in Italy, between the fourteenth and seventeenth centuries, there existed brotherhoods whose raison d'être was to paint instruments of consolation, called *tavolette*. Each *tavoletta* consisted of a two-sided panel (with a little handle for holding): on one side was a painting from the Passion of Christ and on the other a scene of martyrdom. This secondary scene was chosen specifically for the prisoner, meant to relate in some inspirational way to the crime for which execution was the punishment. The brothers would comfort the prisoner on the night before the execution, then carry the *tavoletta* before the condemned man's face so that he could gaze upon it all the way to the place of execution and up until the moment of his death.[1] How extraordinary that a painted image—not the written or spoken word, not even music—would be a thing so powerful that it would offer palpable solace at the most mournful of moments. That an image could be a propitious implement to bridge human existence into the afterlife? Can a painting really do that?

Such is the power of image. And there are innumerable other examples of images that seek to transport the viewer to a spiritual plane: ex voto paintings, Eastern Orthodox icons, pilgrimage devotionalia, the mandalas of Eastern religions. If one doubts the capacity of an image to transform, think of the potency of pornography or political propaganda or advertising. The religions that embrace aniconism understand the force of imagery, or else they would not so stridently ban representations of the spiritual world. Imagery—"out of imagination"—breathes life into the banality of human existence.

If this seems like a dour introduction to the magical and happy portraits in Mark Ryden's series, *Anima Animals*, I agree that Ryden's cheerful creatures, with their doe eyes and gossamer fur, seem more like pictures of toys than devotional objects. But I would argue that Ryden's source material is tapped from the realm of creative chaos where these anima animals originate and spring forth into life through Mark's brush. And I believe that these painted creatures, like other consecrated tokens, have evolved from the plane of pure consciousness into our world to assist us mere mortals during the fraught phenomenon of living during these most challenging times.

If you said you had looked deeply into the eyes of an animal, people would say you were mad. But for the individual
it is an uncanny and profound experience which contains absolute truth. . . .
Carl Gustav Jung

In Ryden's artist statement accompanying this exhibition, he credits an African safari, which he and his wife, Marion Peck, took during the autumn of 2019, as a singular moment when he discovered the awe of observing animals in their natural habitat. After their first day spent in the Nairobi National Park, having seen for the first time in his life rhinos, lions, antelope, baboons, and monkeys outside of a zoo, Ryden had a surreal dream. In it, he was looking up at the mosquito canopy over the bed he was sharing with Peck, but at the crest of the net was a curious hybrid animal, a cross between a cat and a monkey. And before he knew it, the creature was nestled between Ryden and Peck; its presence was calm and loving. Ryden had started his *Anima Animals* series long before his Kenya experience, but his ability to access, and even "communicate" with, a being from his own unconscious is evidence of Ryden's ease in the land of the incorporeal. Ryden believes in the wisdom of animals and is fearless in sharing the wonder inherent in nonhuman beings.

When Ryden is asked if he remembers owning a rubber-faced stuffed animal when he was a child, he admits that he has no special memory of such a toy. But he does say that in depicting certain objects, including the innumerable vintage objects that pique nostalgia in his paintings, he taps into a cache of cultural imagery that dates to his childhood, but is not necessarily

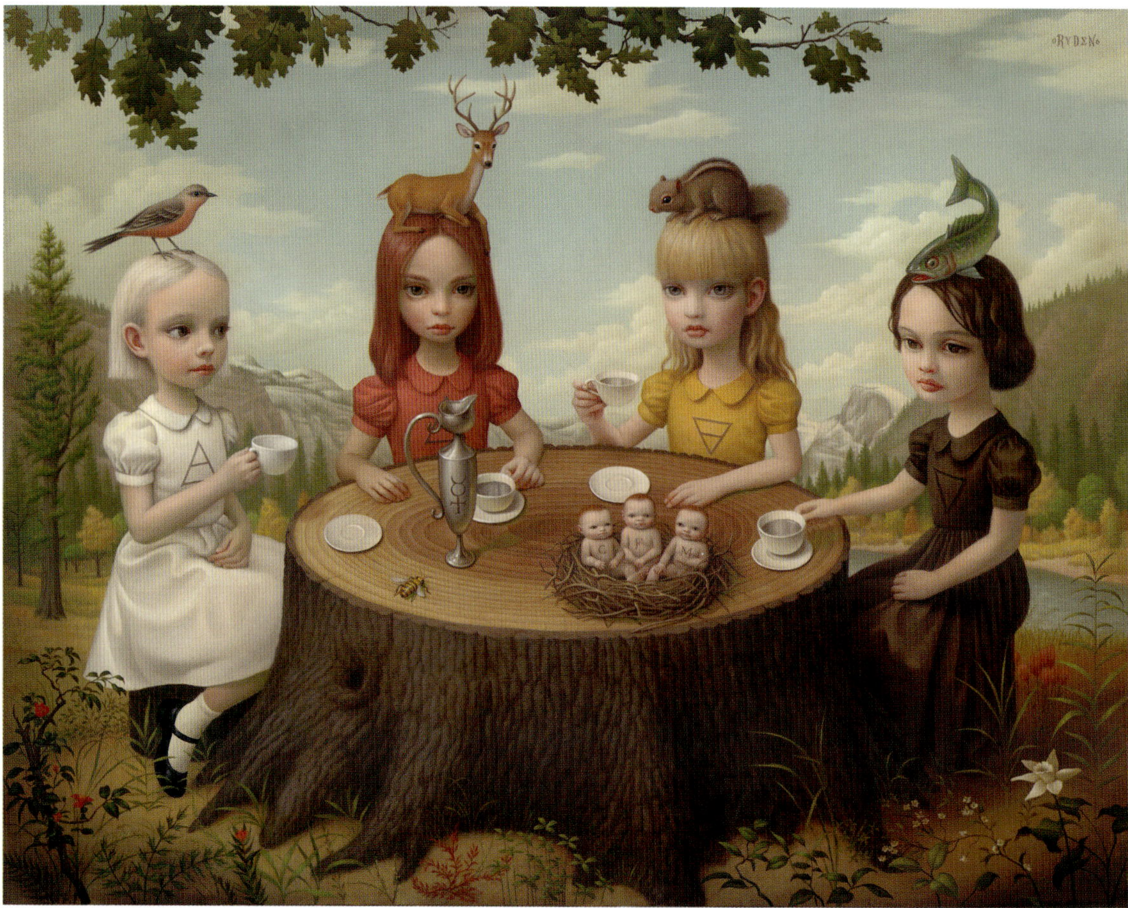

specific to it. Ryden routinely consults the collective unconscious to mine images that are neither personal nor impersonal, but rather *transpersonal*. One might say that Ryden is more Jungian than Freudian. (A comparison of Jung's image of death, *Tod*, from his *The Red Book: Liber Novus* to Ryden's anima animals *Sam* or *Black Yak* convinces me that both artists reliably channel imagery from the not-conscious world of limitless possibility.)

By his own admission, Ryden has his own anima animal. Ryden described this being in his artist statement for *The Meat Show* (1998): "Well, I have to admit I don't really paint my paintings; a Magic Monkey does. He comes to my studio late at night, when it's very quiet . . . Things have to flow from a place that is more subconscious and uninhibited. When you believe and have faith things will flow . . . It's like magic. The Monkey comes tapping at the door, we get the paint and brushes out of the treasure chest and we have a great time making art."

In fact, there *is* a real Magic Monkey in Ryden's studio. Ryden crafted his effigy by sculpting the face in clay and casting it in latex; he designed and sewed the figure's cassock and cape and built and painted the Monkey's pedestal with an all-seeing eye and the invocation "Pray For Us." In the Monkey's four hands are symbolic attributes: a picture of a trilobite, a botanical specimen, a staff surmounted by a skull, and a skeleton key. The sculpture became a sort of personal mascot, yes, but also more importantly it was, and is, a vessel to carry Ryden's true aspirations as an artist. The Magic Monkey has remained in an exalted position in Ryden's studio ever since. When Ryden moved to Portland, Oregon, and established his new studio there, Ryden and Peck even created a performative ritual, documented in a YouTube video, imploring the Monkey to "bless this place with creativity."[2] A version of the Magic Monkey even shows up in a preliminary sketch for *Snow White* (see page 18), before it was eventually replaced by the plastic-faced bunny that administers to the odalisque.

ABOVE

"Allegory of the Four Elements," (#59)

oil on canvas, 28 x 36 inches, 2006

RIGHT PAGE, TOP, LEFT

"Yoshi," (#79)

oil on canvas, 36 x 48 inches, 2007

RIGHT PAGE, TOP, RIGHT

"Cernunnos," (#67)

mixed media, 96 x 48 inches, 2006

RIGHT PAGE, CENTER, LEFT

"Snow Yak," (#87)

oil on canvas, 11 x 15 inches, 2008

RIGHT PAGE, CENTER, RIGHT

"Long Yak," (#86)

oil on canvas, 12 x 30 inches, 2008

RIGHT PAGE, BOTTOM

"Medium Yams," (#102)

oil on panel, 8.5 x 12.5 inches, 2012

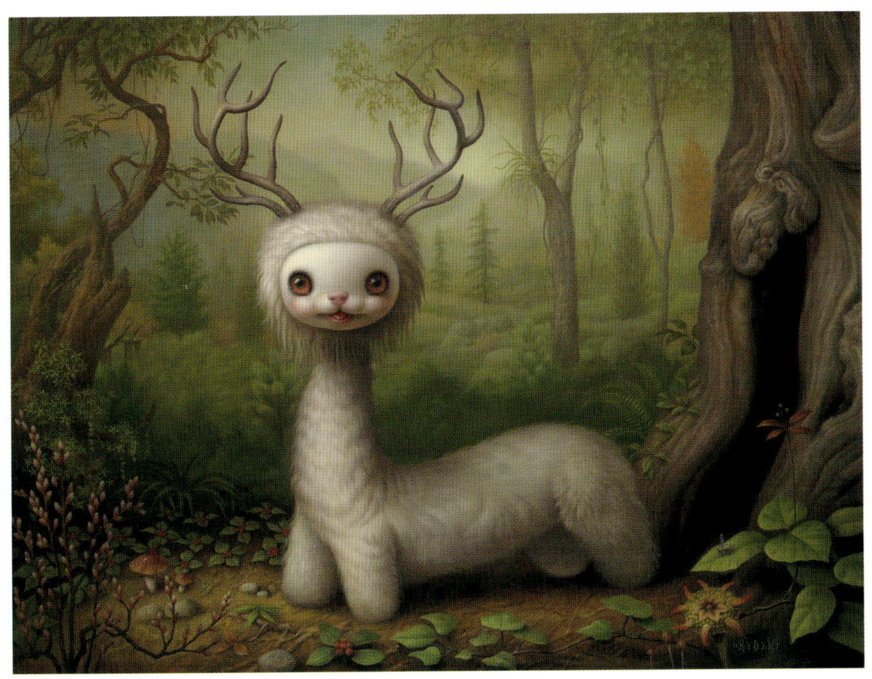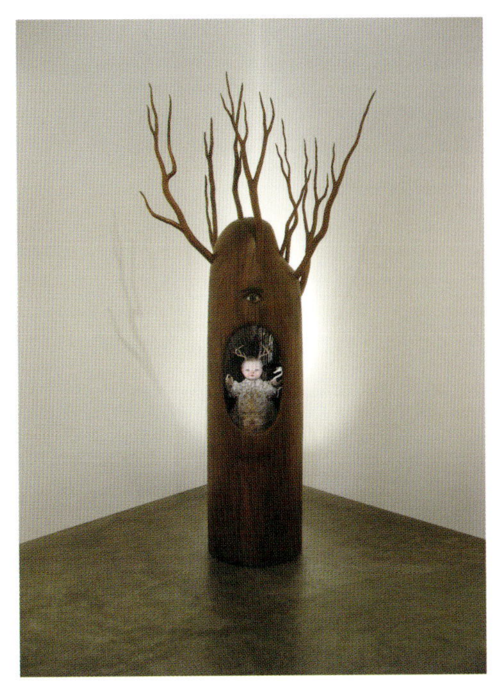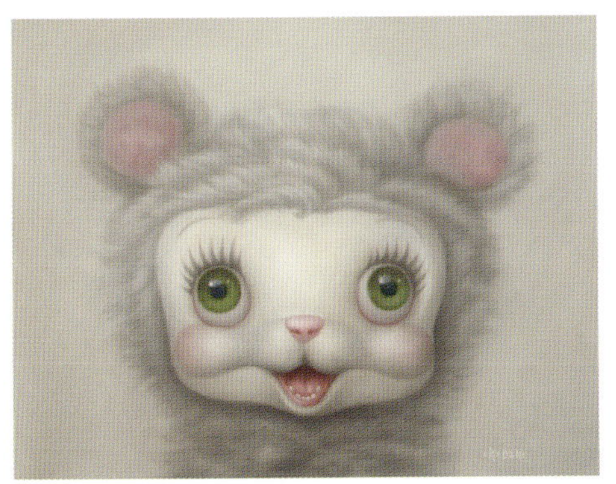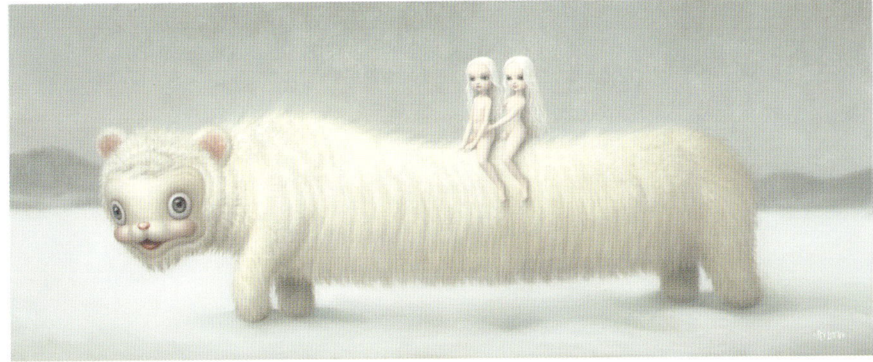

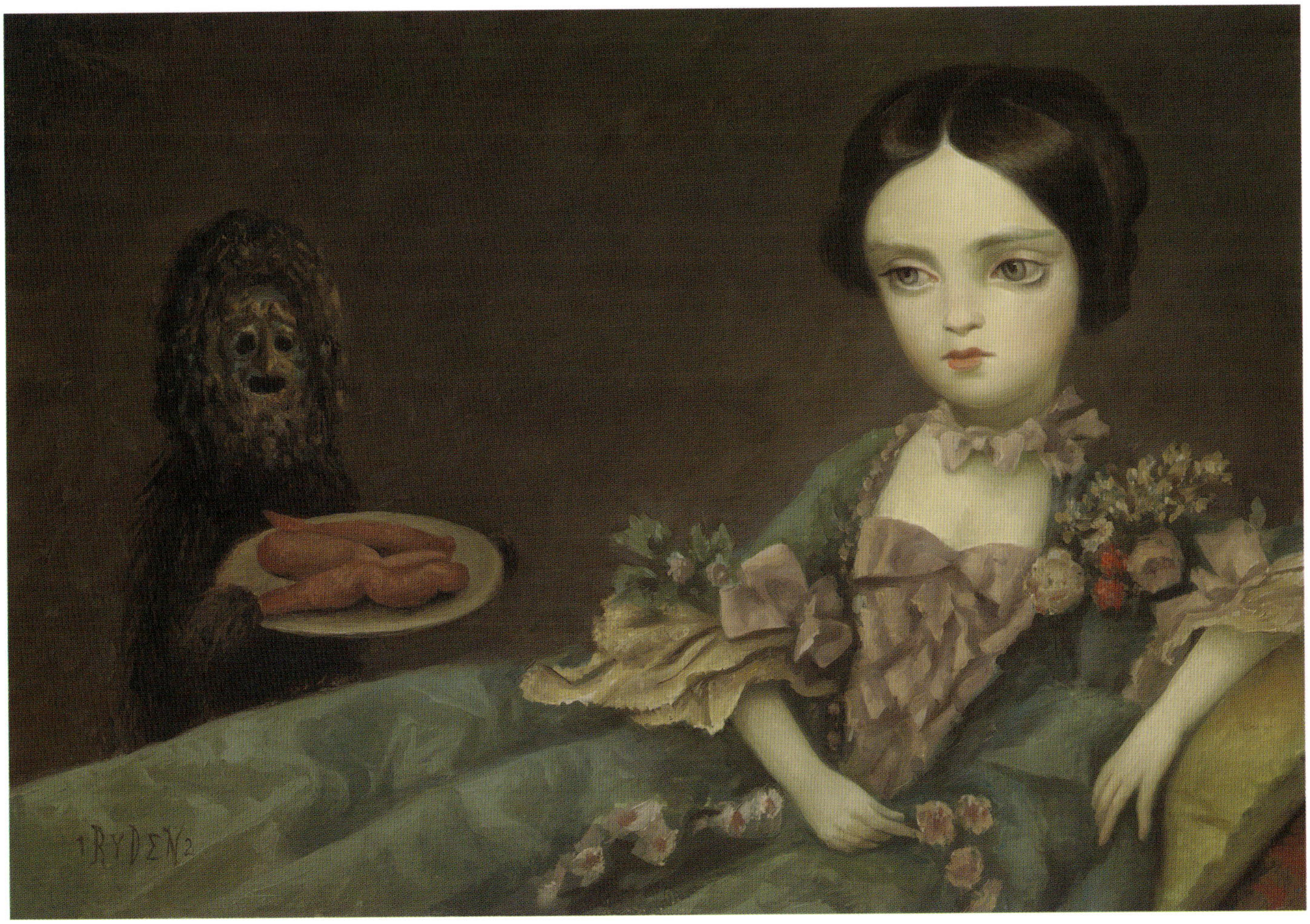

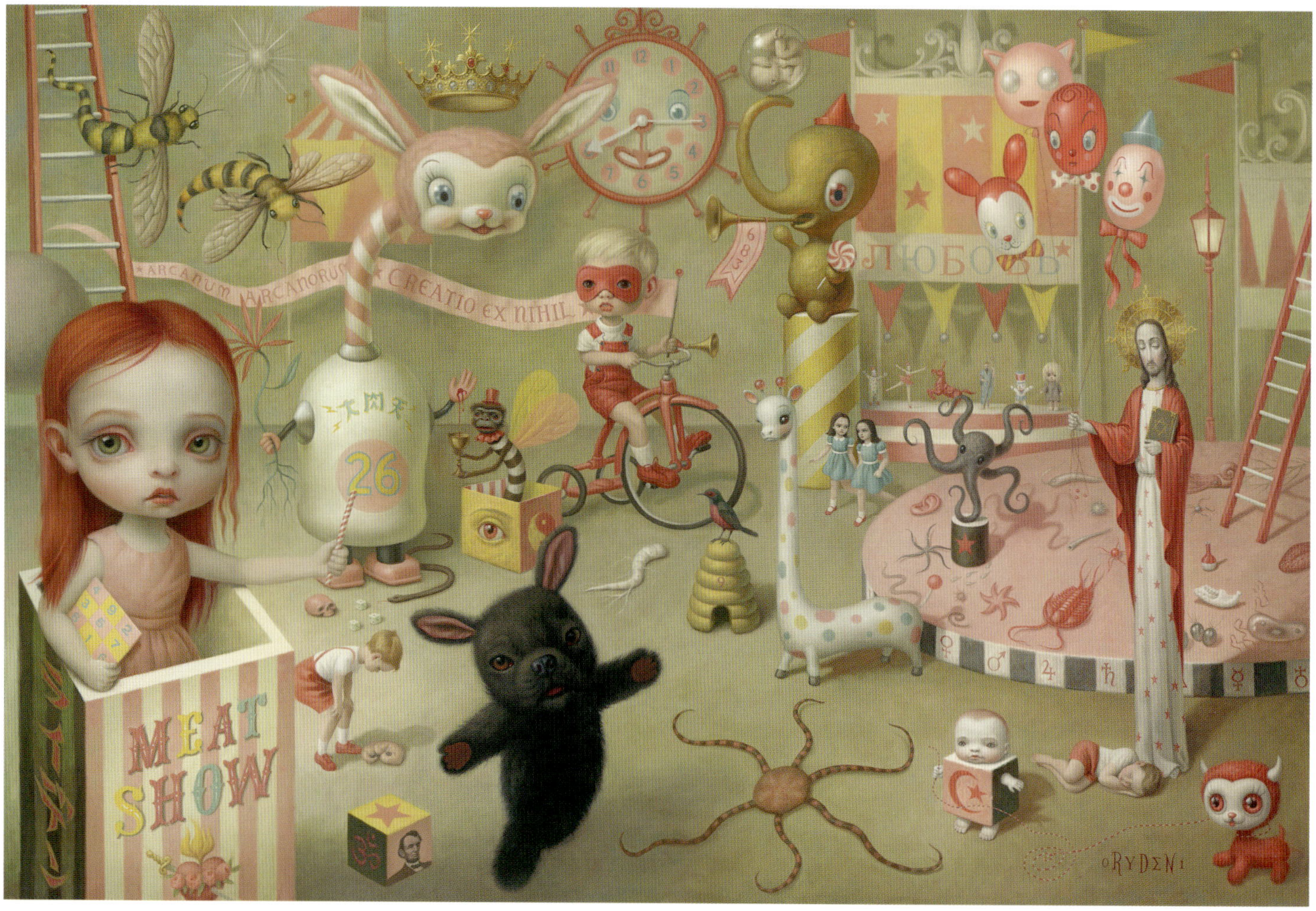

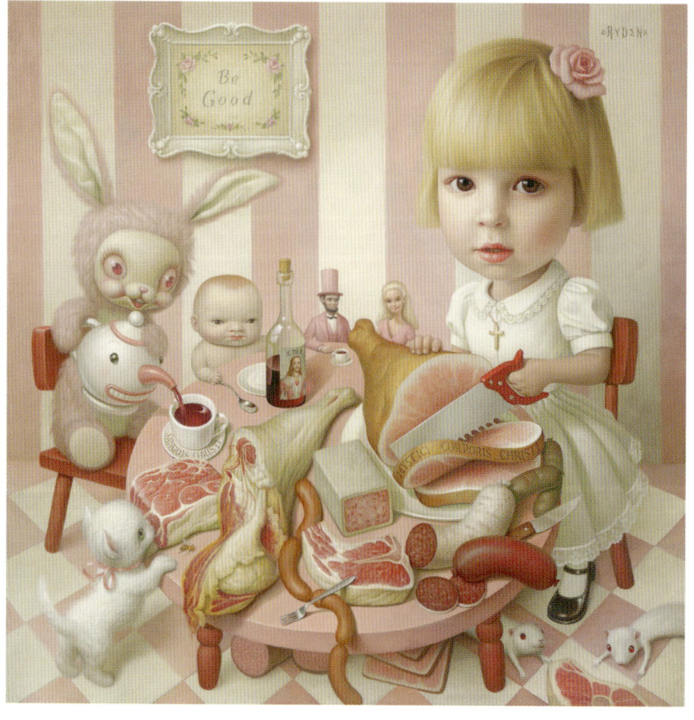

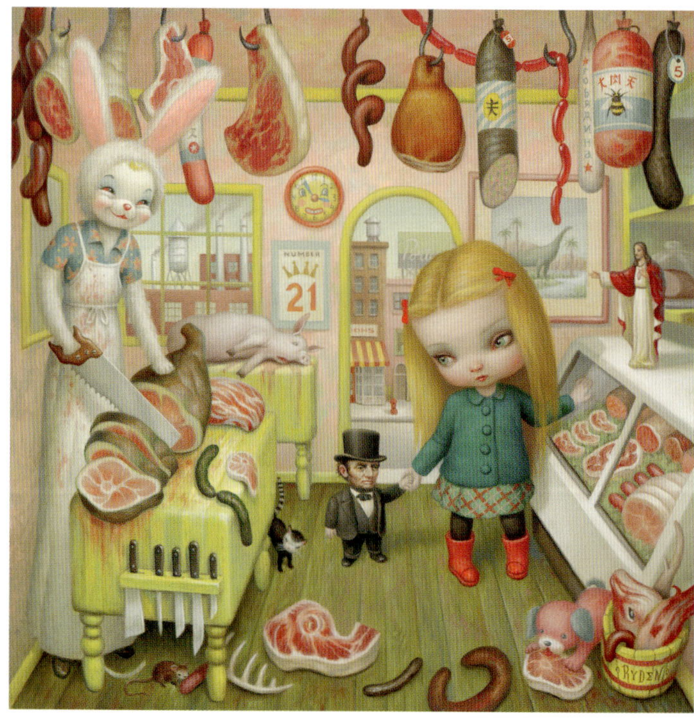

"The Magic Circus," (#26)

oil on canvas, 40 x 60 inches, 2001

"Rosie's Tea Party," (#56)

oil on canvas, 36 x 36 inches, 2005

"The Butcher Bunny," (#21)

oil on panel, 16 x 16 inches, 2000

"Anima animal" is a term used loosely by Ryden in reference to the part of one's psyche that is in touch with the unconscious and the innumerable mystical animals found in many cultures, from dragons in Asian ethnography to Odin's pair of ravens in Nordic mythology to the Mesopotamian lamassu. Ryden has a syncretic view of world cultures, attested to by his entire oeuvre, and variations of anima animals have appeared in Ryden's work for many years. Ryden embraces animism, the idea that objects, places, and creatures possess a spiritual presence; this philosophical foundation breathes reverence and transcendence into his work. *The Tree Show* in 2007 was full of paintings that included spiritual beings, including *Allegory of the Four Elements* (2007), in which each nymph wears an avatar animal on her head (a bird for Air, a deer for Fire, a squirrel for Earth, and a fish for Water). It was in *The Tree Show* where tree stumps have all-seeing eyes, a teddy bear cavorts with a young girl in *Goodbye Bear* (2006), and the friendly, antlered *Yoshi* (2007) appears. Also for *The Tree Show*, Ryden created a magnificent sculptural version of *Cernunnos* (2006), the Celtic god associated with animals and the hunt. Ryden's next exhibition, *The Snow Yak Show,* is an even more ethereal journey into an icy metaphysical realm, a world of celestial whiteness where young maidens dream of gentle yak guides. And in Ryden's *The Gay 90's West* exhibition, the painting *Medium Yams* (2012), in a composition suggested by Édouard Manet's *Olympia*, a wizened and tentative phantom offers a plate of yams (sustenance? spiritual mana?) to the young ingénue. The sympathetic specter's offering suggests the generosity that awaits us from the spirit world, if only we are open to accepting those gifts.

Yet the numinous creatures in *Anima Animals* are in drastic contrast to many of Ryden's earlier paintings. Much of Ryden's oeuvre consists of paintings that are densely packed with imagery—so much so that sometimes his work is described as horror vacui. Many early works, such as *Magic Circus* (2001), *Rosie's Tea Party* (2005), or *The Butcher Bunny* (2000), are so loaded with objects, all seemingly symbolic, that looking at a Ryden painting can feel a little like trying to decipher a mysterious rebus. The anima animals are visual opposites. Each animal is depicted as if it were sitting in Ryden's studio for a traditional portrait. Except for Ryden's pastiche of Leonardo da Vinci's *Salvator Mundi*, an anomaly painted in cerulean blue, the animals are rendered in Ryden's signature palette of pink, cream, and black. Whereas the more image-packed of Ryden's narrative paintings entertain the viewer as their eye pings from curiosity to curiosity, the animal portraits quietly seduce the viewer with the sumptuousness of the details. Pinkie's hair is so voluptuous and silken, the moiré of her dress so tactile, that one can imagine touching her. So, too, are the setae of Bee, the gnarled and boney reach of Messenger's antlers, the plush of Pink Bunny's fleece. Each animal's eyes are arresting as well. Make no mistake, their eyes do not have the verisimilitude of reality in the sense that they could belong to a living animal; they mostly look like the eyes one would find on a child's stuffed animal. But each animal gazes so directly at the viewer that one feels like a conversation might ensue. Ryden has commented that making these paintings was particularly challenging; because the compositions are so deceptively simple, the more important it is to imbue life into every little tuft of fur.

Ryden's titles are deceptively succinct as well. Some of the portraits are simply identified by the species—*Bee,* for example, and the various yak portraits, *Pink Yak, Pretty Yak, Green Eyed Yak, Black Yak,* and *Black Tie Yak*. But other portrait titles point to Ryden's love of language, and his fascination with lesser-known denizens of the animal kingdom. *The Stoat,* for example, is another name for an ermine, and the *Numbat,* as fanciful as that word sounds, is a marsupial native to Western Australia. *Dowradu* is an even more imaginative play on words, as it is a riff on the Portuguese term *mico-leão-dourado*, for the golden lion tamarin monkey. But Ryden's reach for cultural references is vast. *Makkuro* means "pitch black" in Japanese, but it is also the name for the animated Soot Sprites in the Studio Ghibli animé film *Spirited Away* (2001).

I love the idea of a painting being so precious it becomes sacred.
Mark Ryden

Virtually every essay written about Ryden describes the enchantment of visiting this artist's studio. Ryden loves objects—he is such a serious collector that his home is an idiosyncratic cabinet of curiosities. He acquires all manner of old toys, Little Golden Books and other volumes of children's literature, photographs, anatomical models, taxidermy, didactic and instructional charts, religious artifacts, vintage paper ephemera, Lincoln figures and memorabilia, Colonel Sanders replicas, entomological specimens, shells, masks, thrift store paintings, and more. He describes finding inspiration at flea markets, but he does not search for any particular thing—only to identify the secondhand object that is somehow energized by a visceral "spiritual charge" that makes the object stand out from the morass of other "stuff." He often remarks that being surrounded by these objects is an important aspect of his creative process.

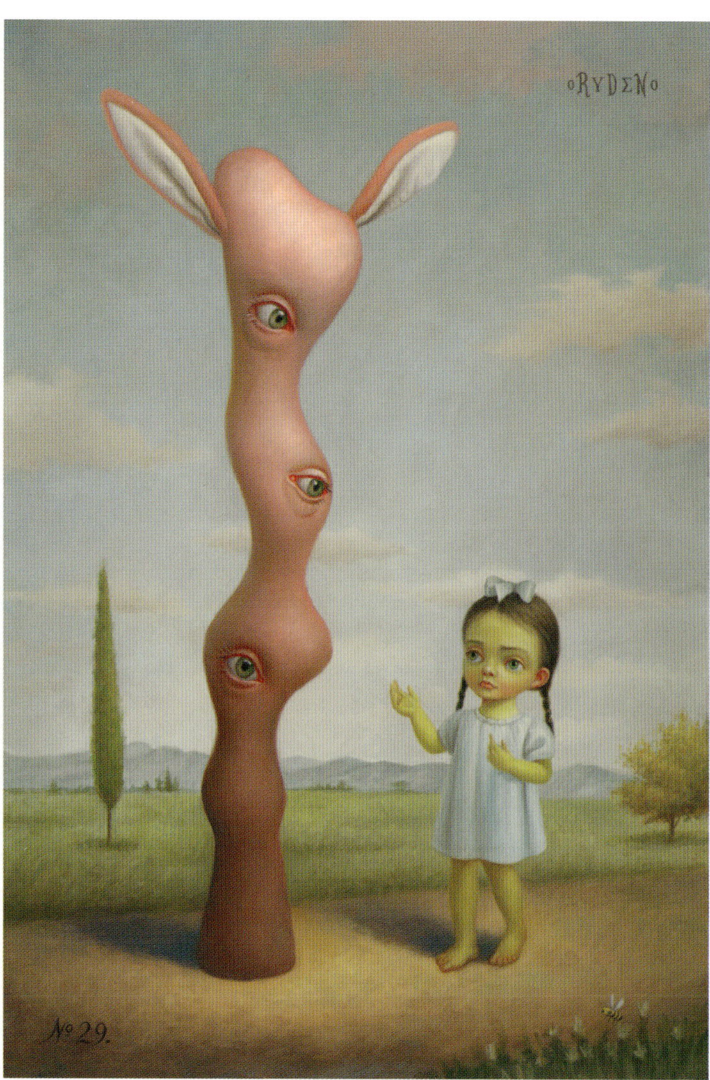

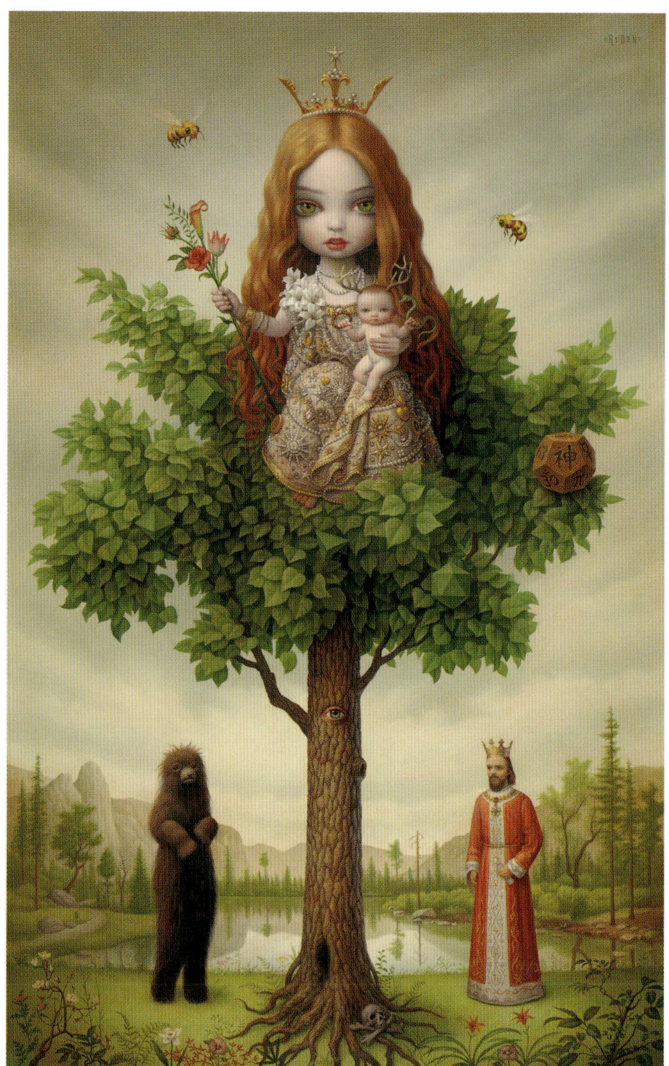

Evidence of Ryden's perception that his paintings are objects—a philosophy that sets Ryden apart from many of his contemporaries—is that he carefully designs his own frames with the most assiduous attention to detail. Ryden spends an inordinate amount of time on each frame, creating many sketches of the molding, illustrating his ideas at different angles and in cross section, then he carefully directs the carving. The frame reinforces the idea that his painting is an *object*, equal and opposite to the flat surface image, and that the frame is essentially the reliquary encasing a holy relic. Each frame in the *Anima Animals* series was crafted specifically for the painting.

Ryden creates sculptures as well as paintings, and when working on a series, it is not uncommon for him to manifest three-dimensional work in concert with his paintings. His painting *The Angel of Meat* (1998) from *The Meat Show* evolved into the tabletop-size porcelain figure, *The Angel of Meat* (2007, edition of 30), and the marvelous porcelain *Meat Dress* (2012, edition of 9) came after he painted *Incarnation* (2009). Such is Ryden's interest in multiples that he established his own imprint, Porterhouse Fine Art Editions, which offers a panoply of objects based on Ryden's studio output. One interesting antecedent to the *Anima Animals* series is the *YHWH* vinyl figures that evolved out of Ryden's painting, *YHWH* (2000). The urban vinyl figure is a slightly lumpy, totem pole–like creature with ears and multiple eyes. Given the title, the tetragrammaton of Yahweh (the Hebrew name of God transliterated in four letters), both the painting and the columnar sculpture have a distinctly shamanic connotation.

Included in the *Anima Animals* series is Ryden's latest porcelain sculpture, the figure known as *Bos*. "Bos" is not a make-believe word; it is the name of the genus to which yaks belong. The Bos figures come in an edition of thirty, ten each in the colors bistre, blush, and buff—pale colors that, together, make one think of Neapolitan ice cream. The creatures have long, columnar bodies and short legs; their truncated arms outstretch as if offering a hug. They are covered head to toe with shaggy fur, so like their long-haired namesake; their sunny faces have dappled cheeks and button eyes.

"YHWH," (#29)

oil on canvas, 10 x 14 inches, 2000

"The Tree of Life," (#63)

oil on canvas, 66 x 42 inches, 2006

Bos is not a new creature in the Ryden pantheon. A cursory line drawing of this figure appears in the marginalia of a graphite preparatory drawing of *The Magic Circus* (2001). Bos most notably appears as an attendant in *The Tree of Life* (2006), opposite a wise, old wizard king. Even *Parfait Man* (2017), one of Ryden's costume designs for the American Ballet Theatre's production of Richard Strauss's *Whipped Cream,* bears a certain visual relationship to the *Bos* figures, and the costume's oval aperture for the performer's face mirrors the rubber face of the vintage stuffed animals.

I cannot bear the tragedy of the present time. I want to create joy.
Richard Strauss

Ryden does not deny the absurdist quality in these paintings, and he means for viewers to have fun in the experience of looking at them. Some of Ryden's portrait sitters are humbly pious—*God Yak* and *Messenger*—while others are a little silly. The carnivalesque and buzzy, pipe-smoking *Jack Rabbit* is even comical. *Salvator Mundi*, though, with its pink, wall-eyed gaze, an uplifted paw in a gesture of blessing, and holding a crystal sphere, may be the standard bearer of this series. These works are evidence that a central theme in this series is sanctity, a subject notably absent in today's contemporary art world, where religious-themed art is often ghettoized and dismissed as anti-intellectual. Yet Ryden has chosen to bestow considerable devotion to these fantastic and lyrical beings. There is a message in Ryden's discipline for the rest of us; it may be as simple as an invitation to see the world in a nonconventional way.

What do Ryden's lighthearted anima animals mean for today's world? These talismans were painted at the precipice of an intensely dark time in human history. The portraits were originally meant to be shown at Perrotin Shanghai in March 2020, just at the moment when international travel collapsed due to COVID-19 and the world turned inward in quarantine. Now that the exhibition has been rescheduled to open in July 2020, the world is an entirely different place than it was when Ryden made these paintings. Not only are humans suffering the uncertainty borne of a global pandemic, but in the U.S. the murder of George Floyd and other Black Americans have focused an inexorable light on the injustices of racism that have been a pervasive component of American culture. Add to this the disastrous widespread environmental degradation that poises humankind— and innumerable other species—on the brink of extinction. Individuals and collectives are being called upon to be agents of drastic change. But what is the way forward?

The French art theorist, Bertrand Rougé, likens the experience of viewing a powerful painting to a shaman going on a spiritual journey; that a work of art can be a "bridge that makes it possible to be transported to another side of experience, away from real life."[3] There is little disagreement that answers to the dire dilemmas of our day are not likely to be found in the anemic solutions of the past. But perhaps, like the Italian *tavolette*, the power of Ryden's imagery might serve to transport the viewer into an exalted realm, if even for a moment. It may be that only by assenting to a nonhuman source can humankind recalibrate its place in nature. Ryden's unabashedly joyful *Anima Animals* represents another intelligence, an alternate sentience, made tangible in these sacred portraits.

—Linda Tesner

Linda Tesner is an independent curator and writer living in Portland, Oregon. She has served as the interim director of the Jordan Schnitzer Museum of Art at Portland State University and as the director and curator at the Ronna and Eric Hoffman Gallery of Contemporary Art at Lewis & Clark College (1998–2019). She was formerly the assistant director of the Portland Art Museum and the director of the Maryhill Museum of Art in Goldendale, Washington. She received her BA in art history from the University of Oregon and her MA in the history of art from Ohio State University.

Endnotes

1. David Freedberg, *The Power of Images: Studies in the History and Theory of Response* (Chicago: The University of Chicago Press, 1989), pp. 5-9.

2. Mark Ryden, "Invoking the Magic Monkey in my new studio," www.youtube.com/watch?v=ye18kpuRx5w

3. James Elkins, *Pictures & Tears* (New York: Routledge, 2001), pp. 71-72.

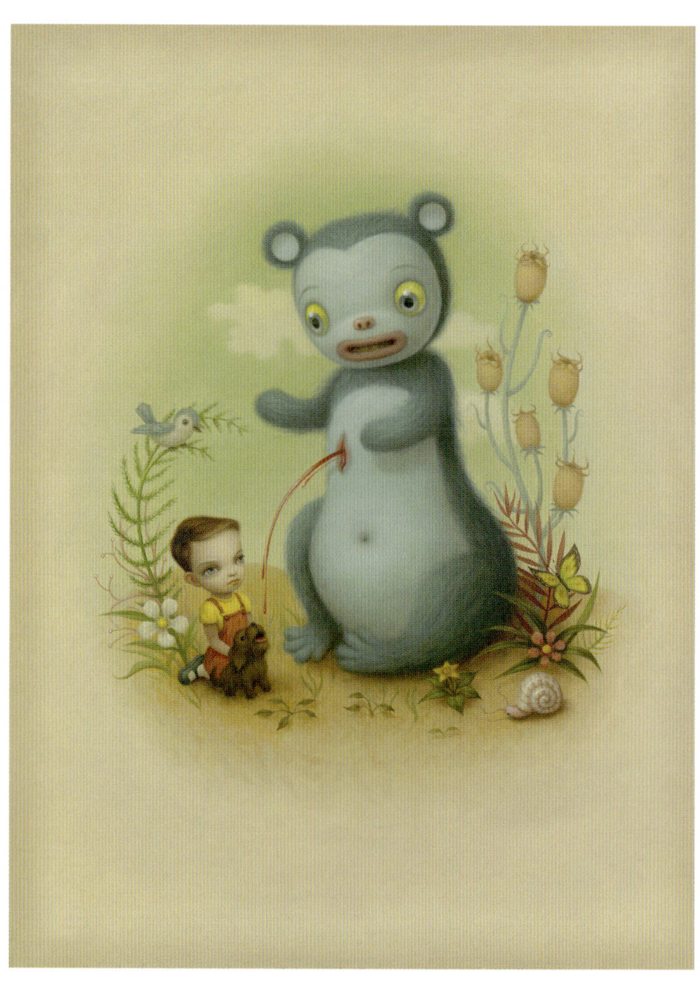

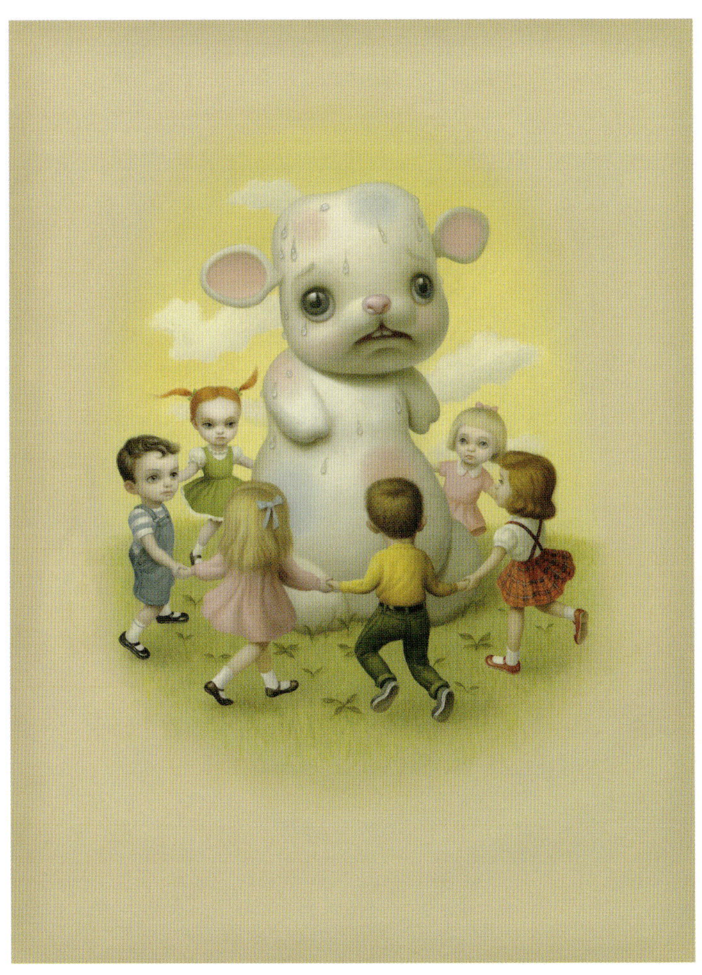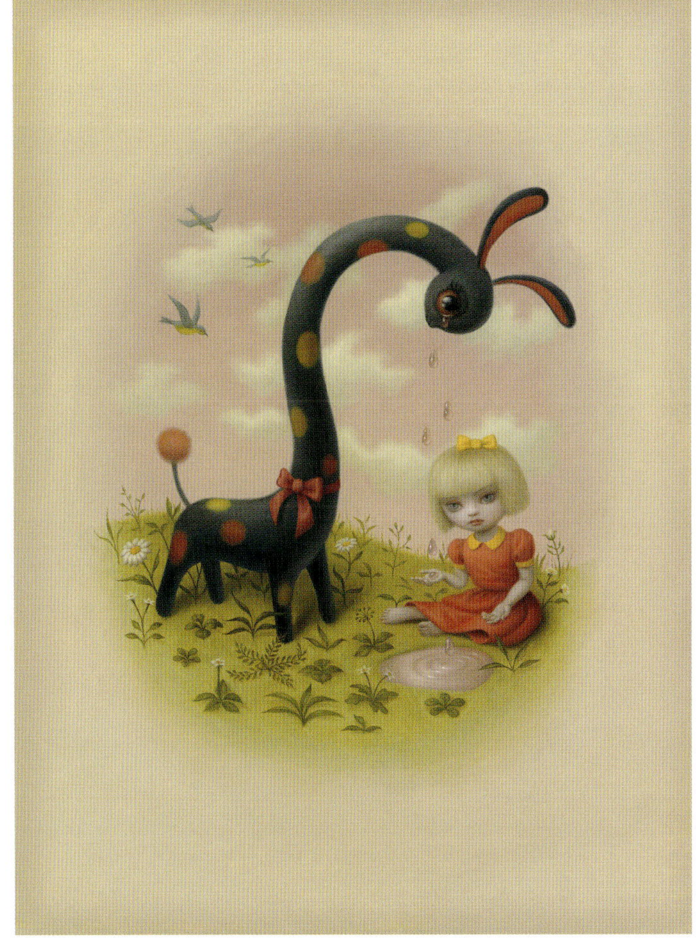

THIS SPREAD

"Blood, Sweat & Tears,"

oil on board, 24 x 18 inches each, 2005

NEXT SPREAD, LEFT

"Inside Sue," (#8)

oil on panel, 15 x 11 inches, 1997

NEXT SPREAD, RIGHT

"California Brown Bear," (#60)

oil on canvas, 20 x 16 inches, 2006

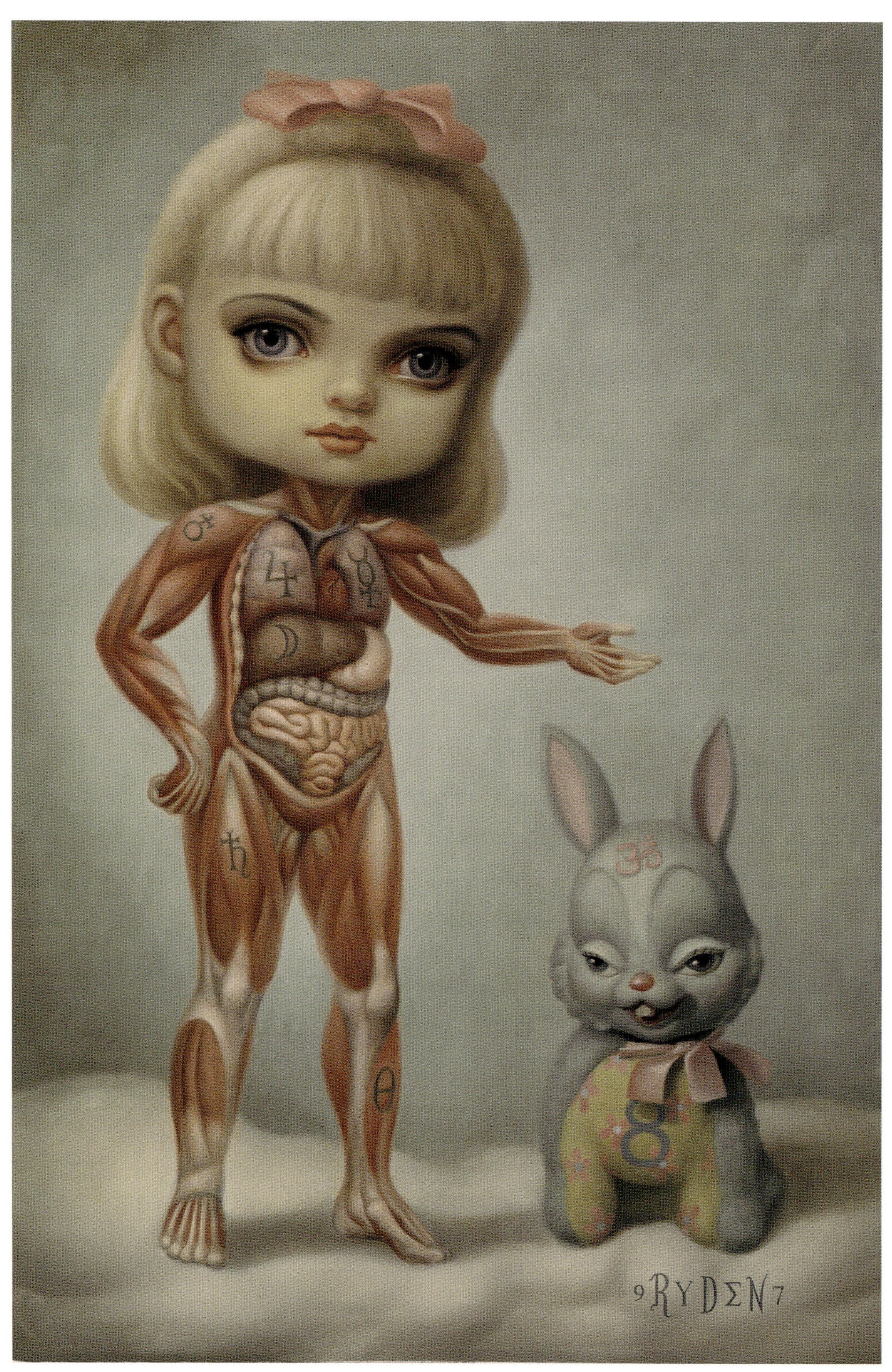

9RYDEN7

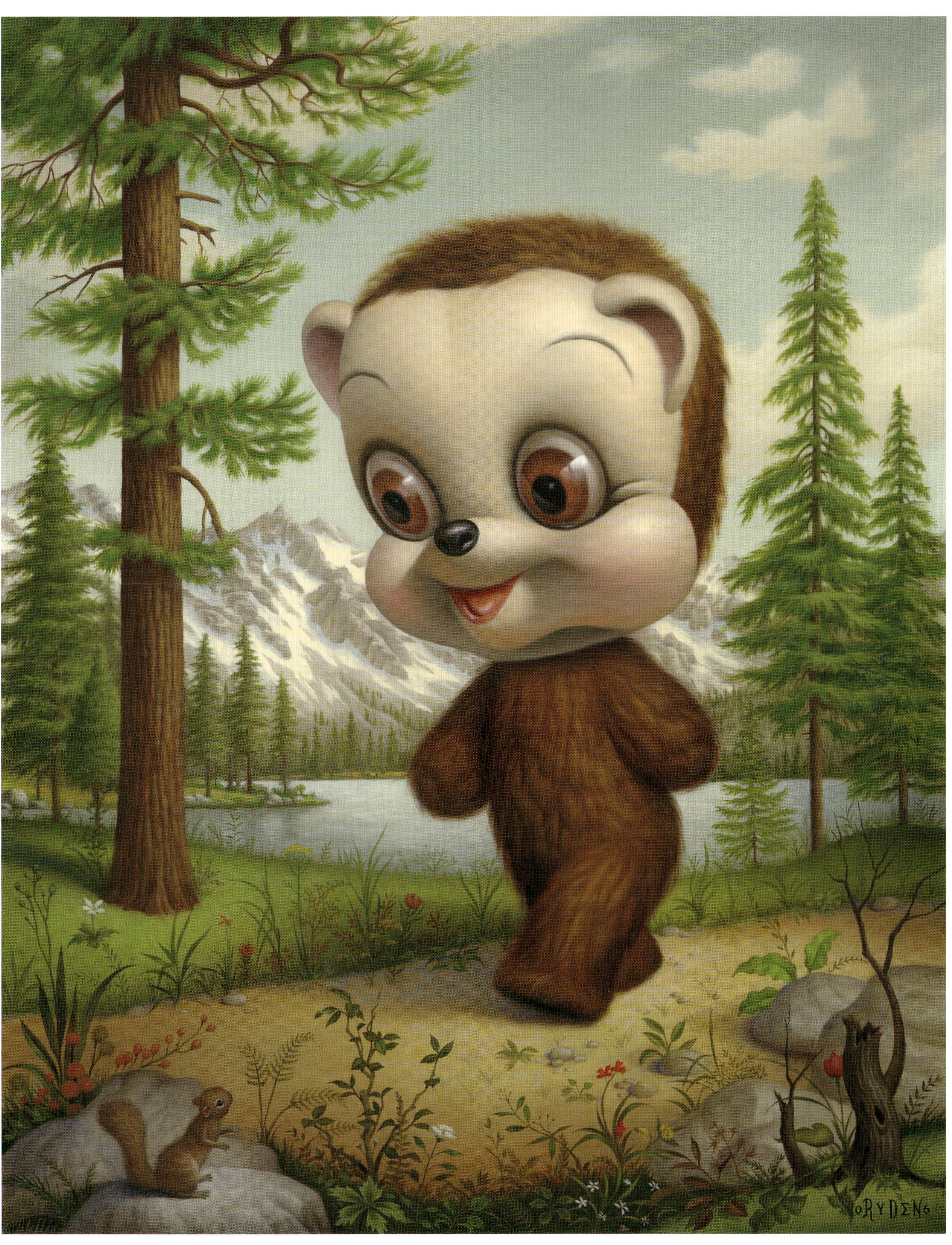
oRYDENo

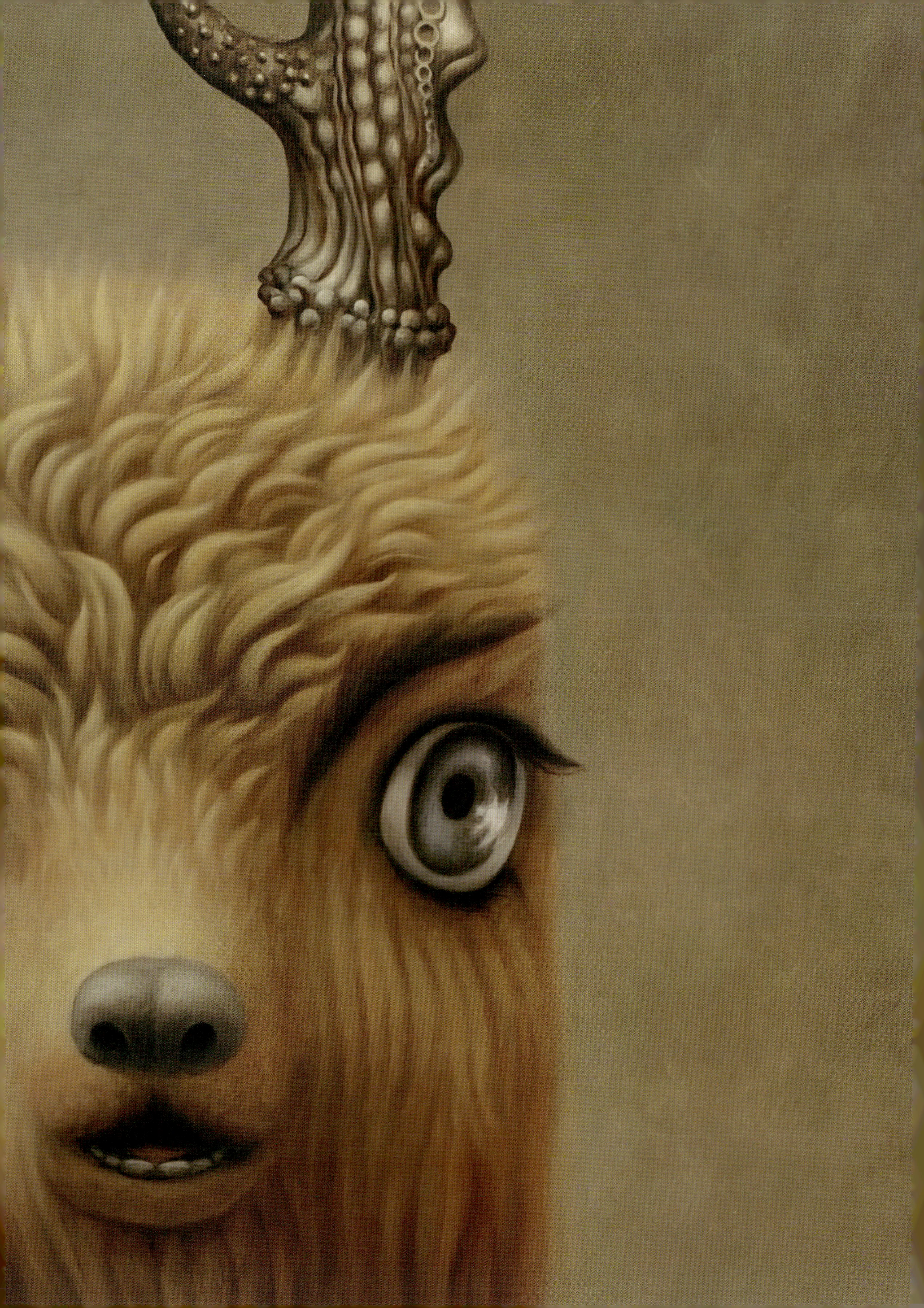

PAINTINGS

No 136
PINK YAK

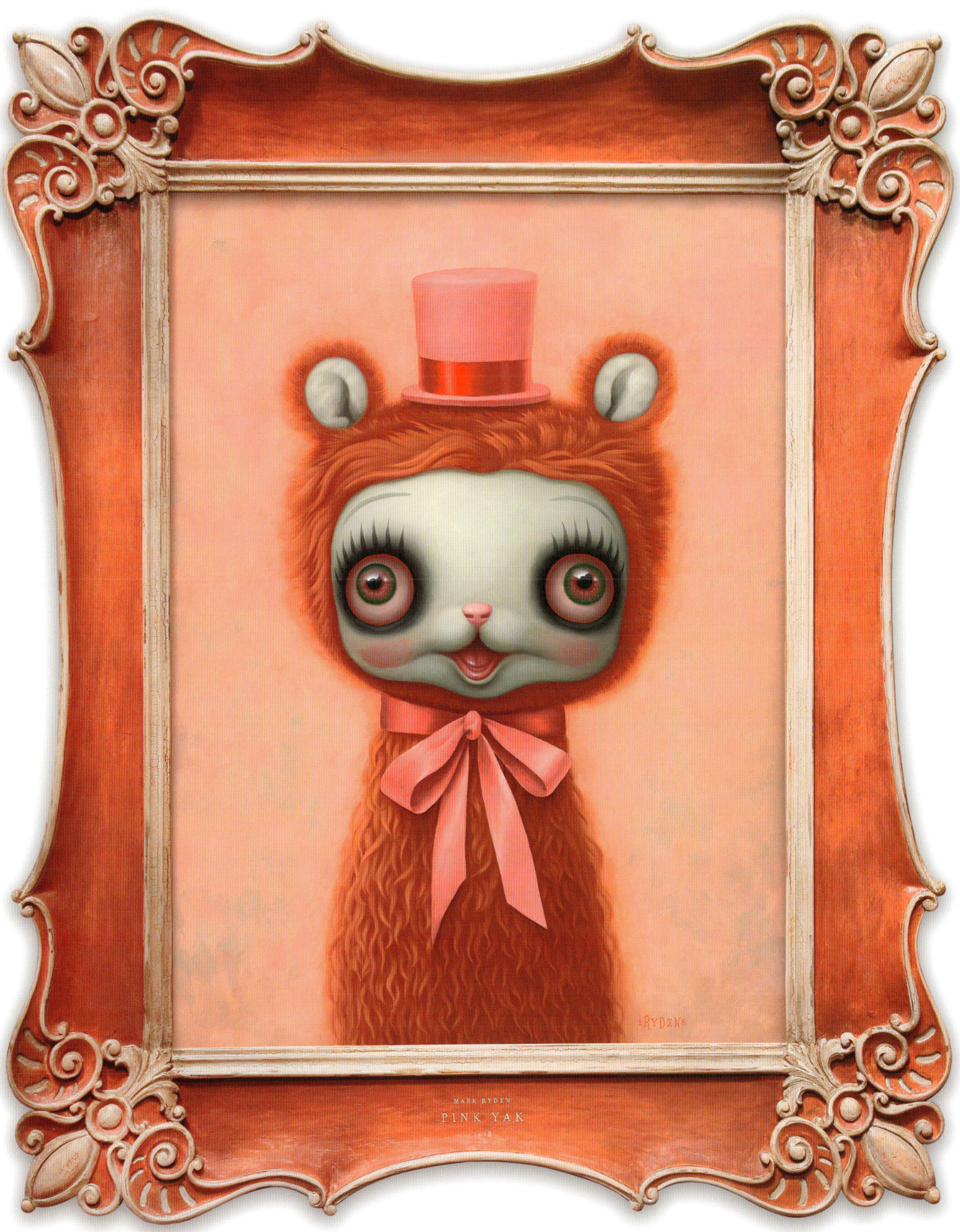

MARK RYDEN
PINK YAK

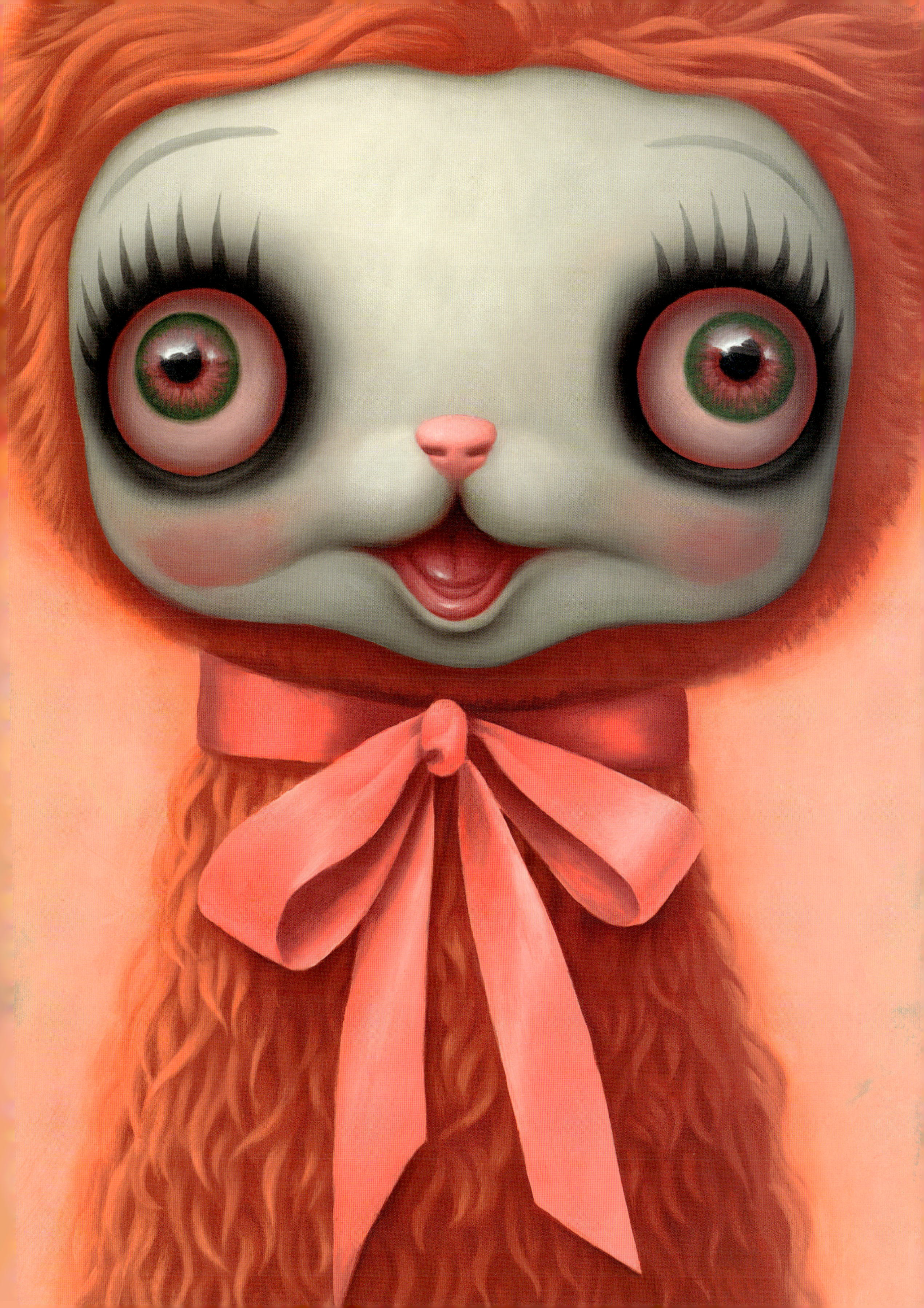

SALVATOR MUNDI

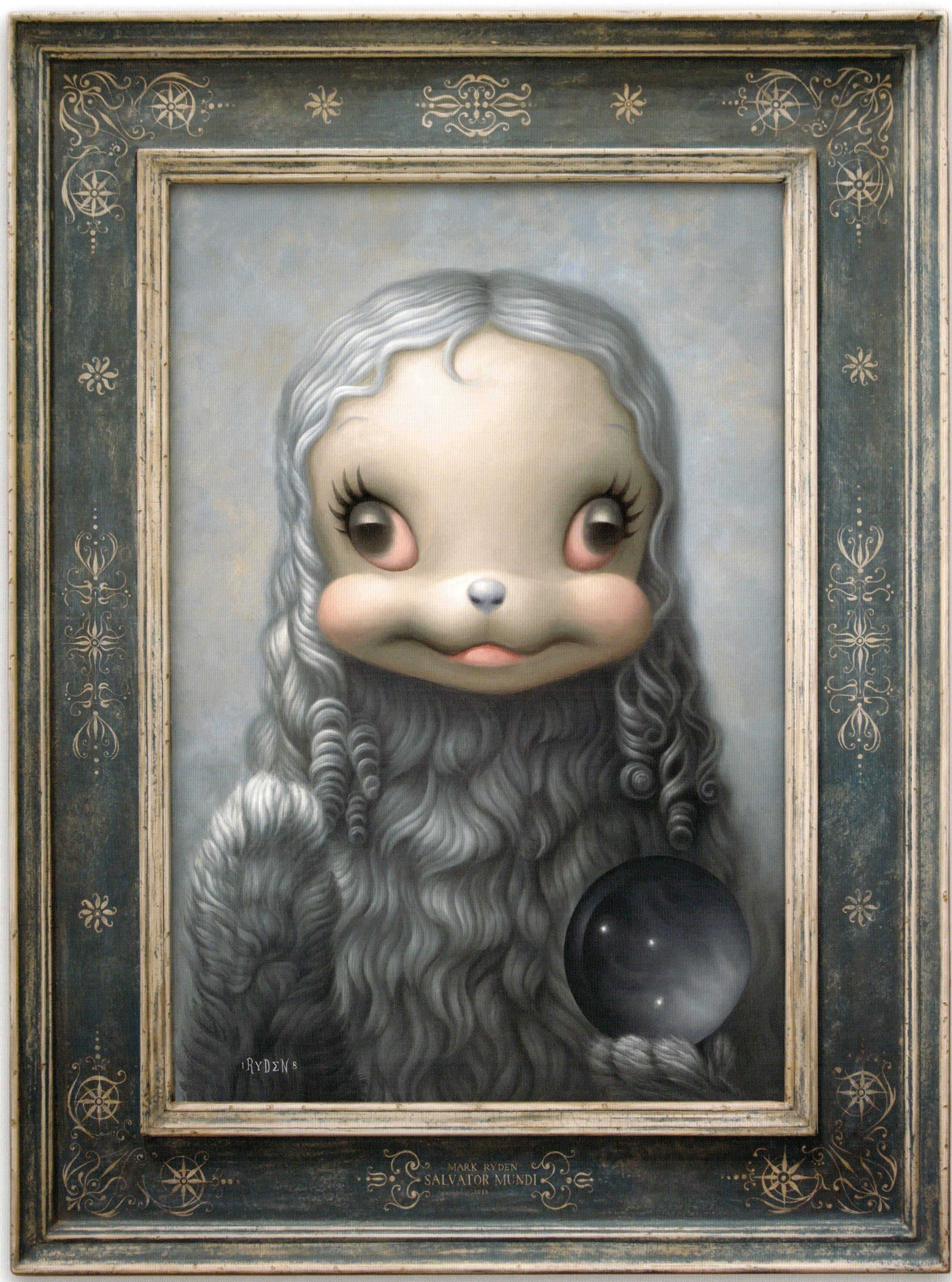
RYDEN
MARK RYDEN
SALVATOR MUNDI

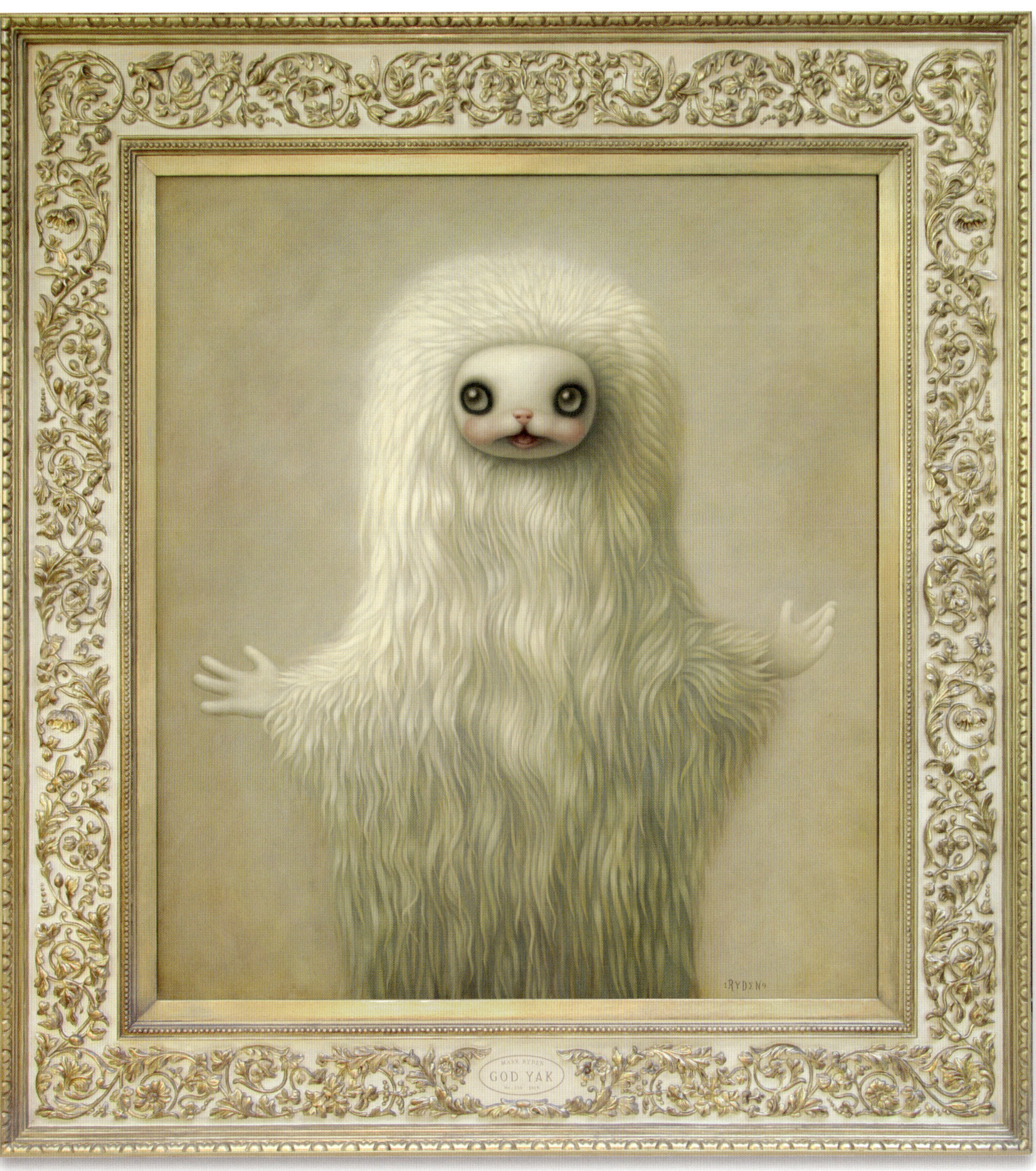
MARK RYDEN
GOD YAK
RYDEN

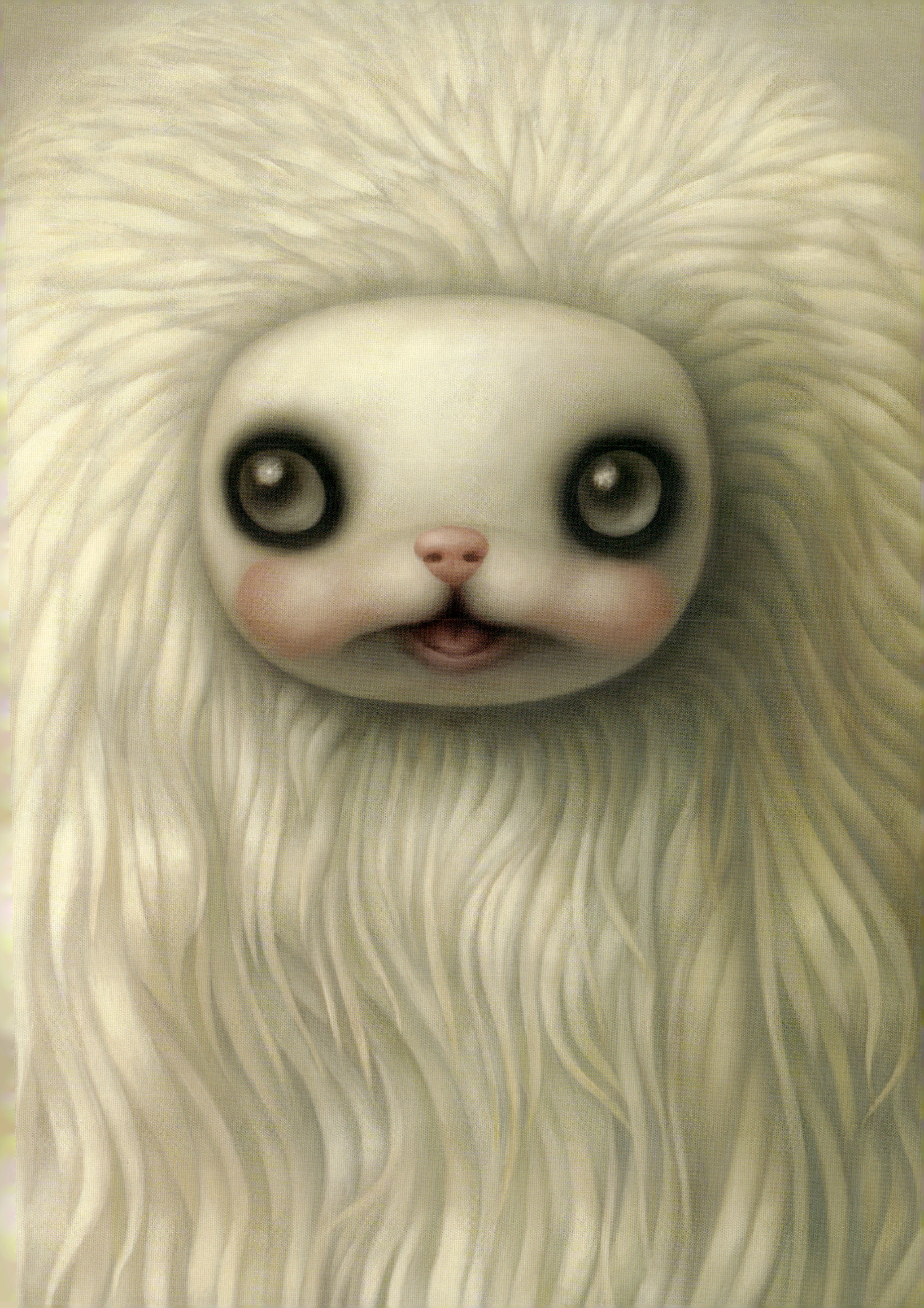

No 139
PRETTY YAK

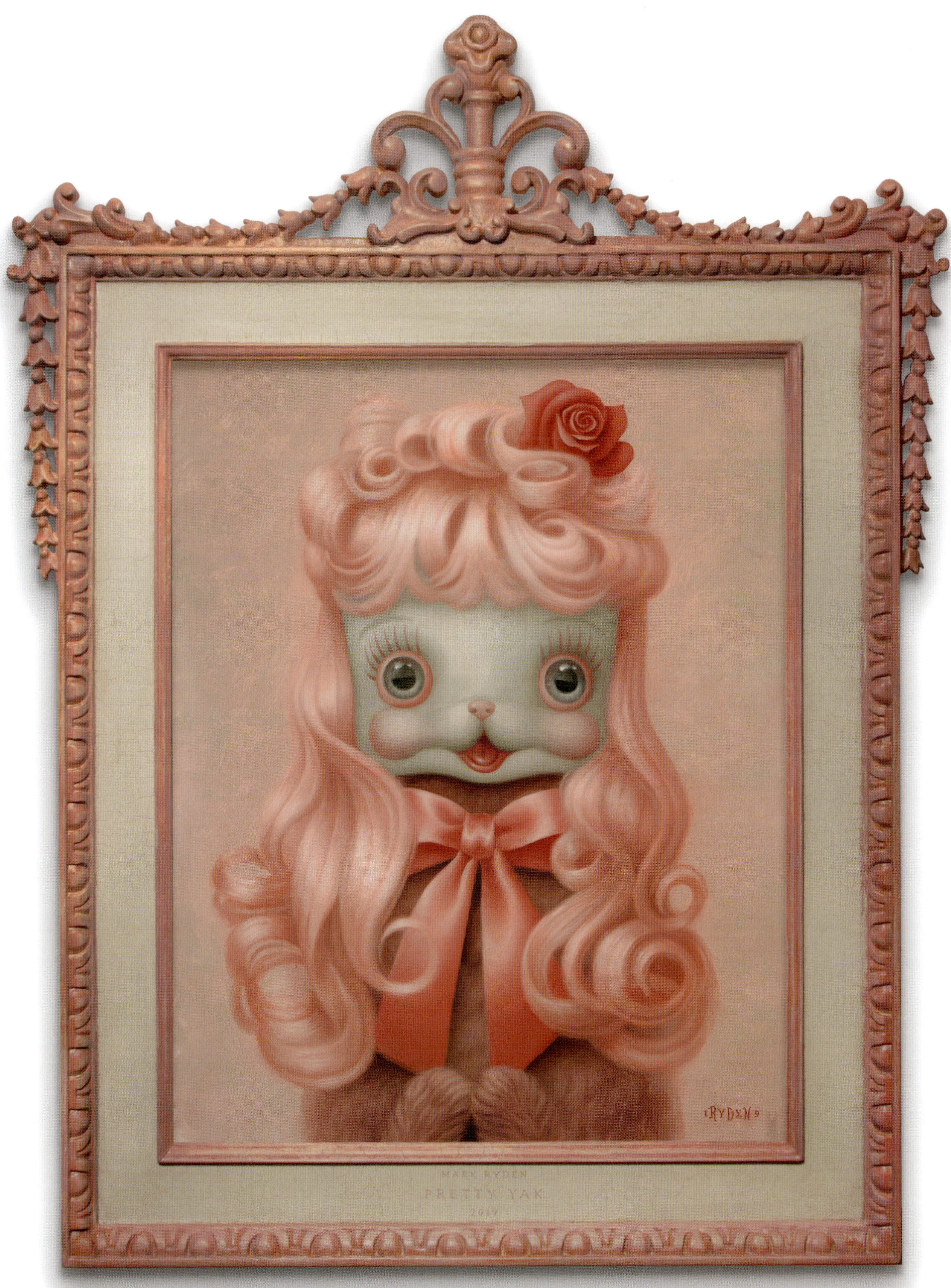

MARK RYDEN
PRETTY YAK
2019

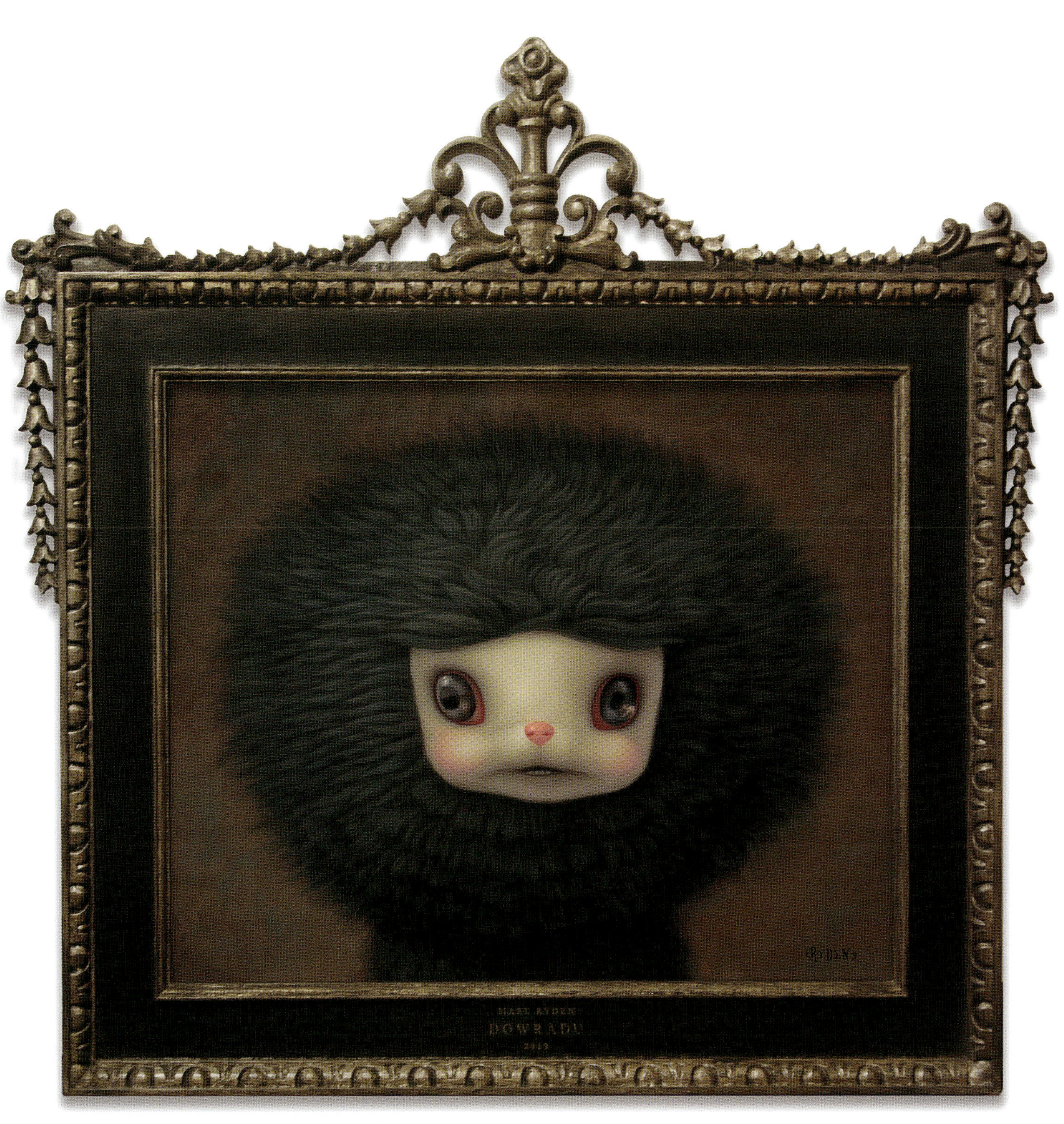

MARK RYDEN
DOWRADU
2019

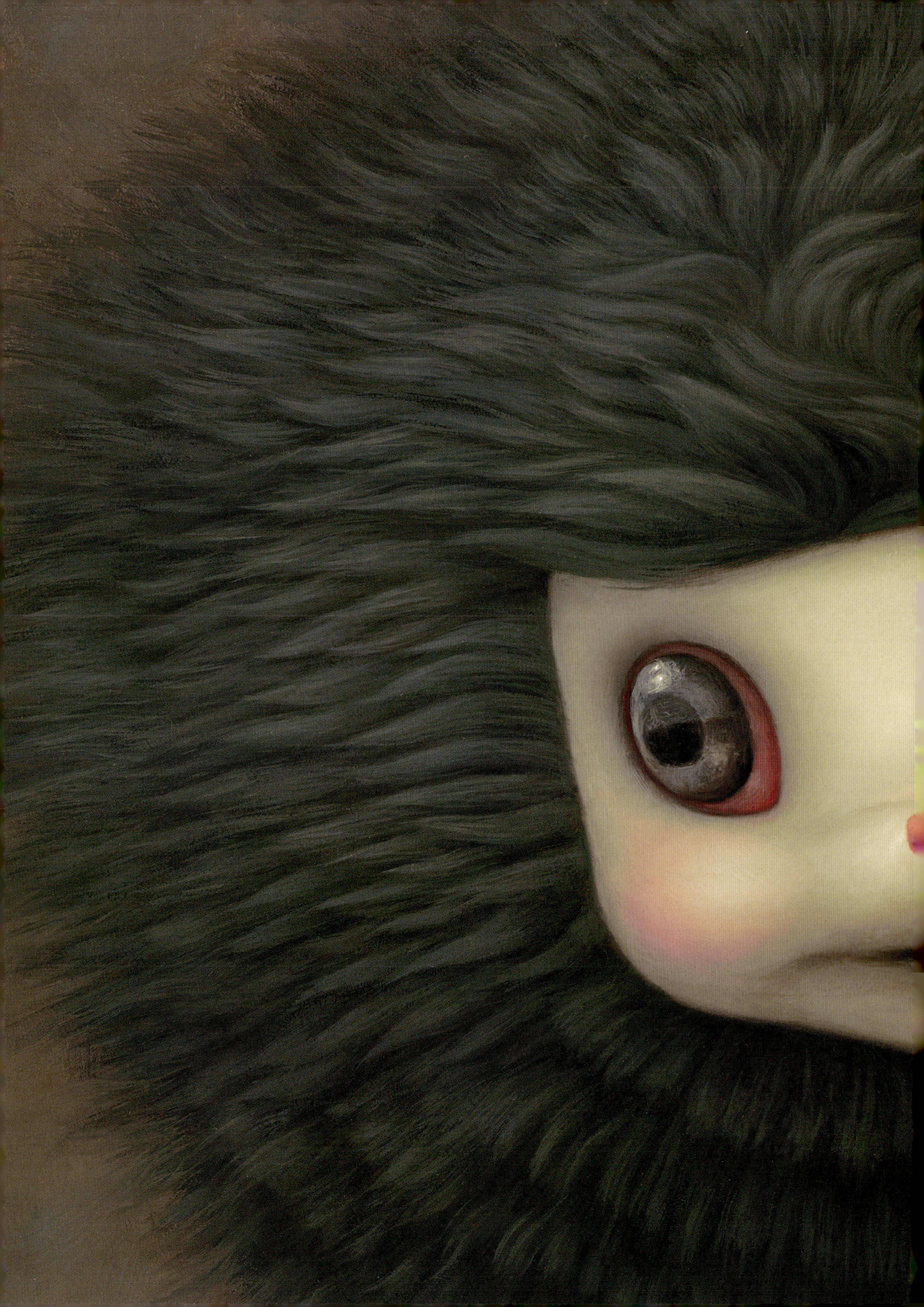

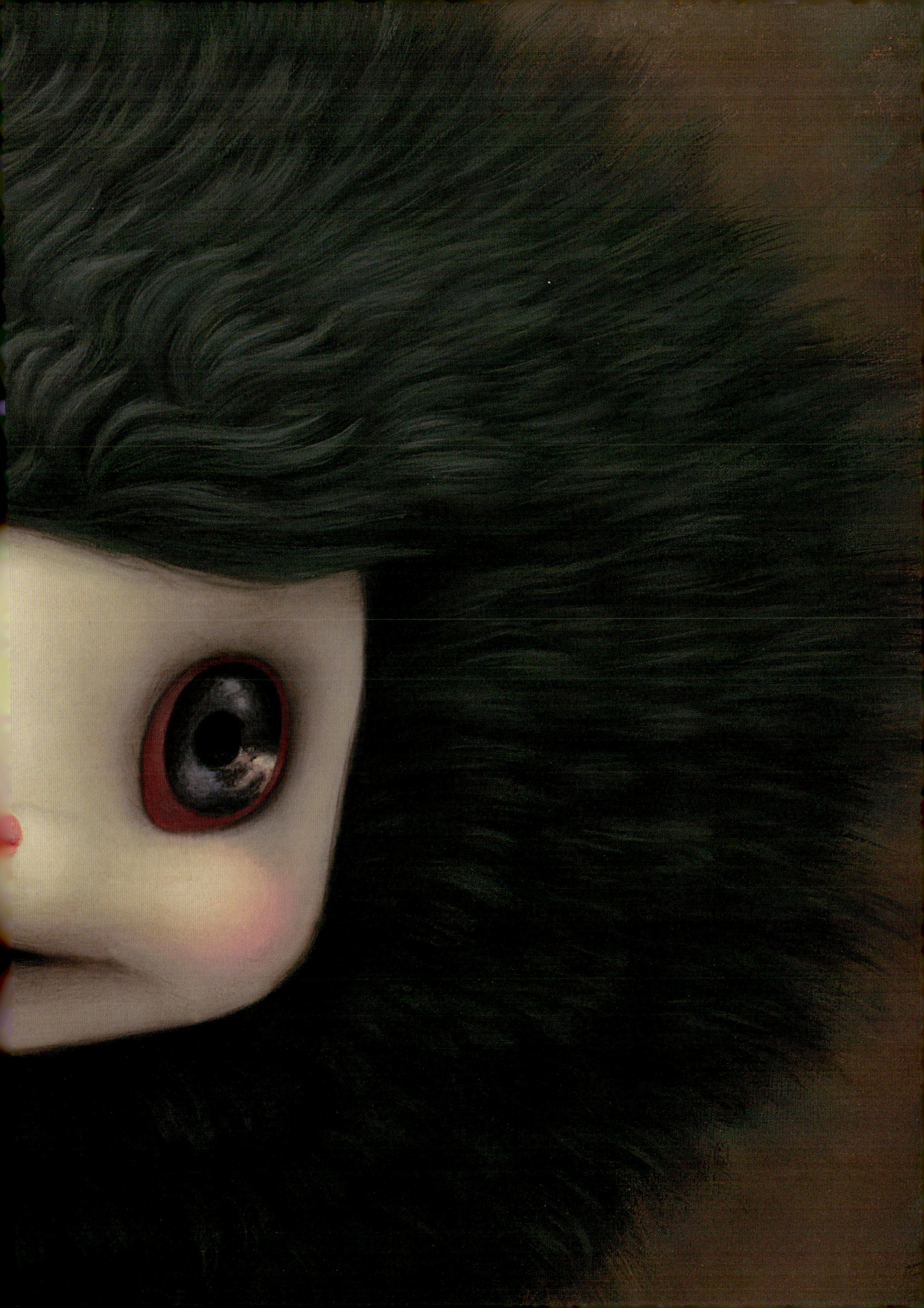

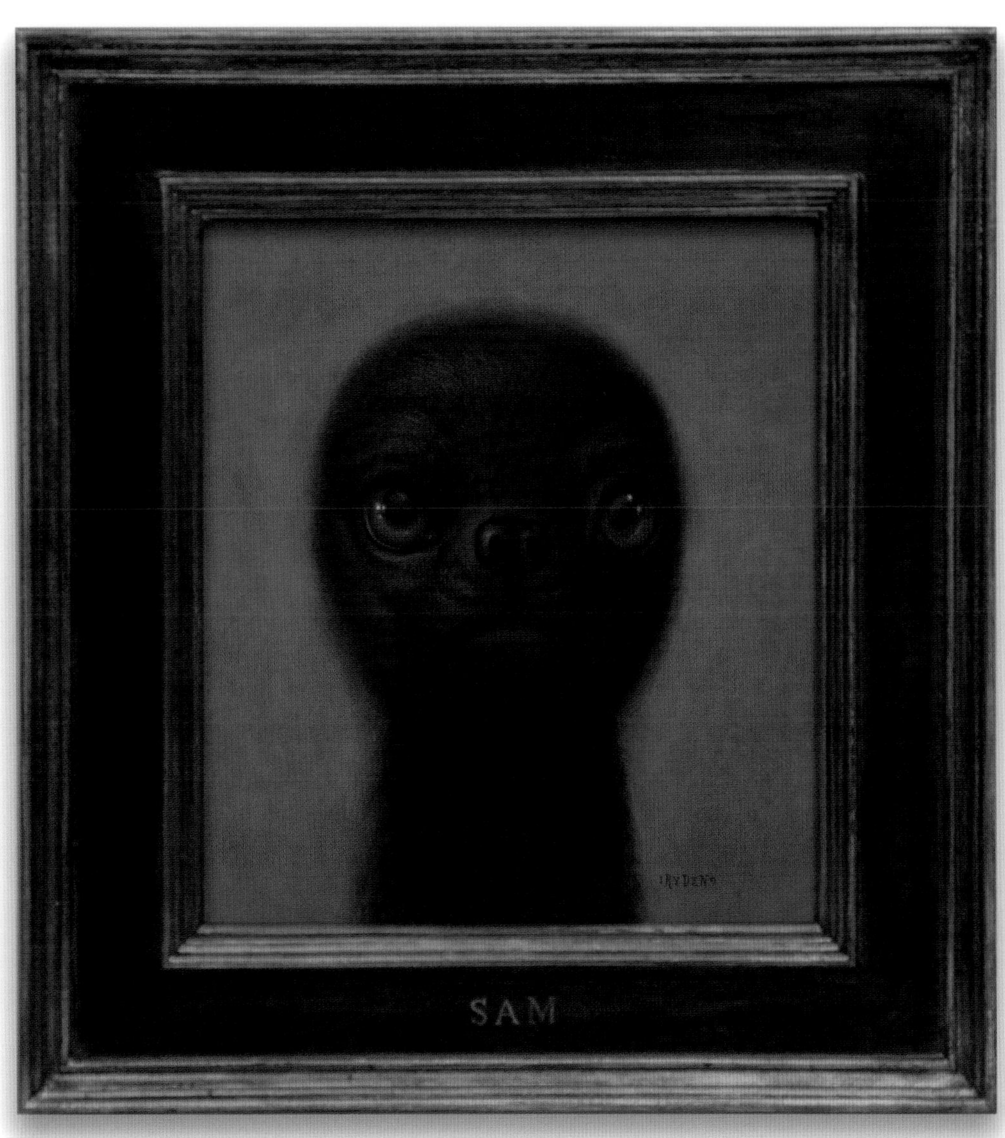
SAM

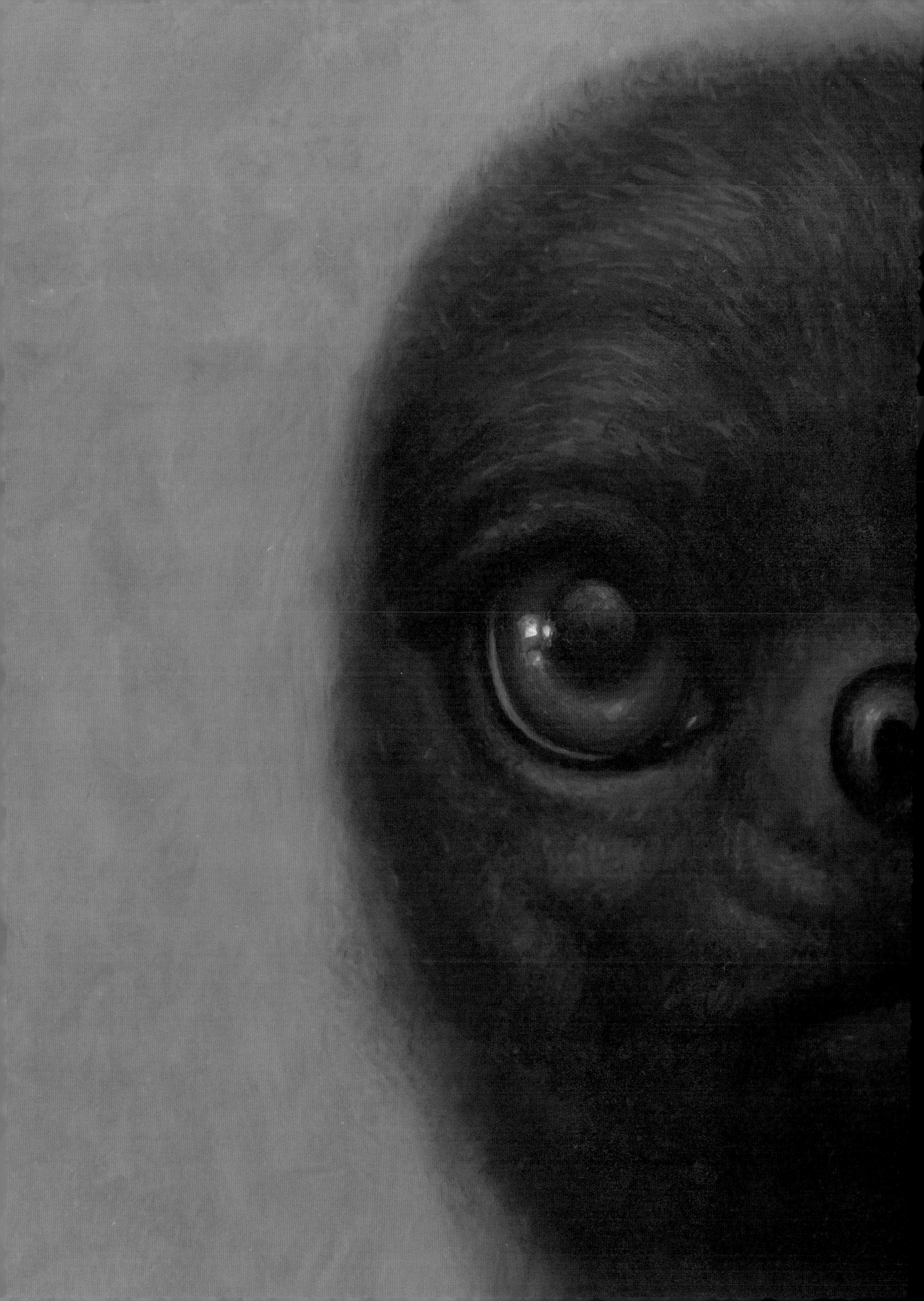

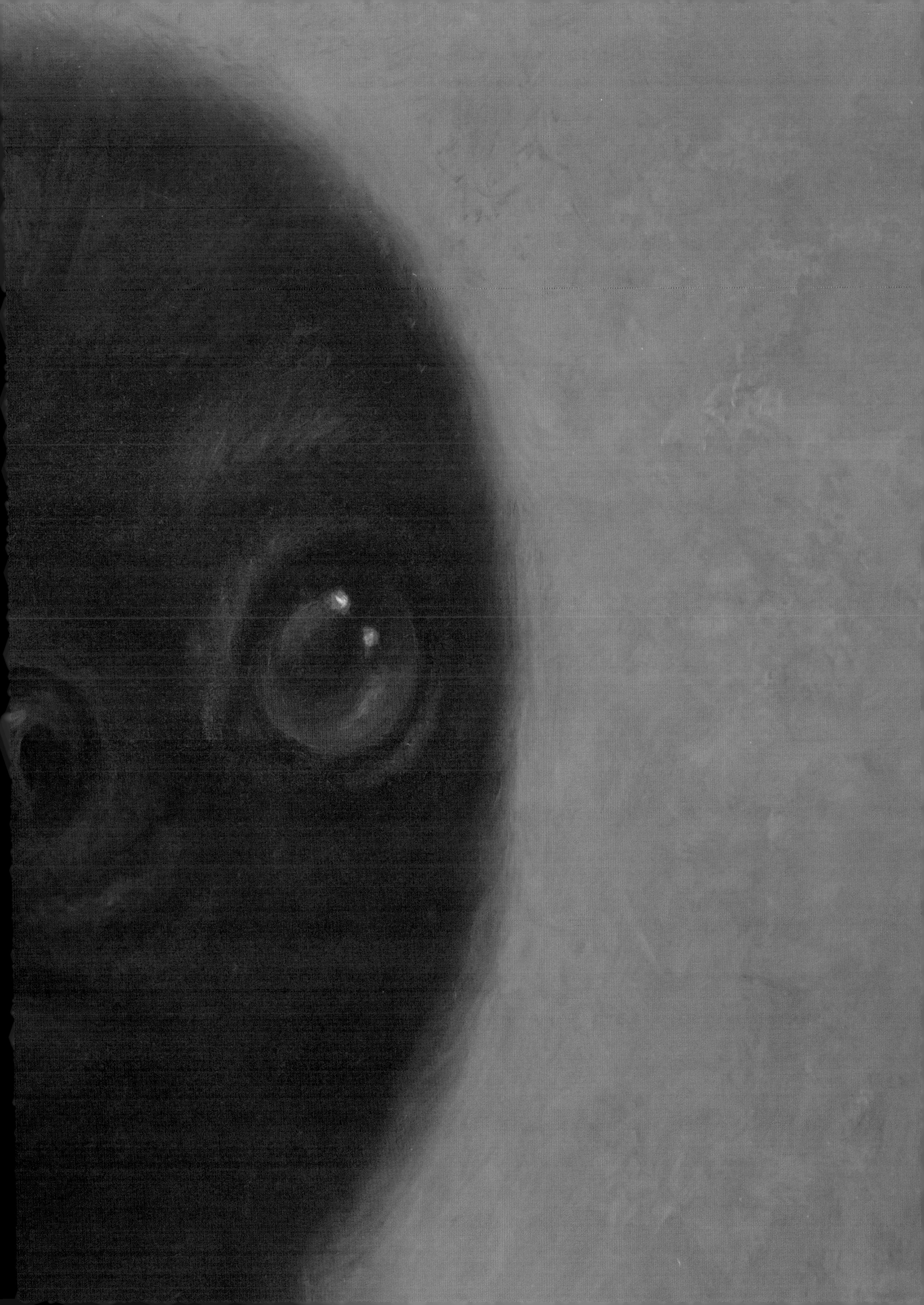

No 142

NUMBAT

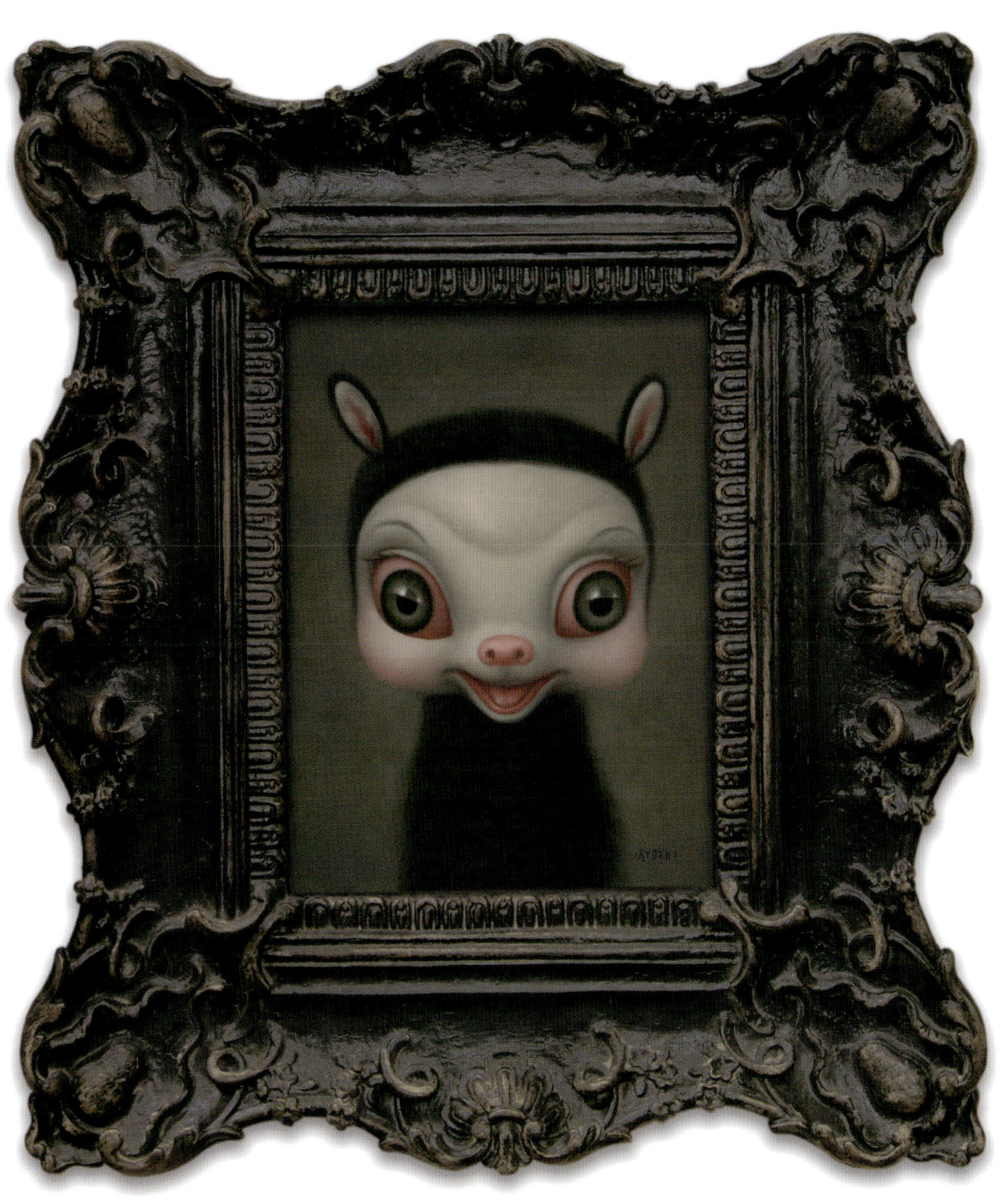

No 143

MAGIC BEAR

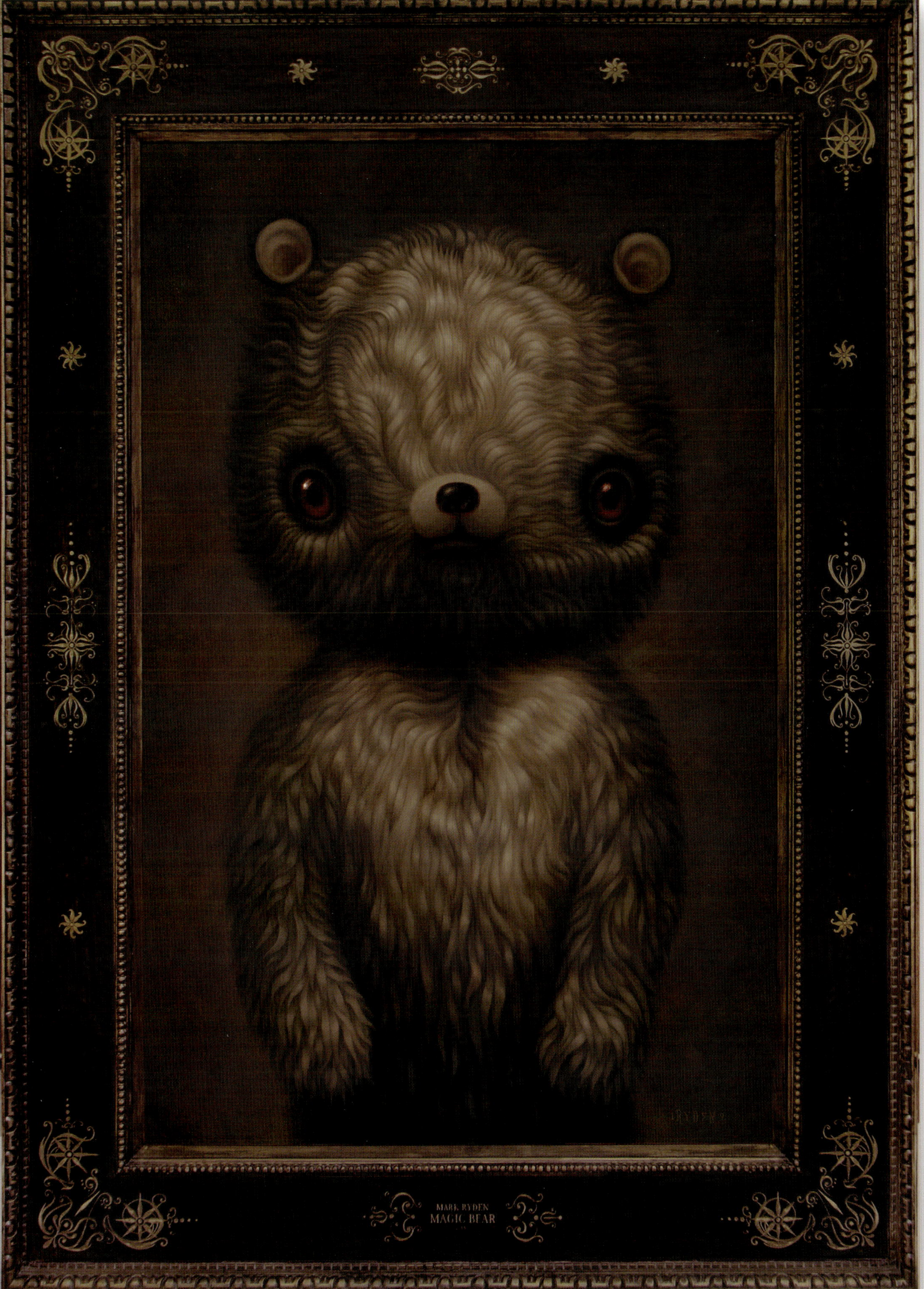

MARK RYDEN
MAGIC BEAR

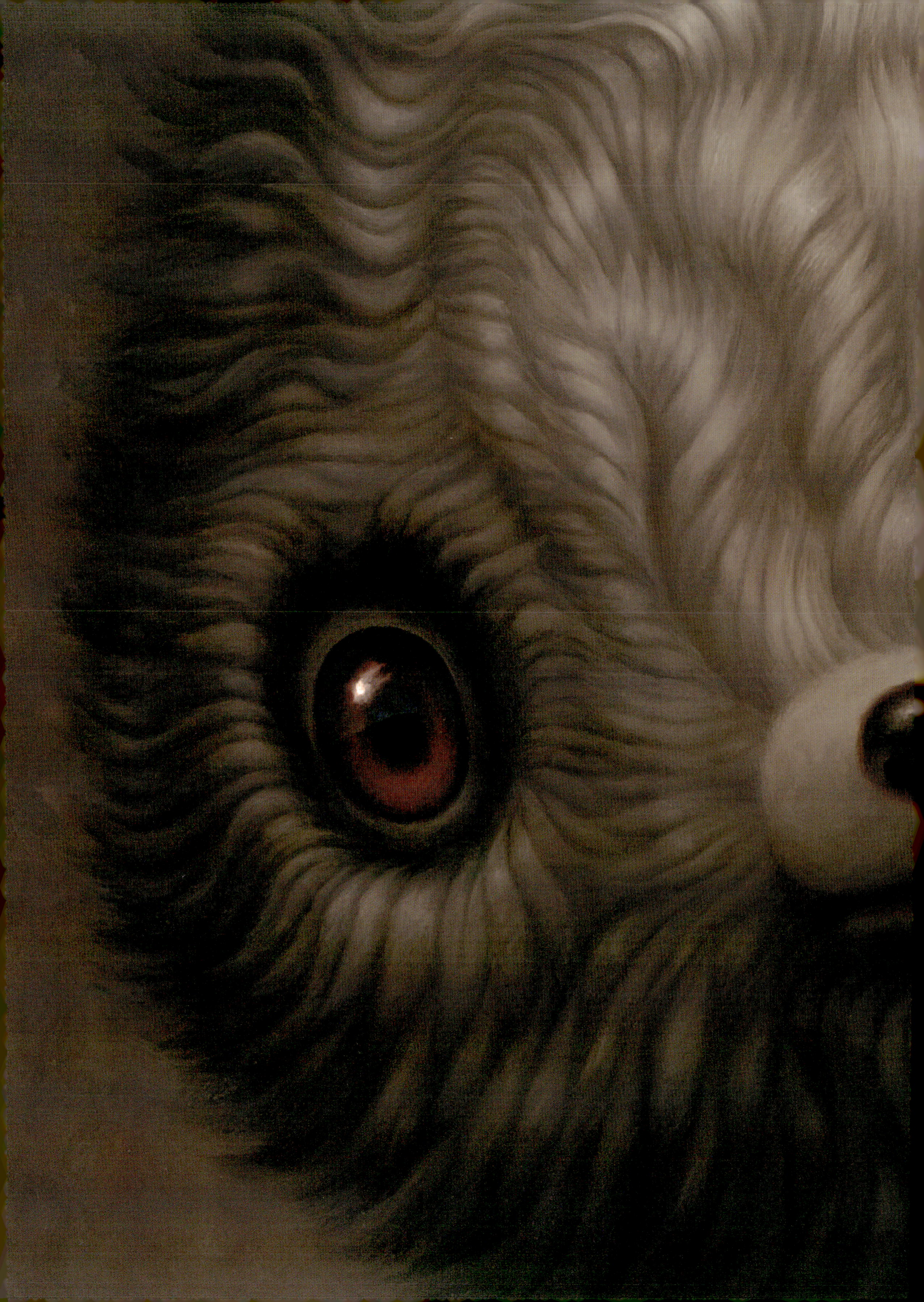

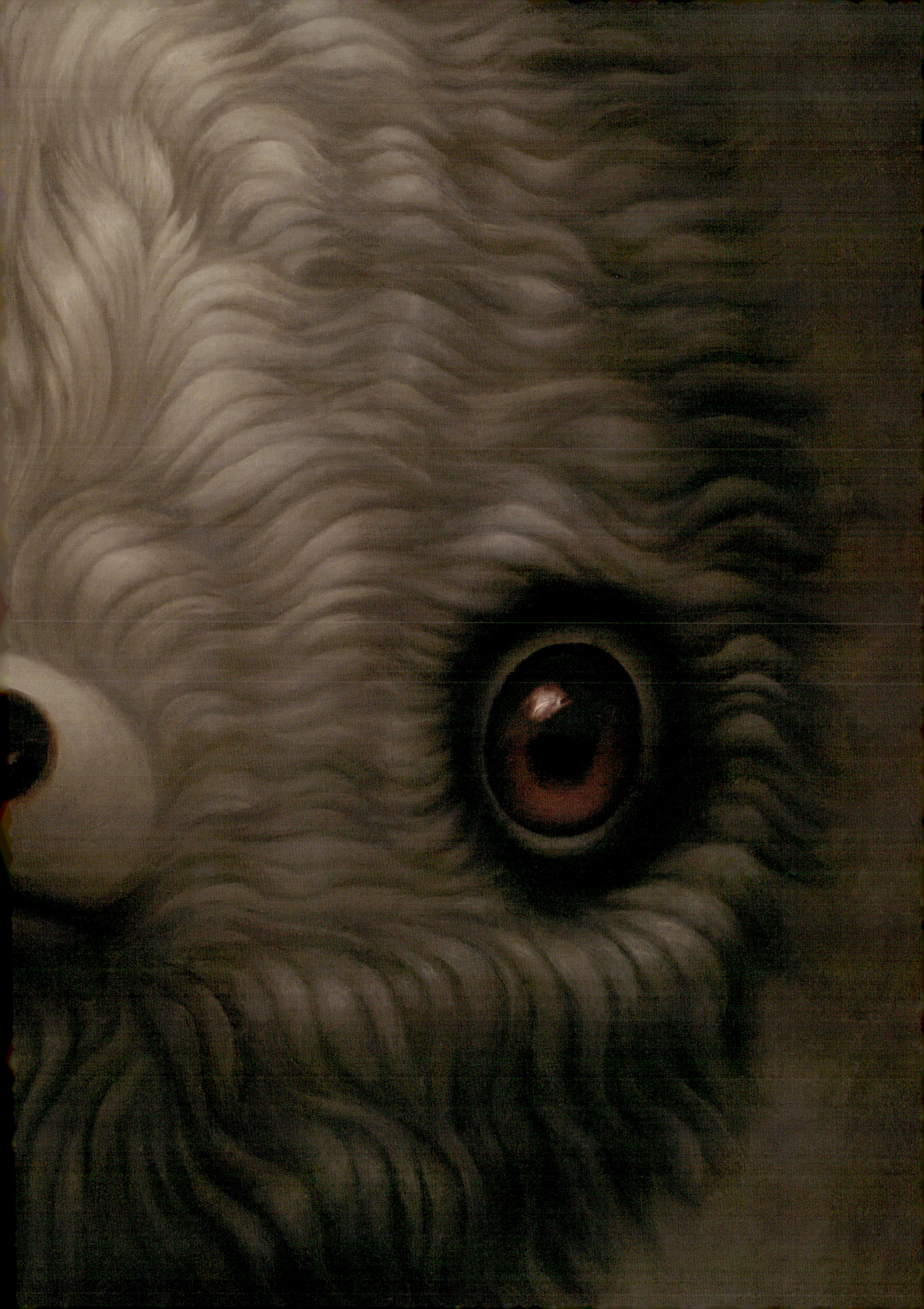

No 144
BEE

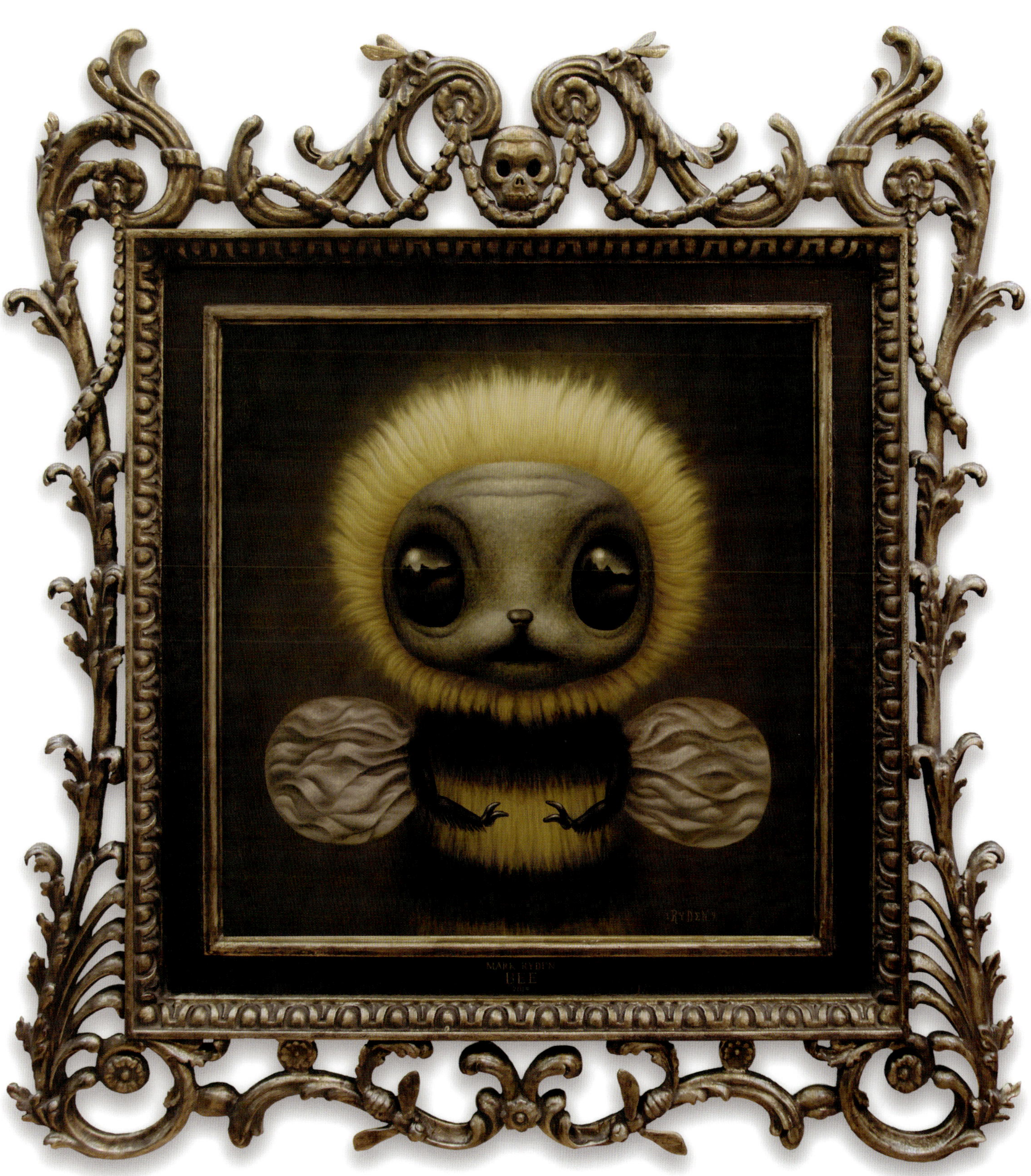

MARK RYDEN
BEE

No 145
PINK BUNNY

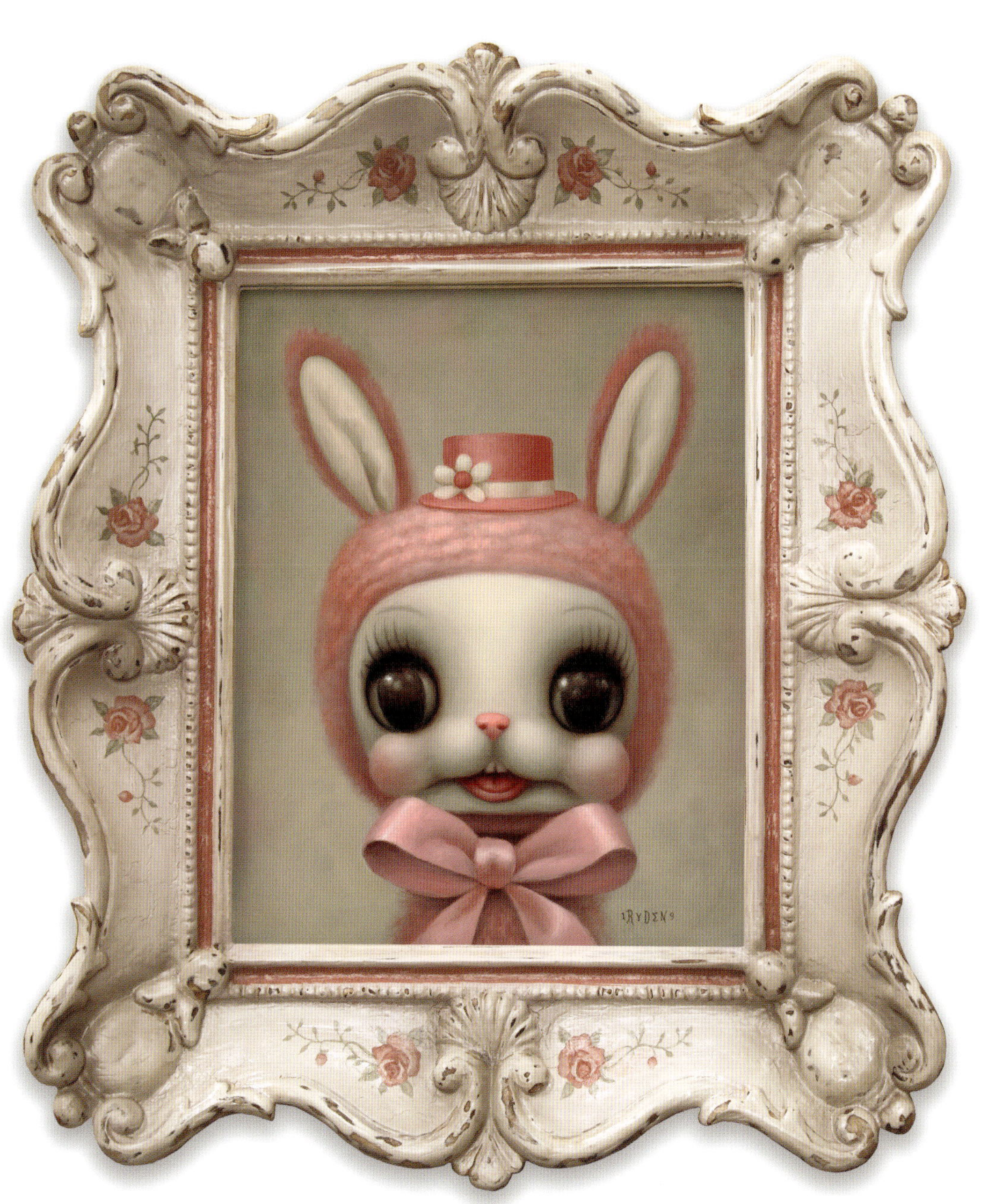

No 146
GREEN EYED YAK

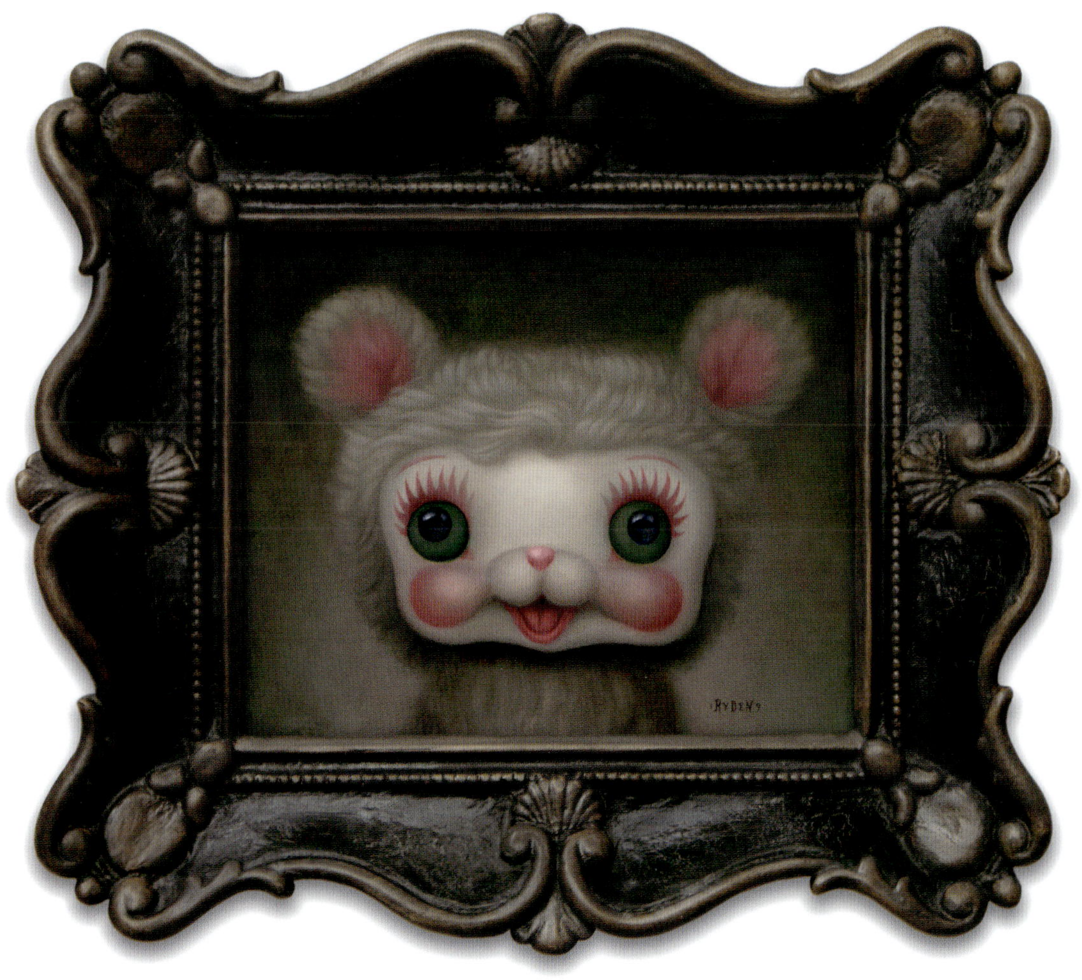

No 147

BLACK YAK

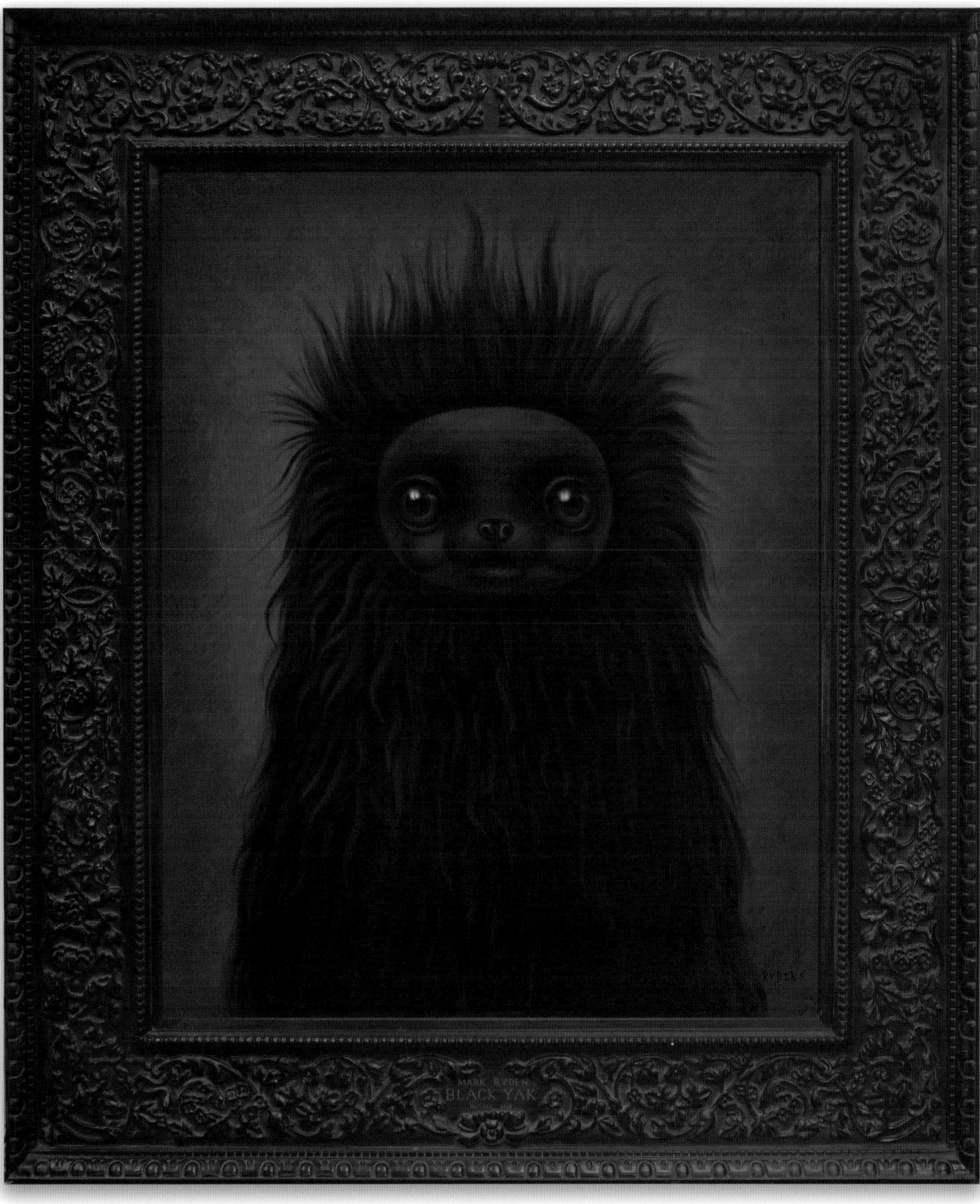
MARK RYDEN
BLACK YAK

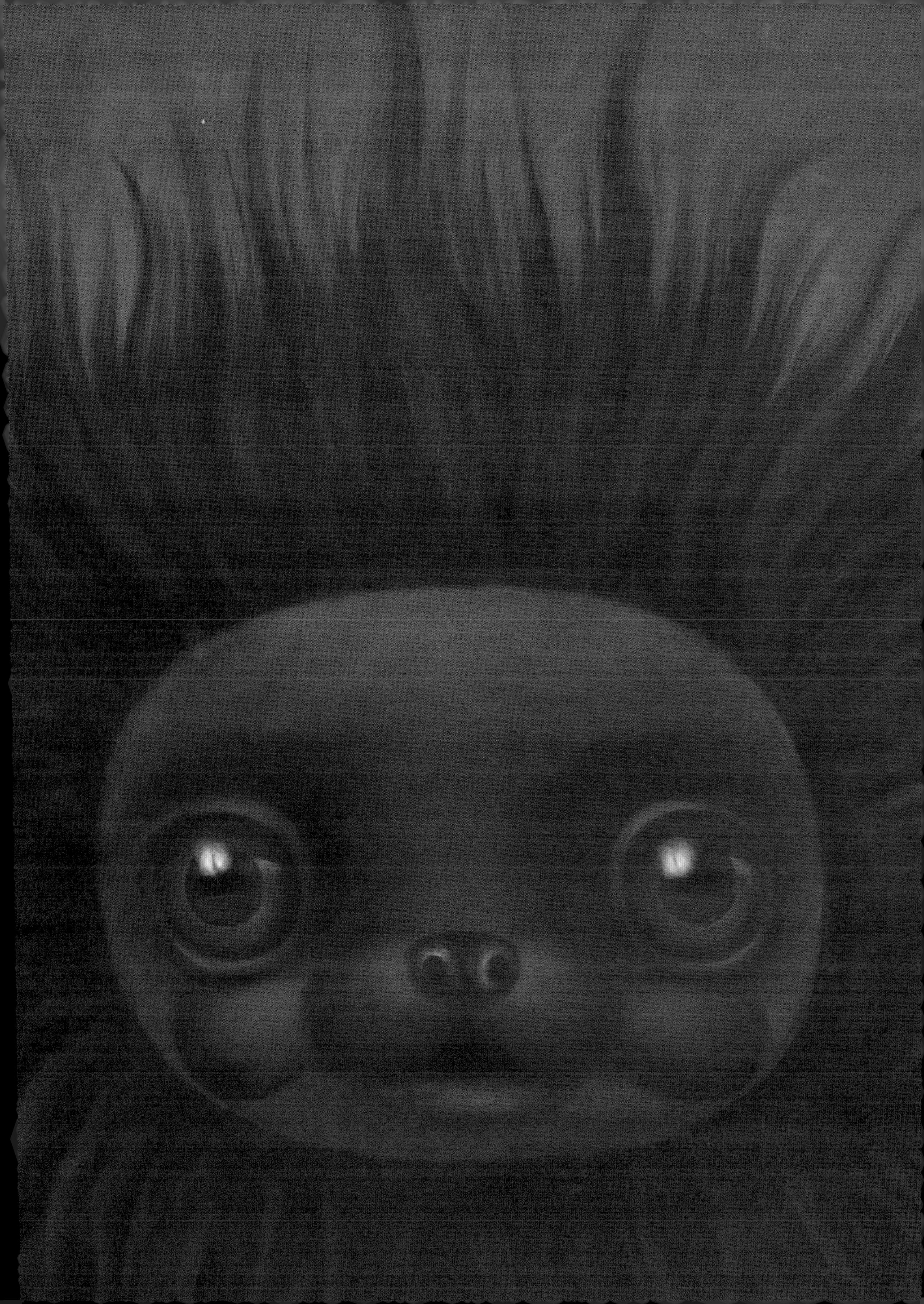

No 148

MESSENGER

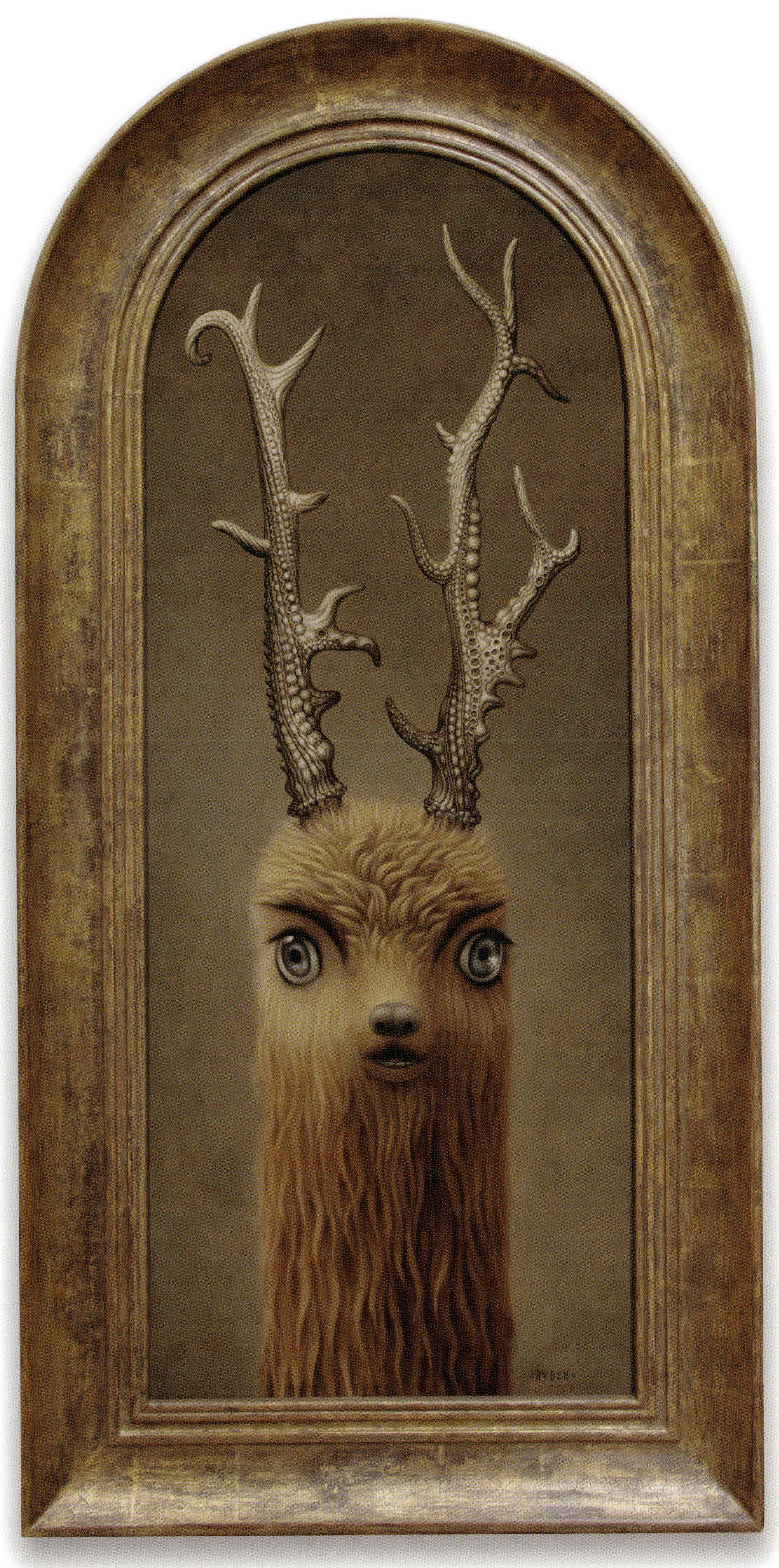

No 149
THE STOAT

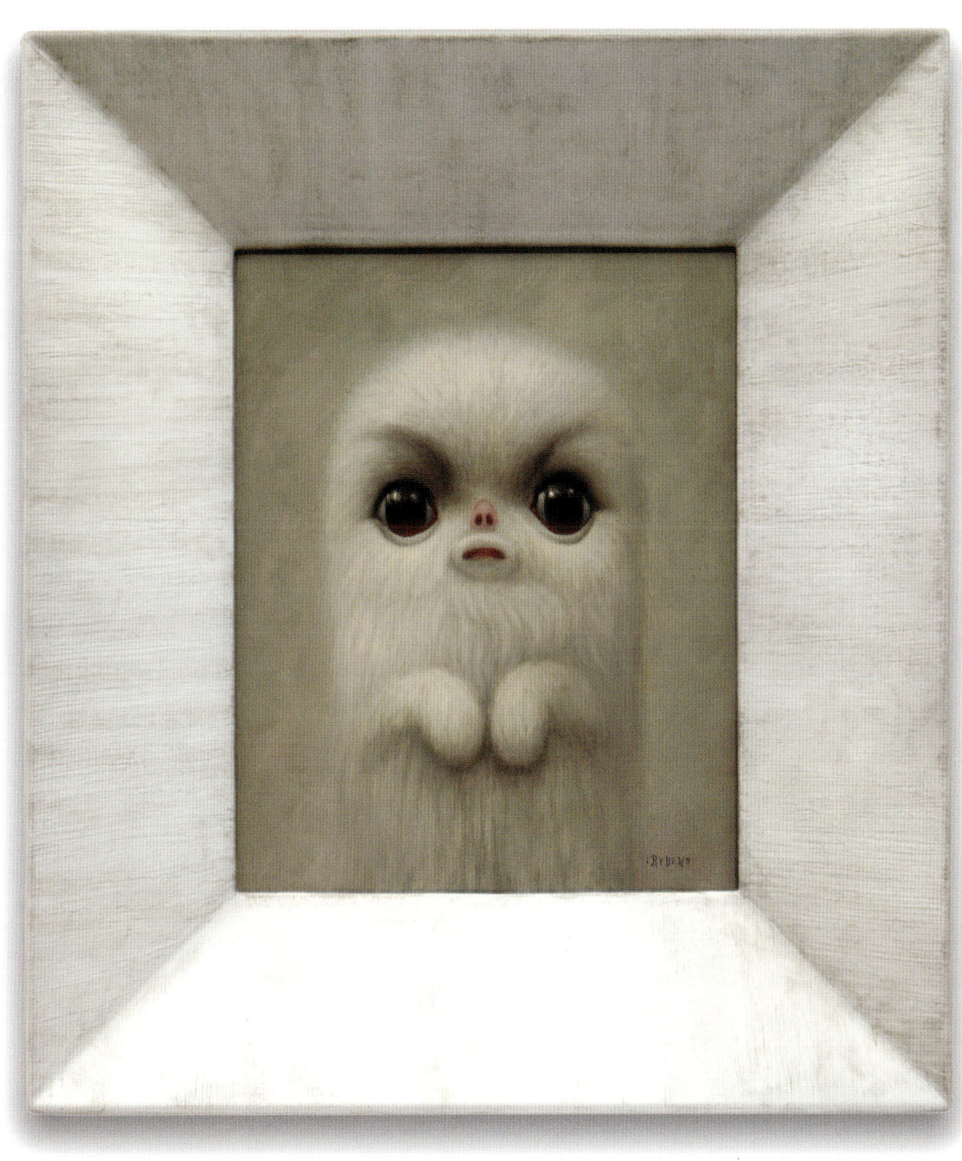

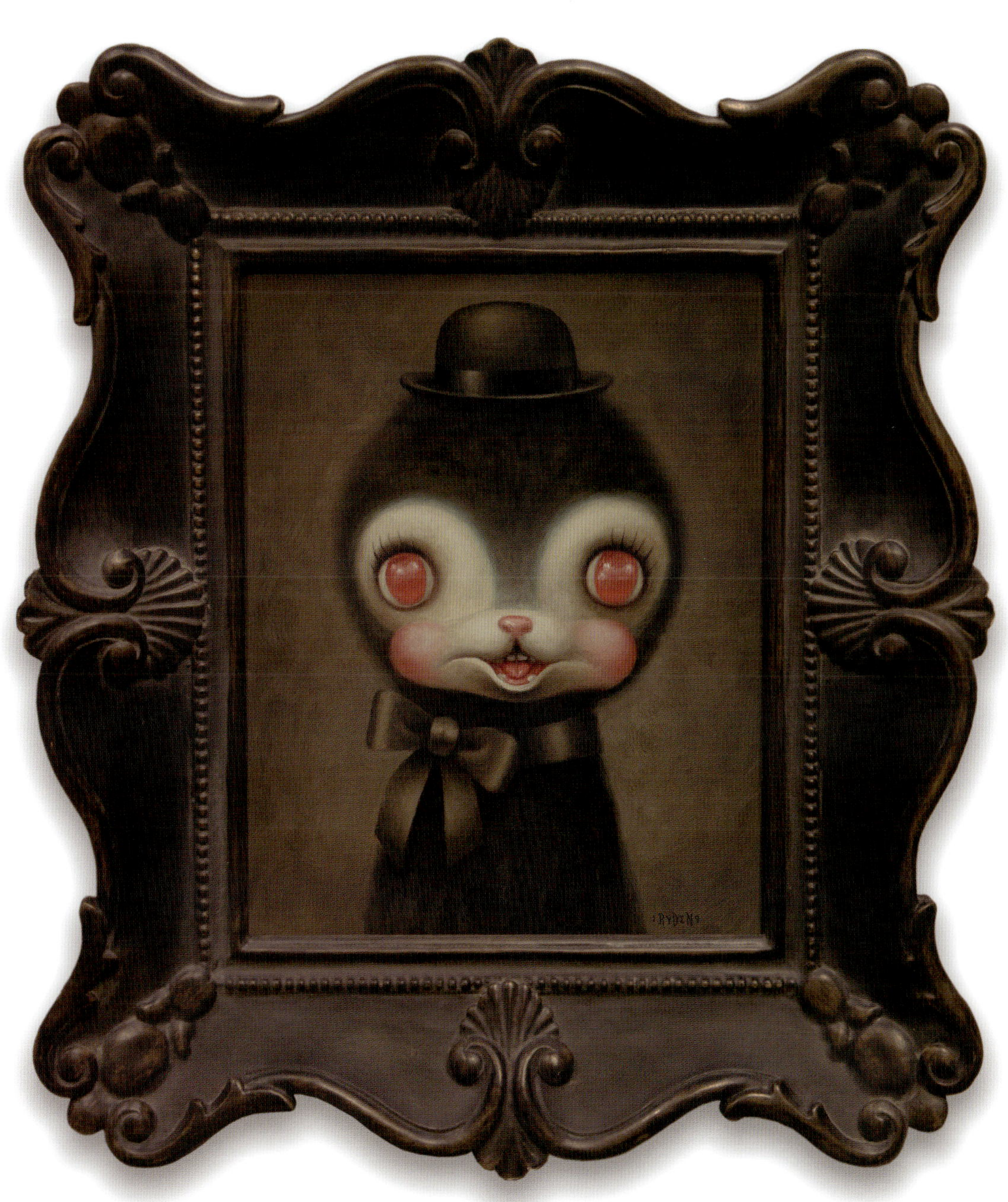

No 151

JACK RABBIT

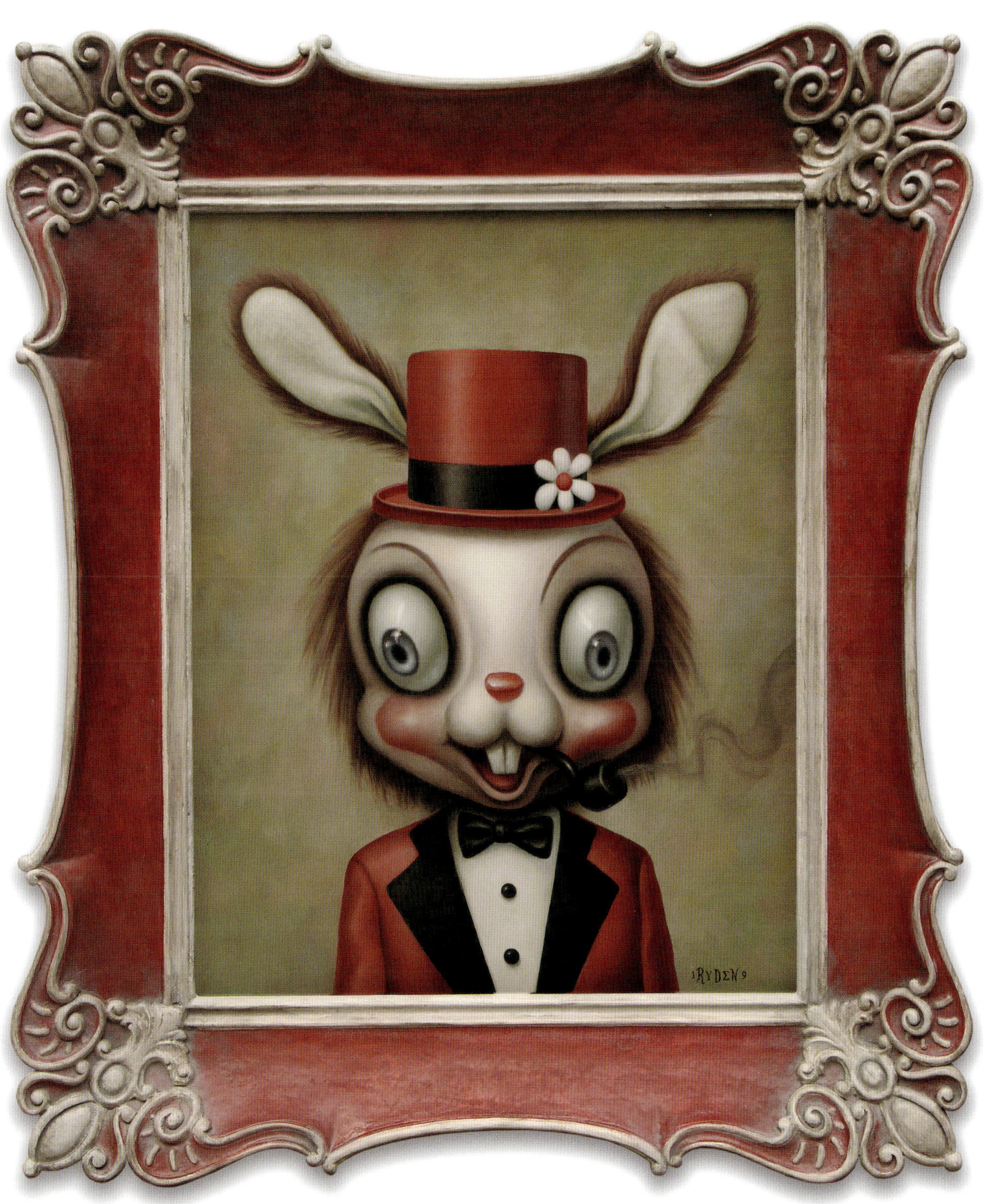

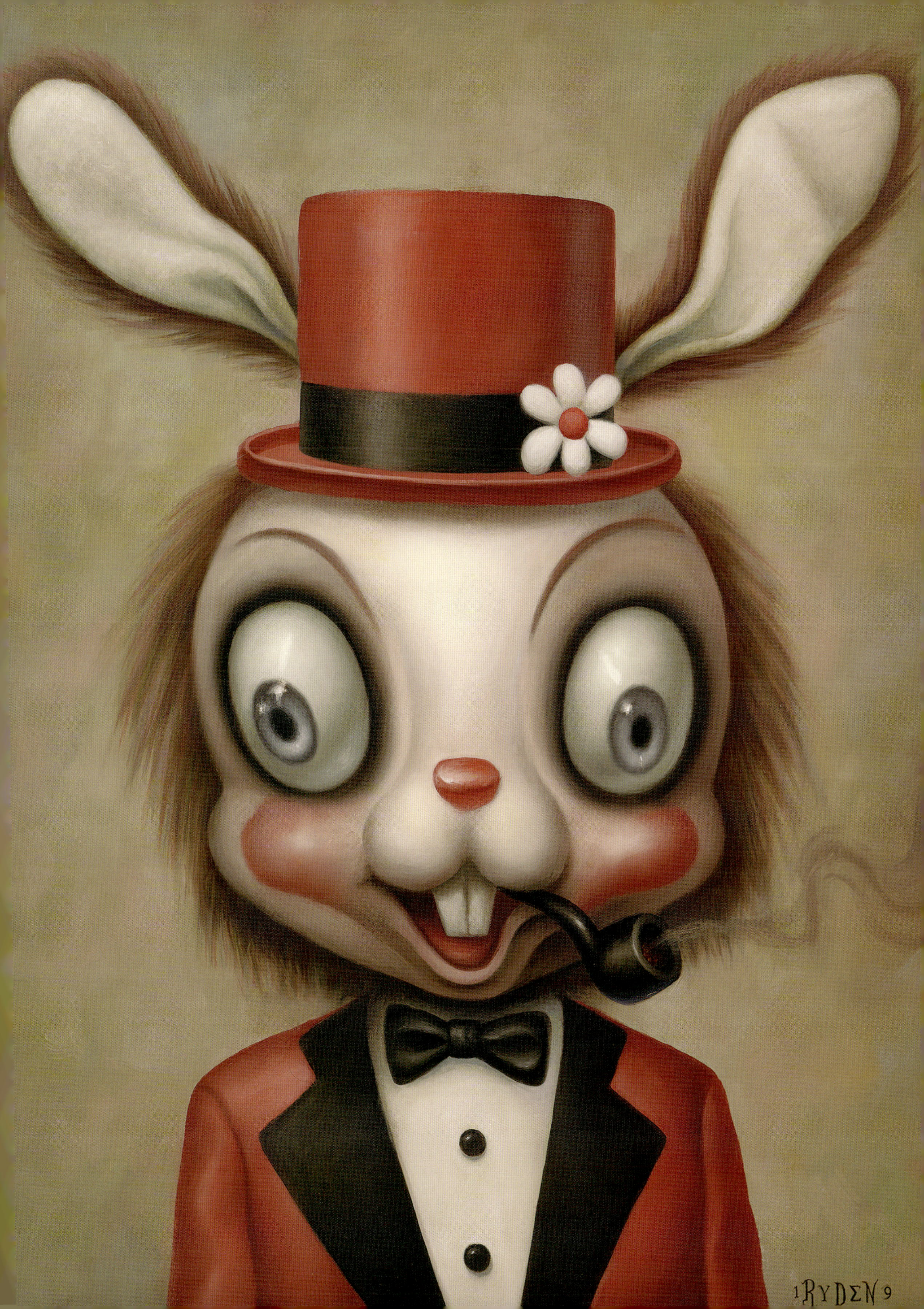

RYDEN

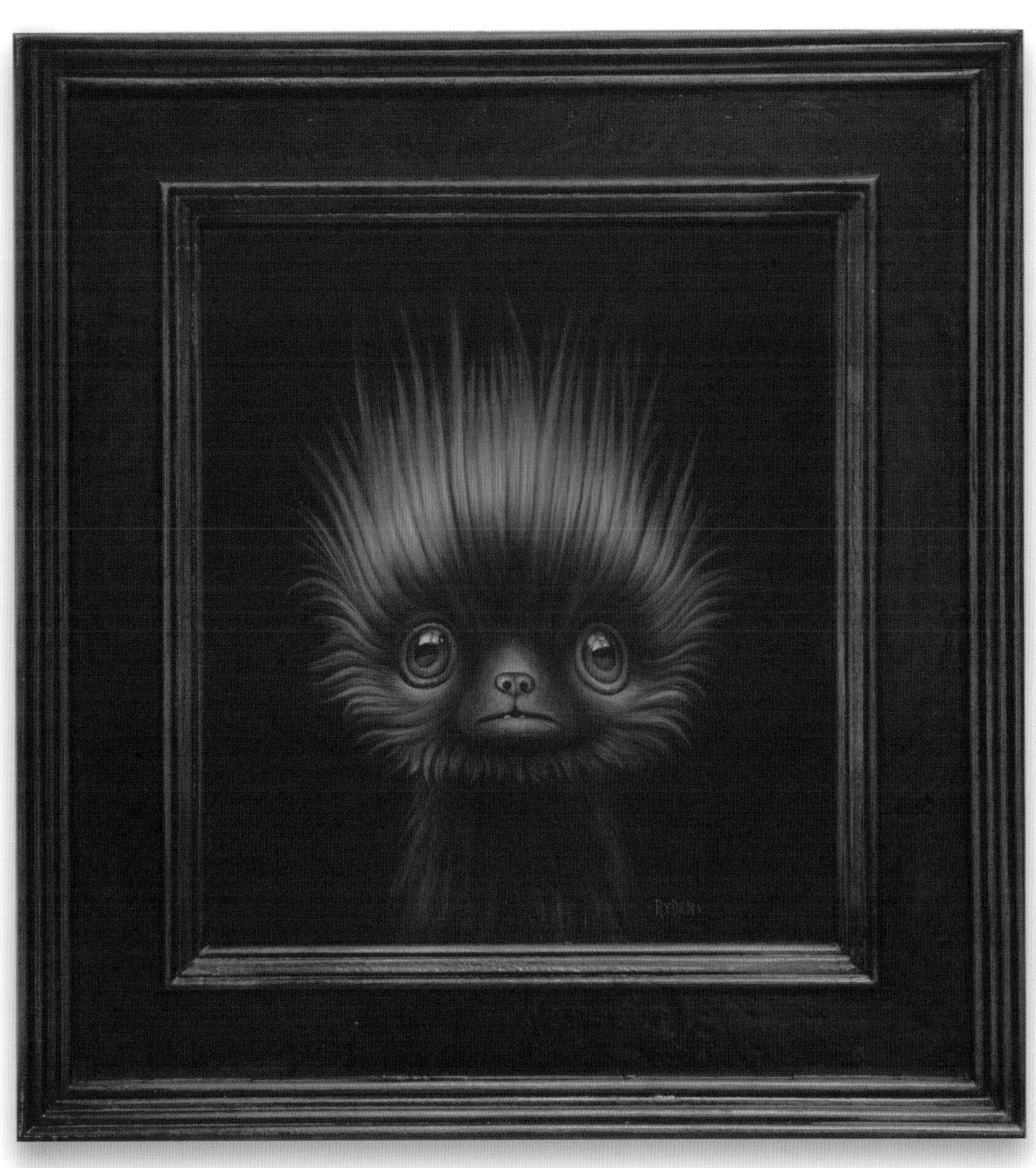

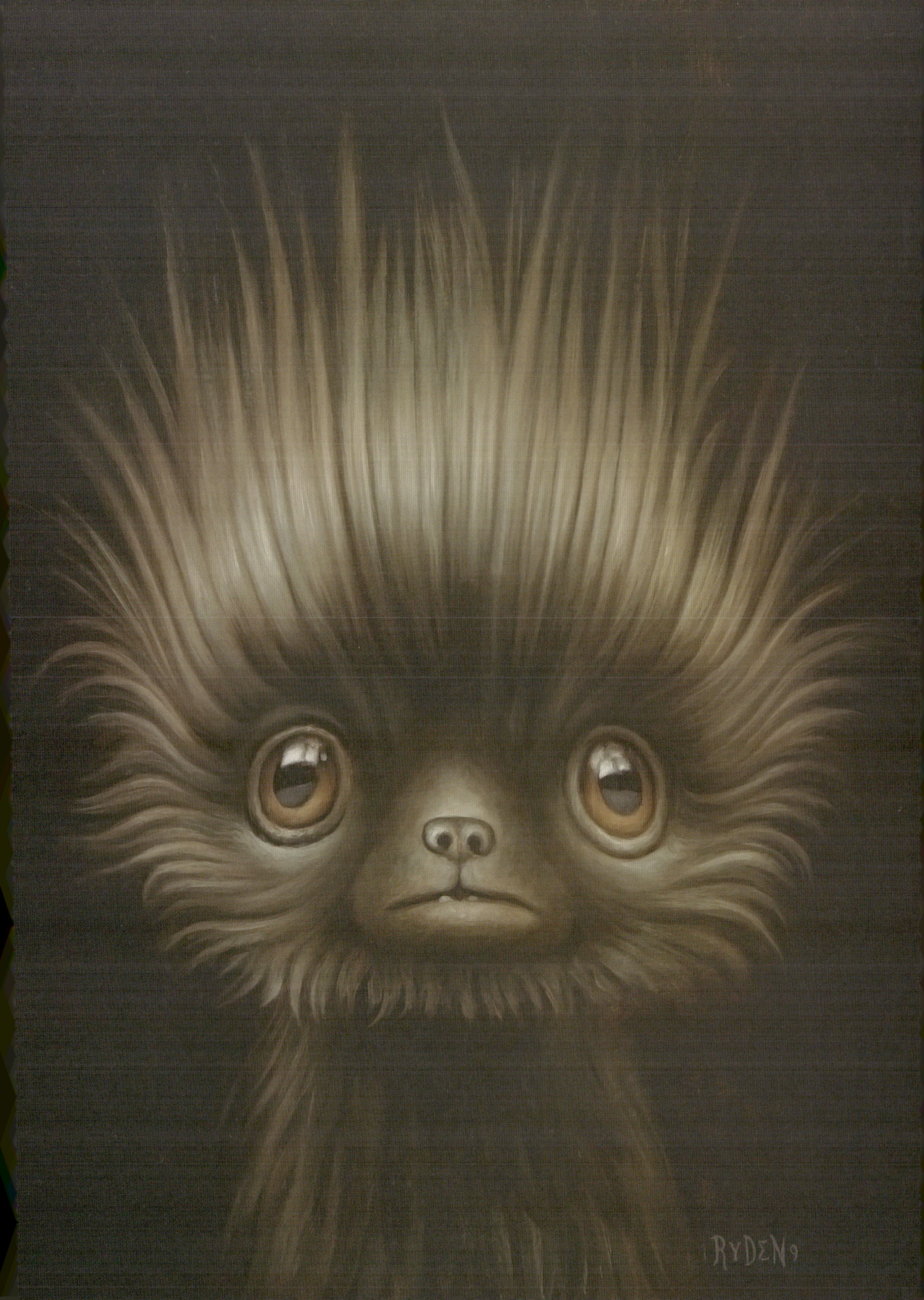

RYDEN9

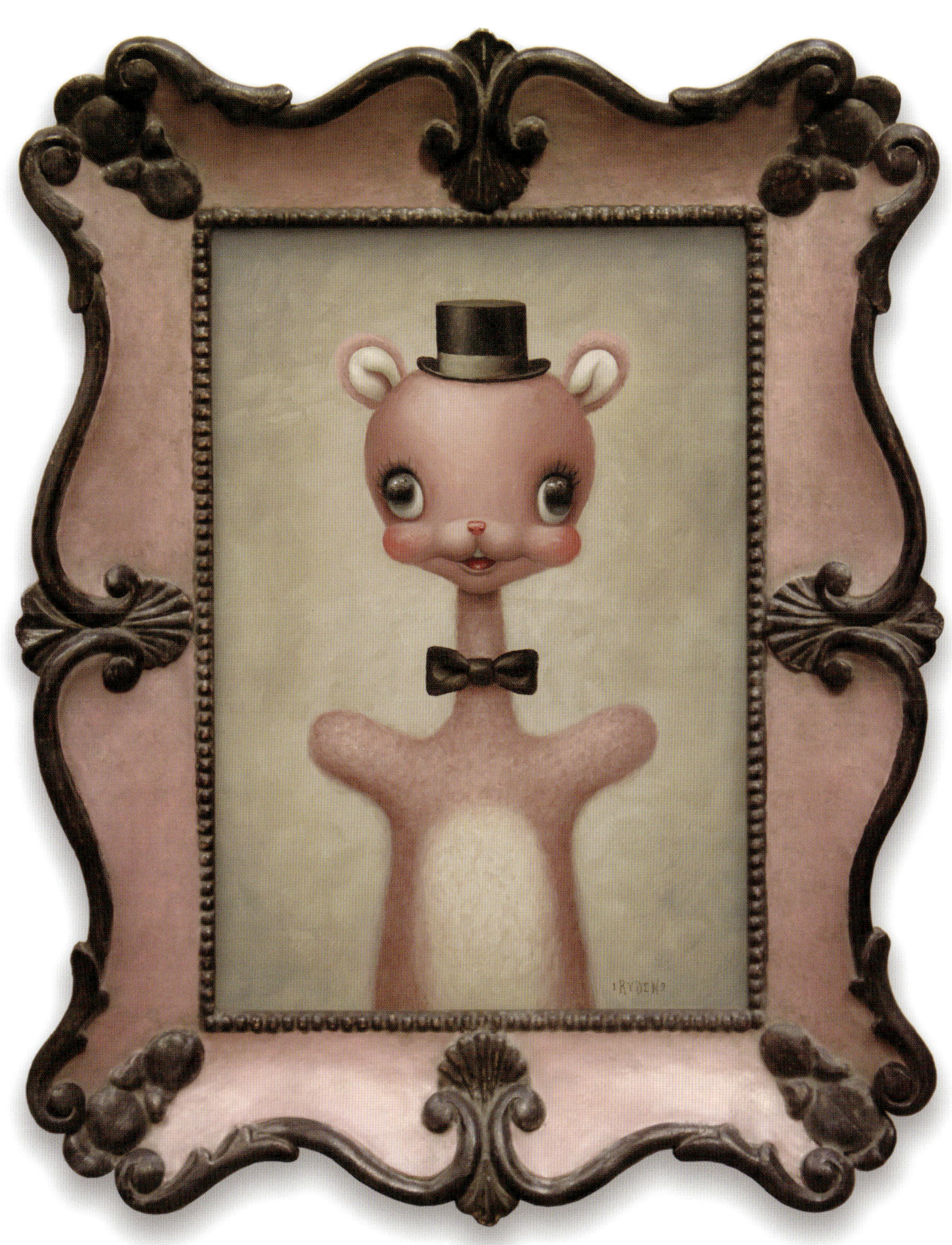

No 154
PINKIE

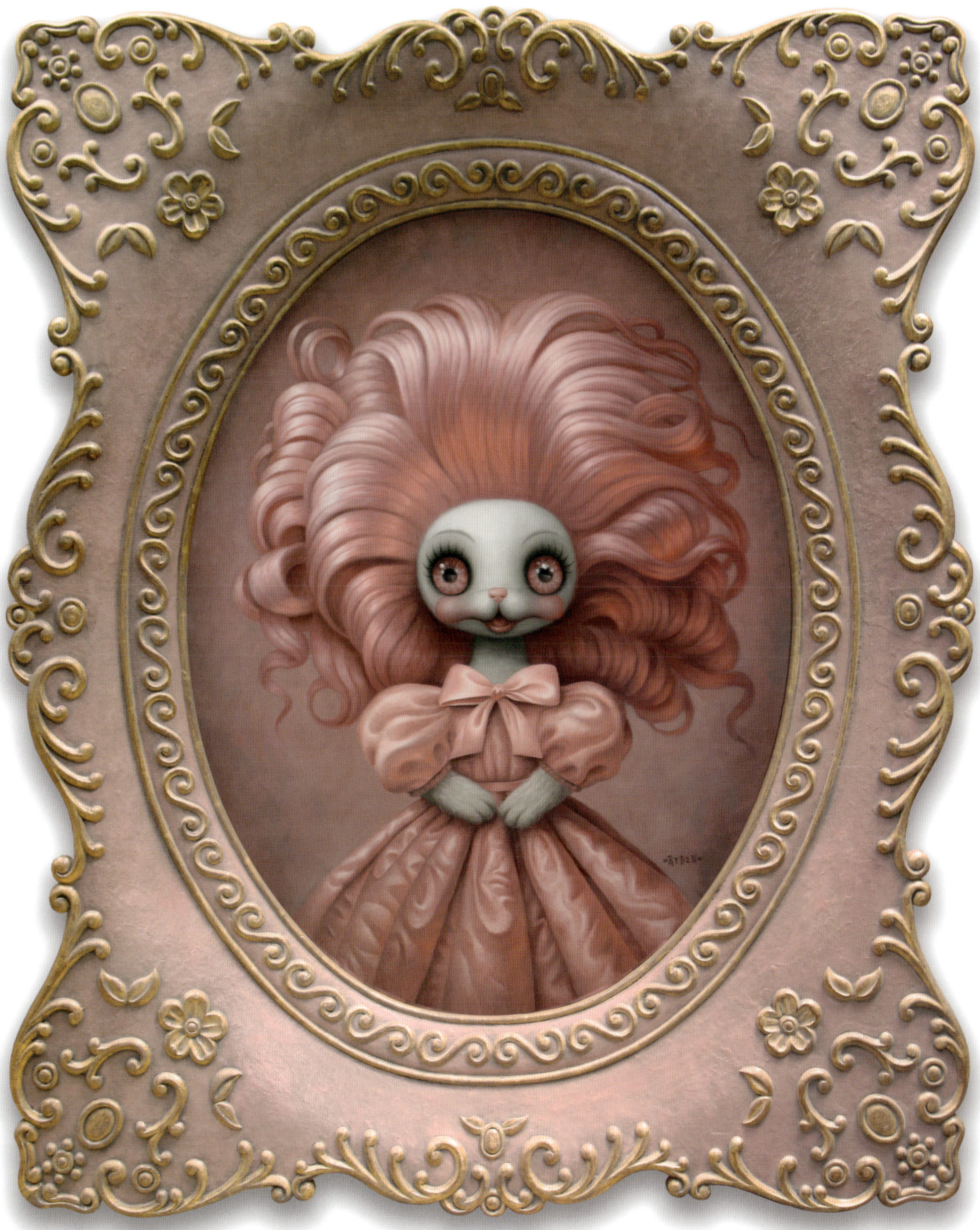

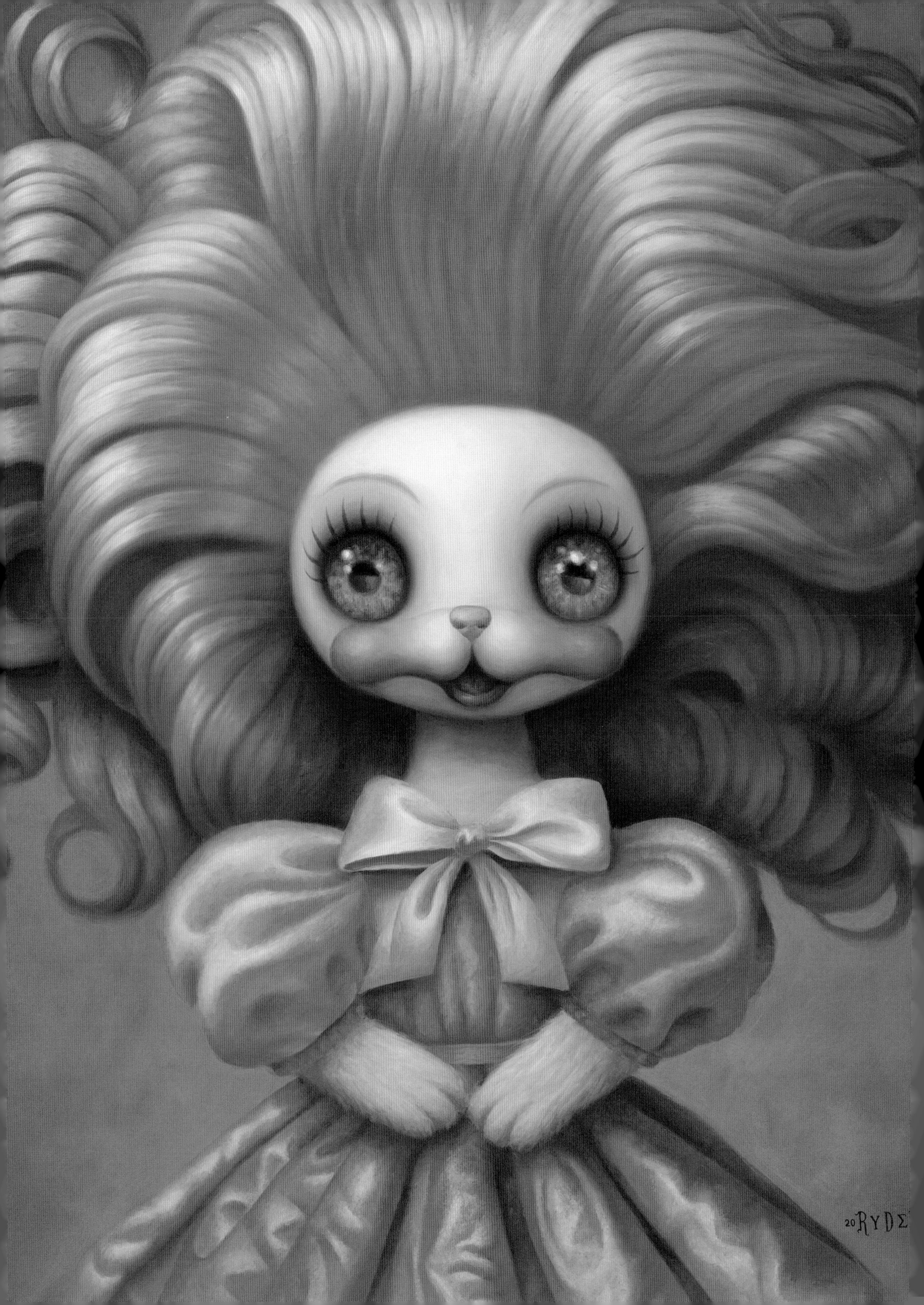

20RYDE

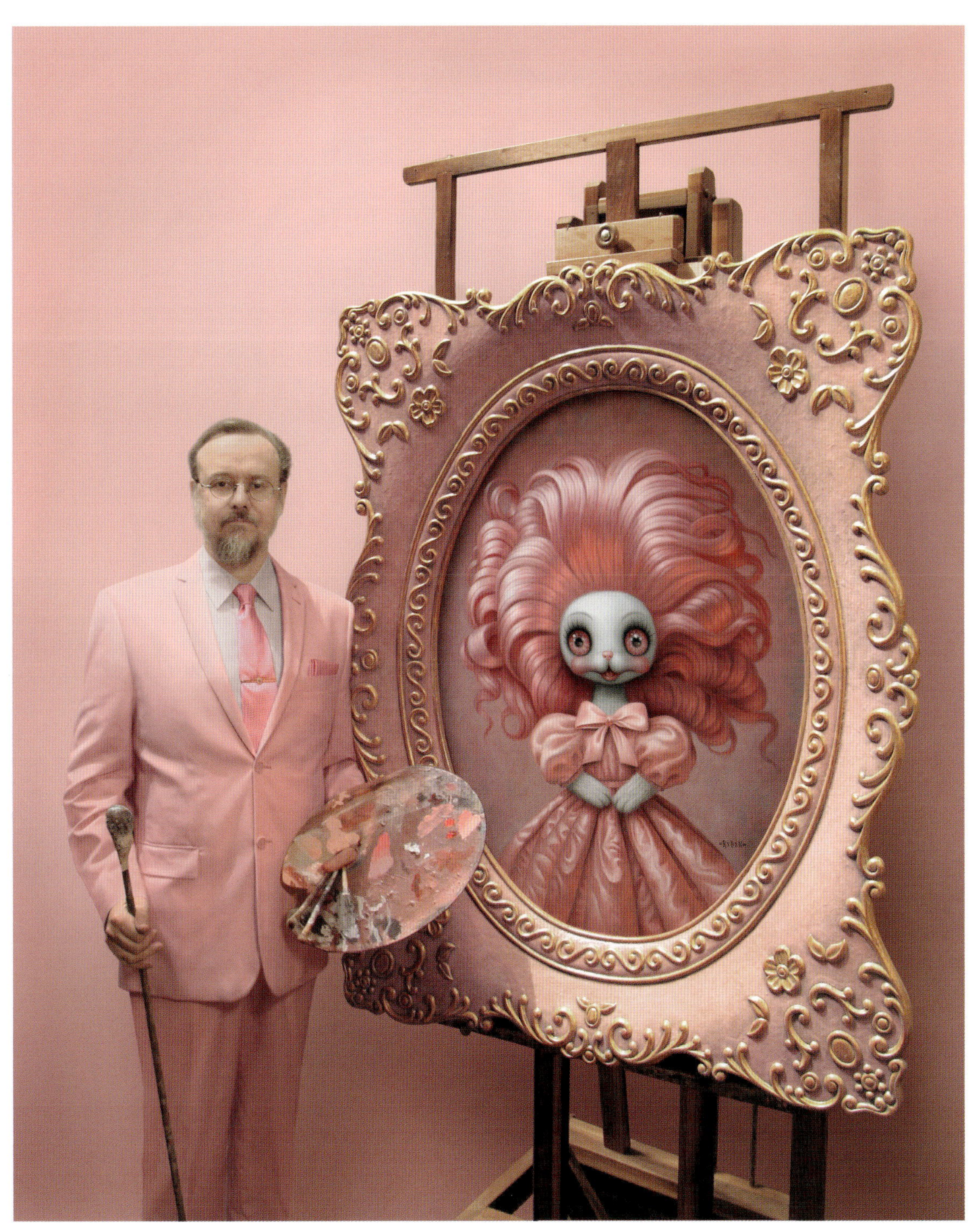

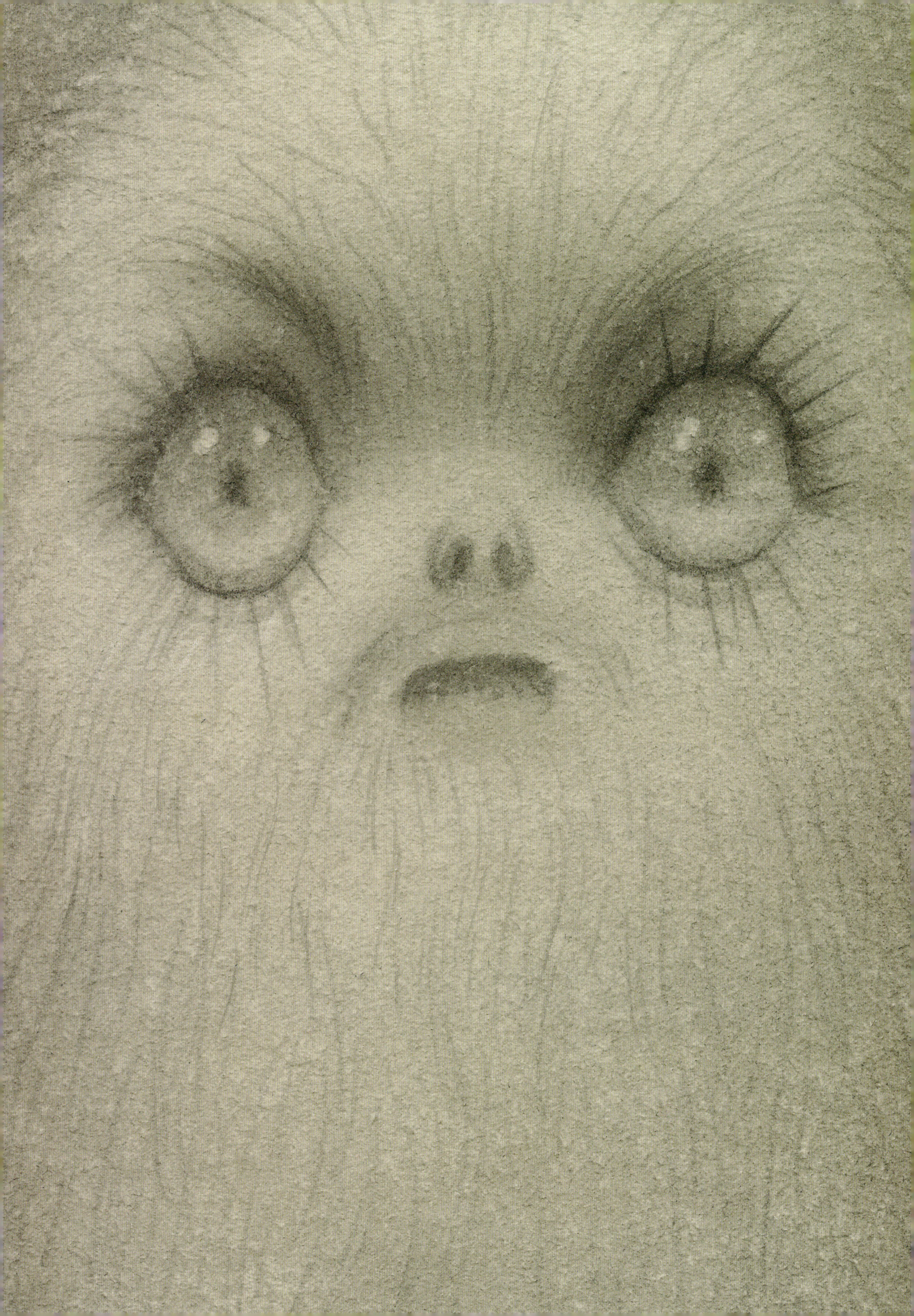

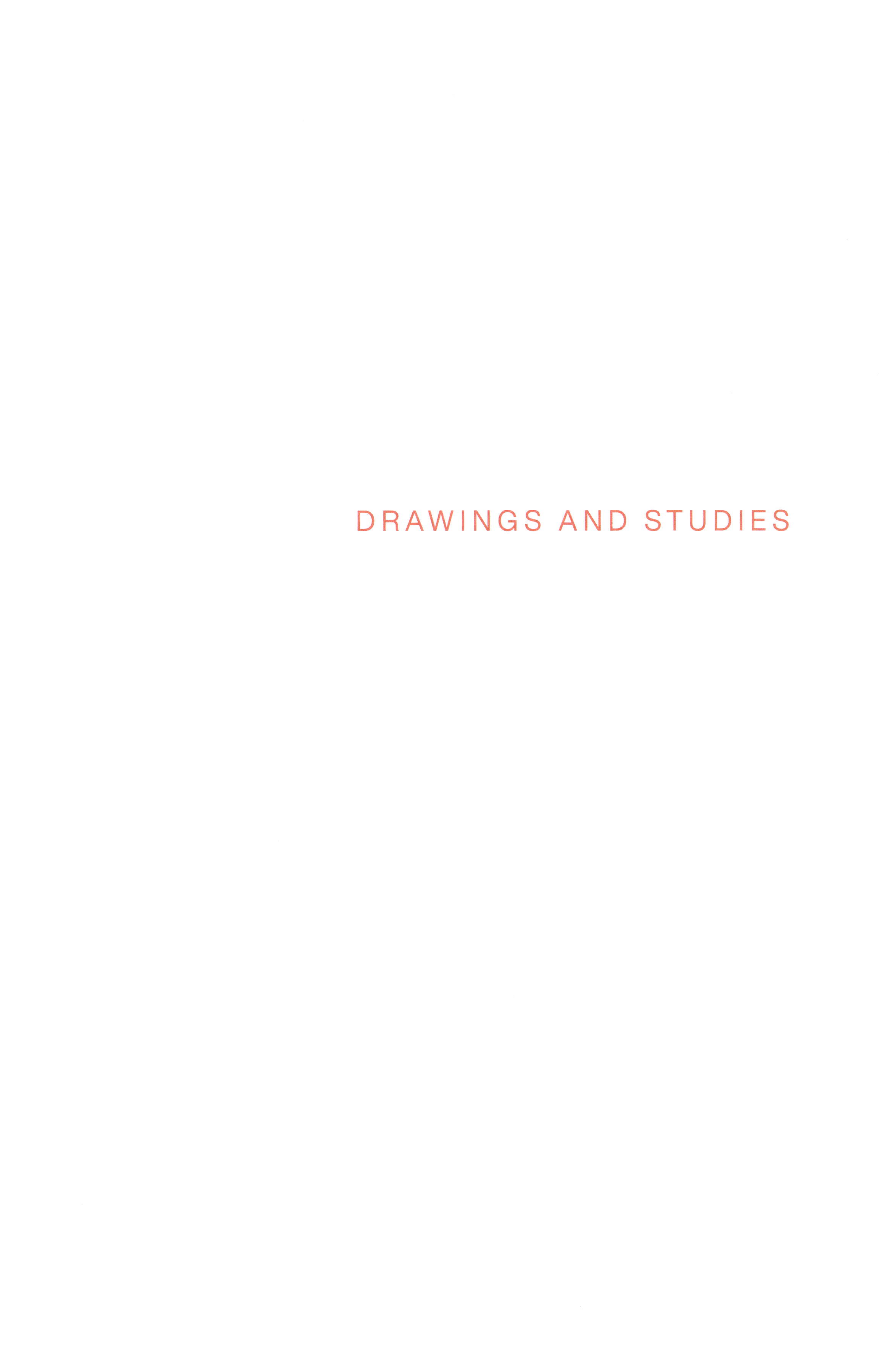

DRAWINGS AND STUDIES

DIVOC

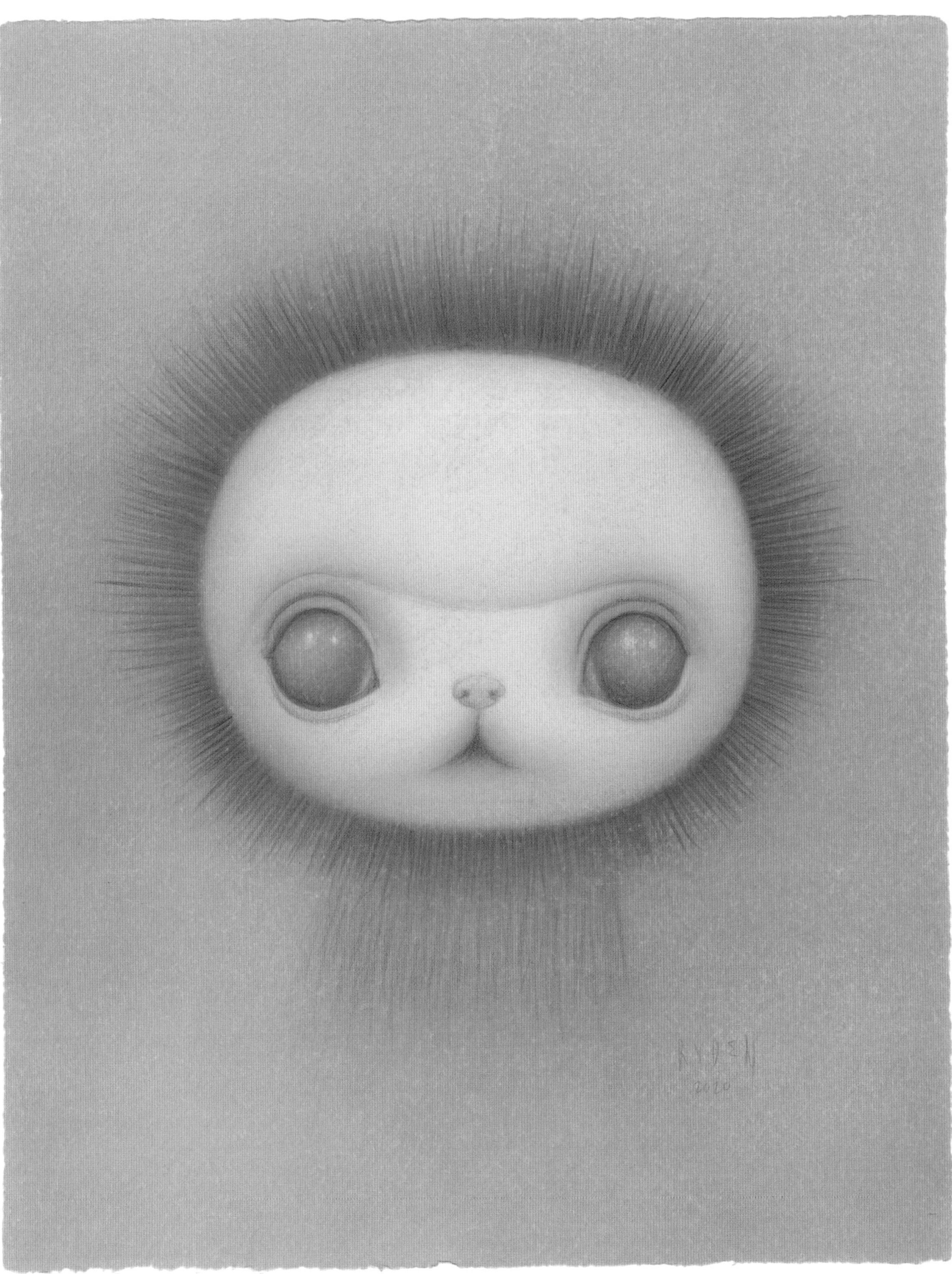

SHAG

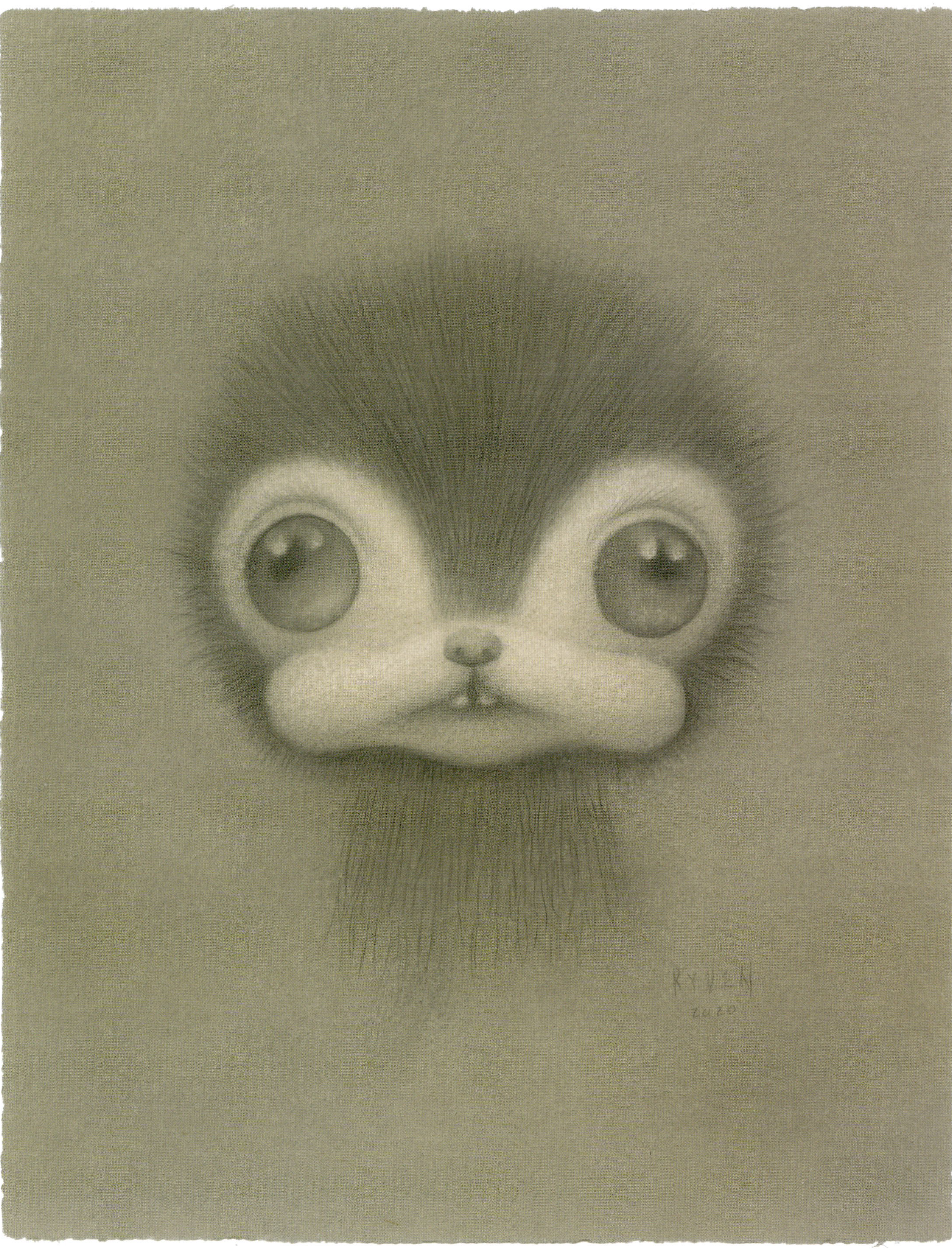

LOUIE

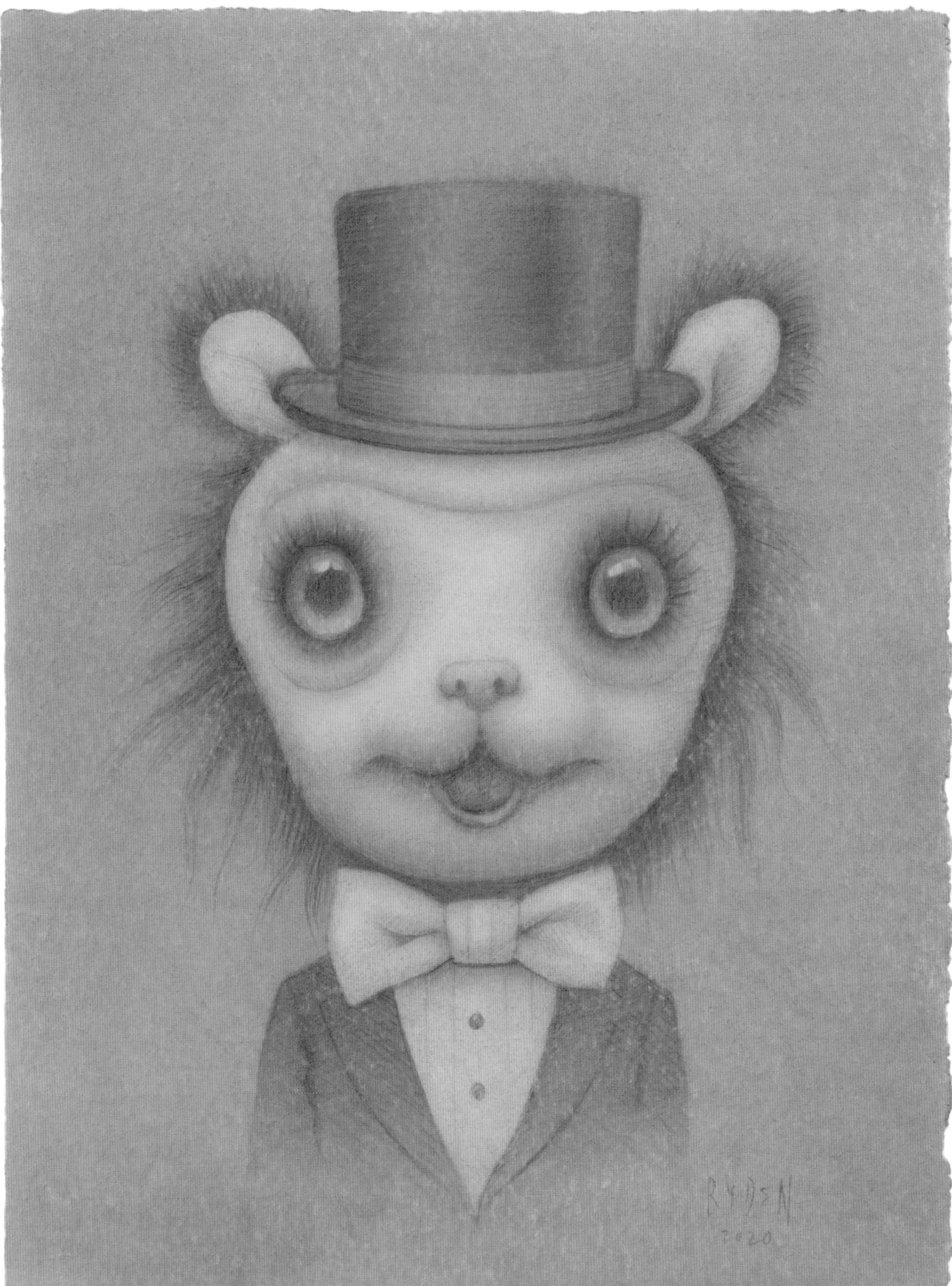
RYDEN
2020

MAKKURO

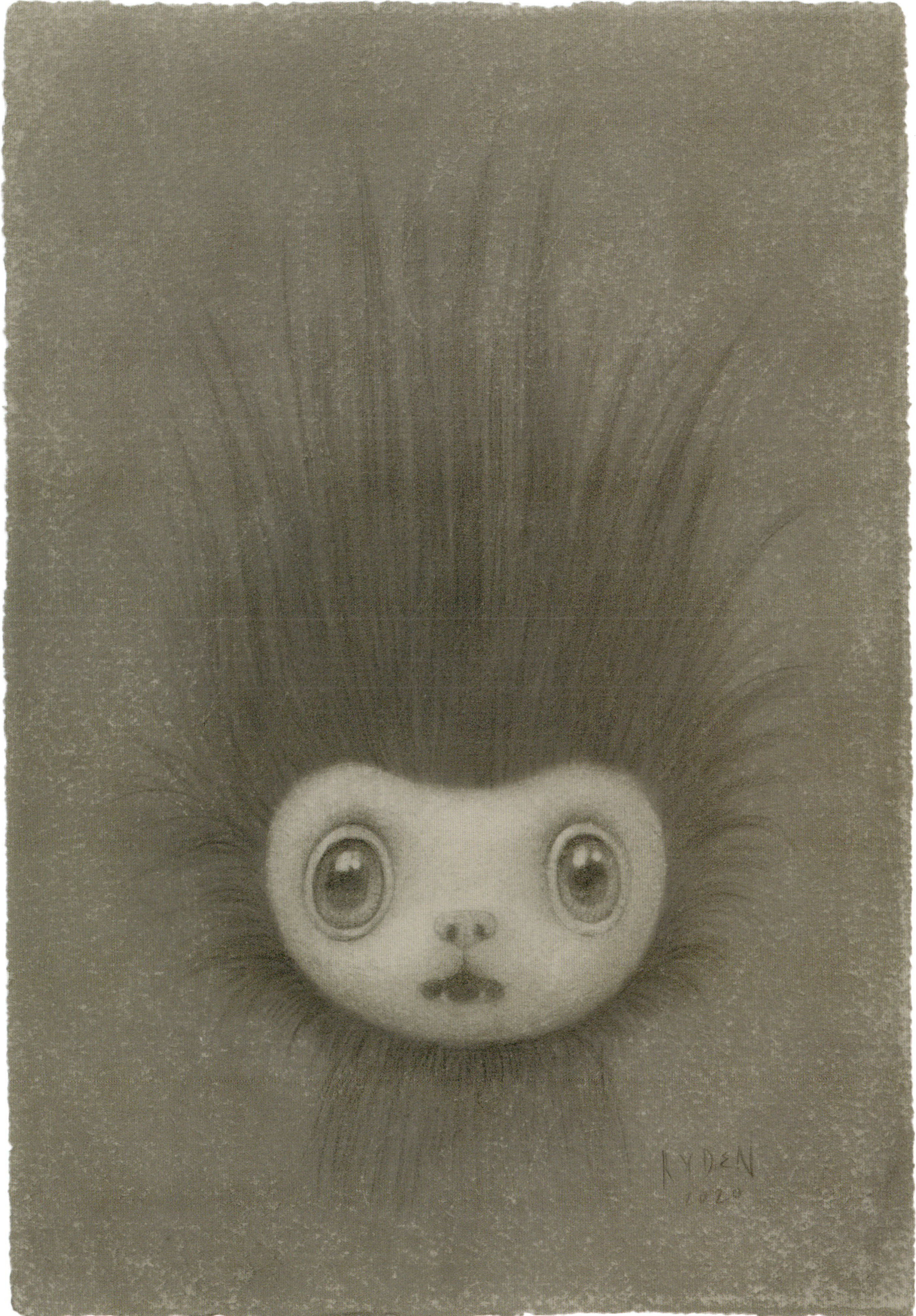
RYDEN
2020

DIRTY GIRL

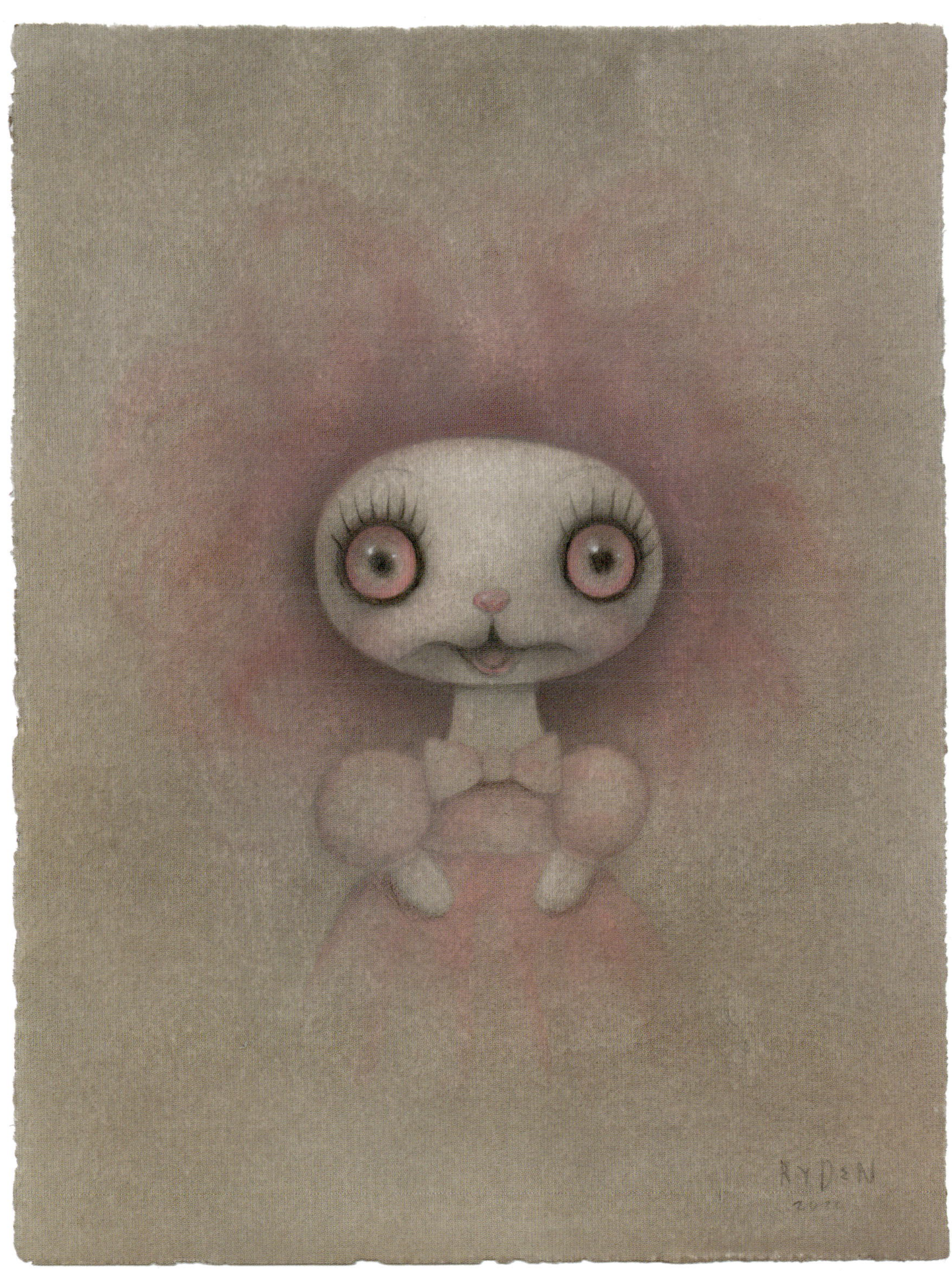

PINKIE

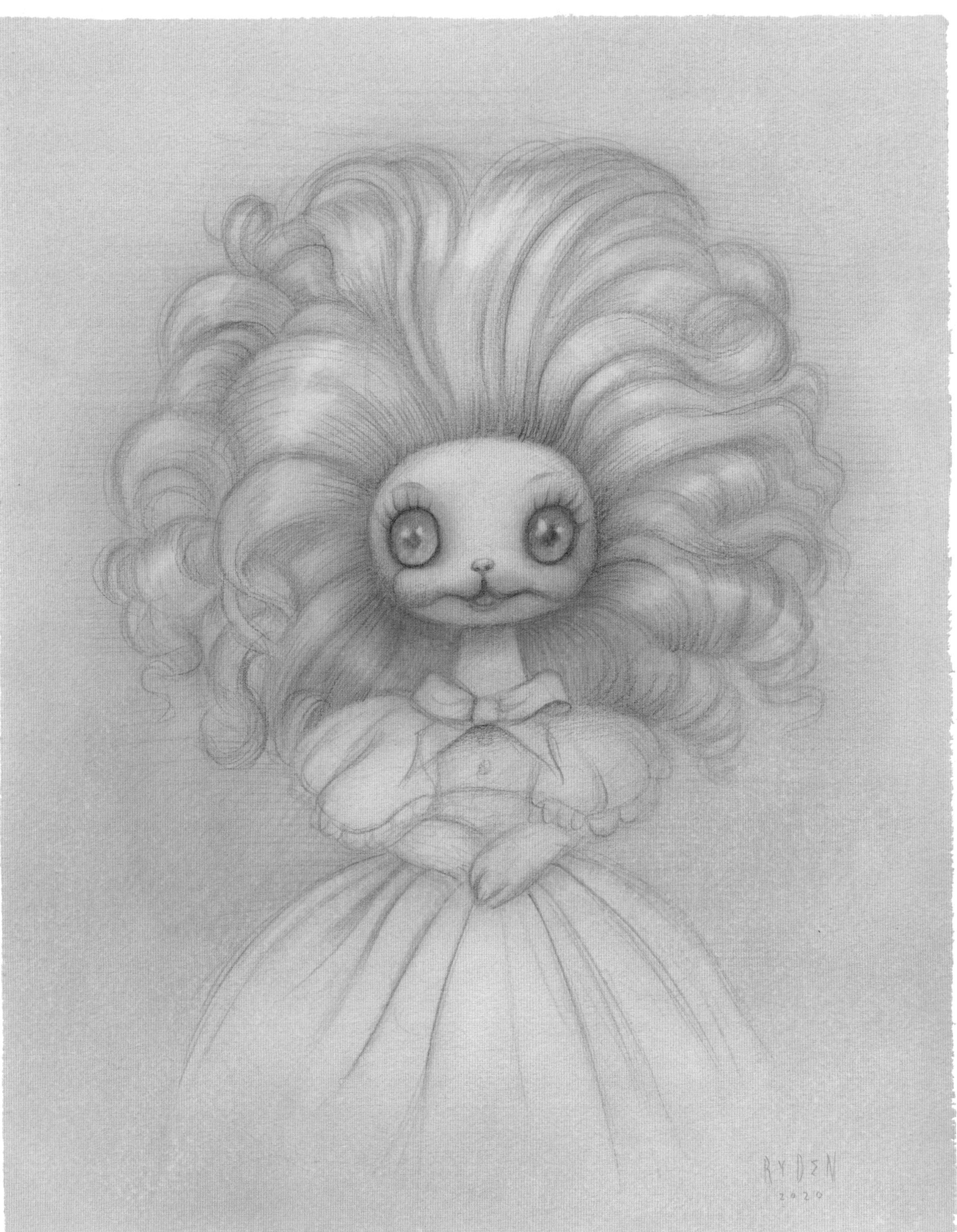

DOWRADU

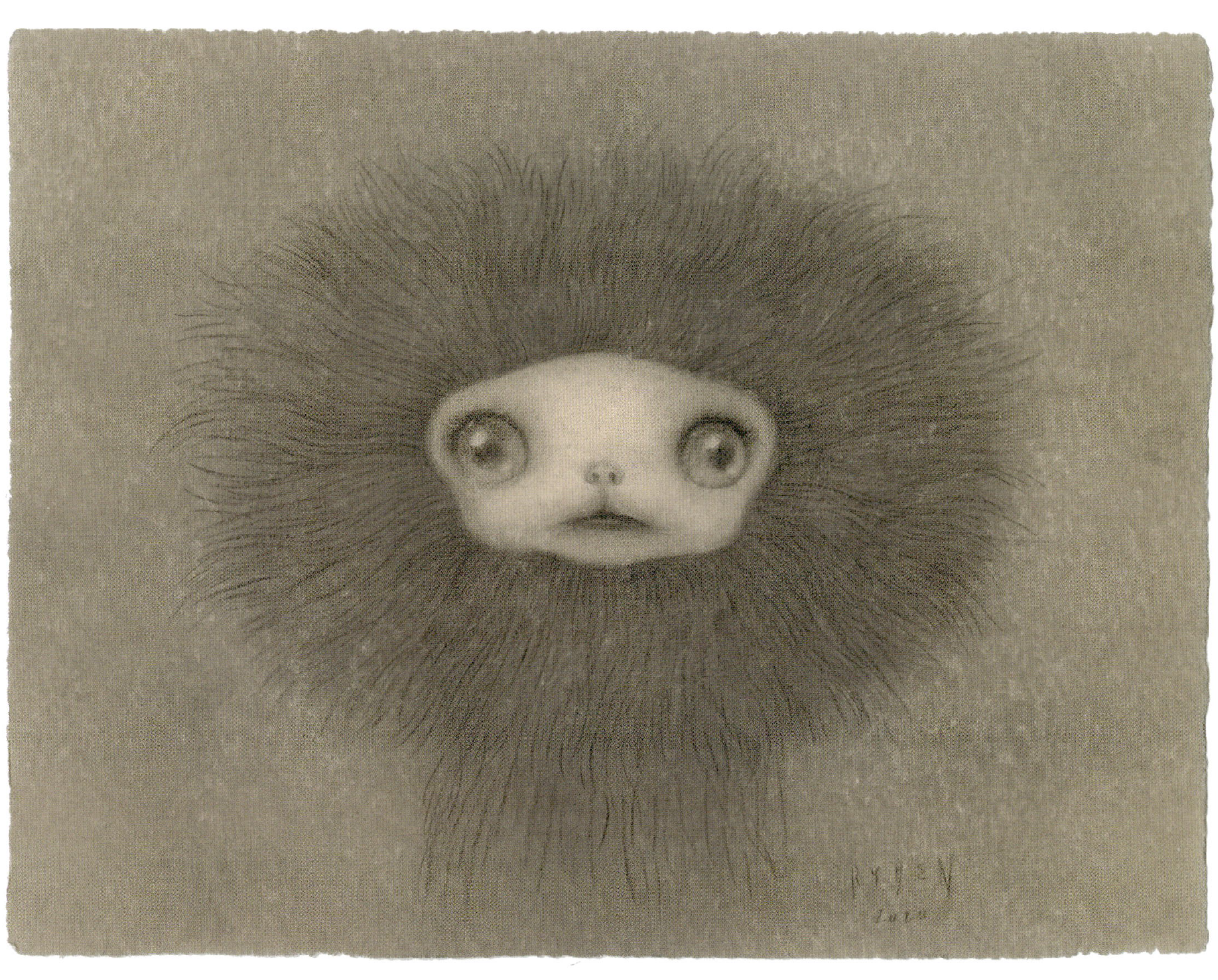

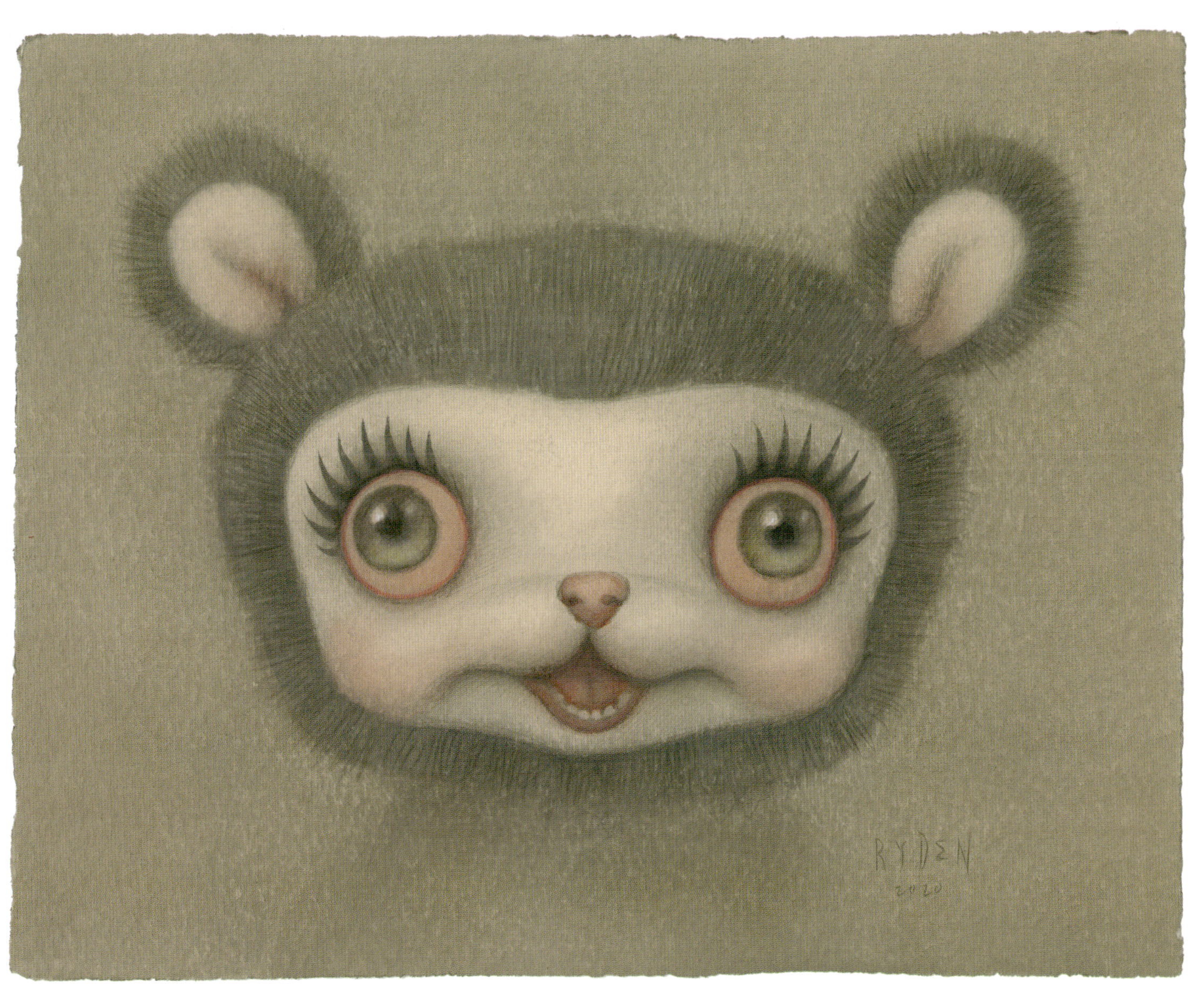

RYDEN
2020

STANDING YAK

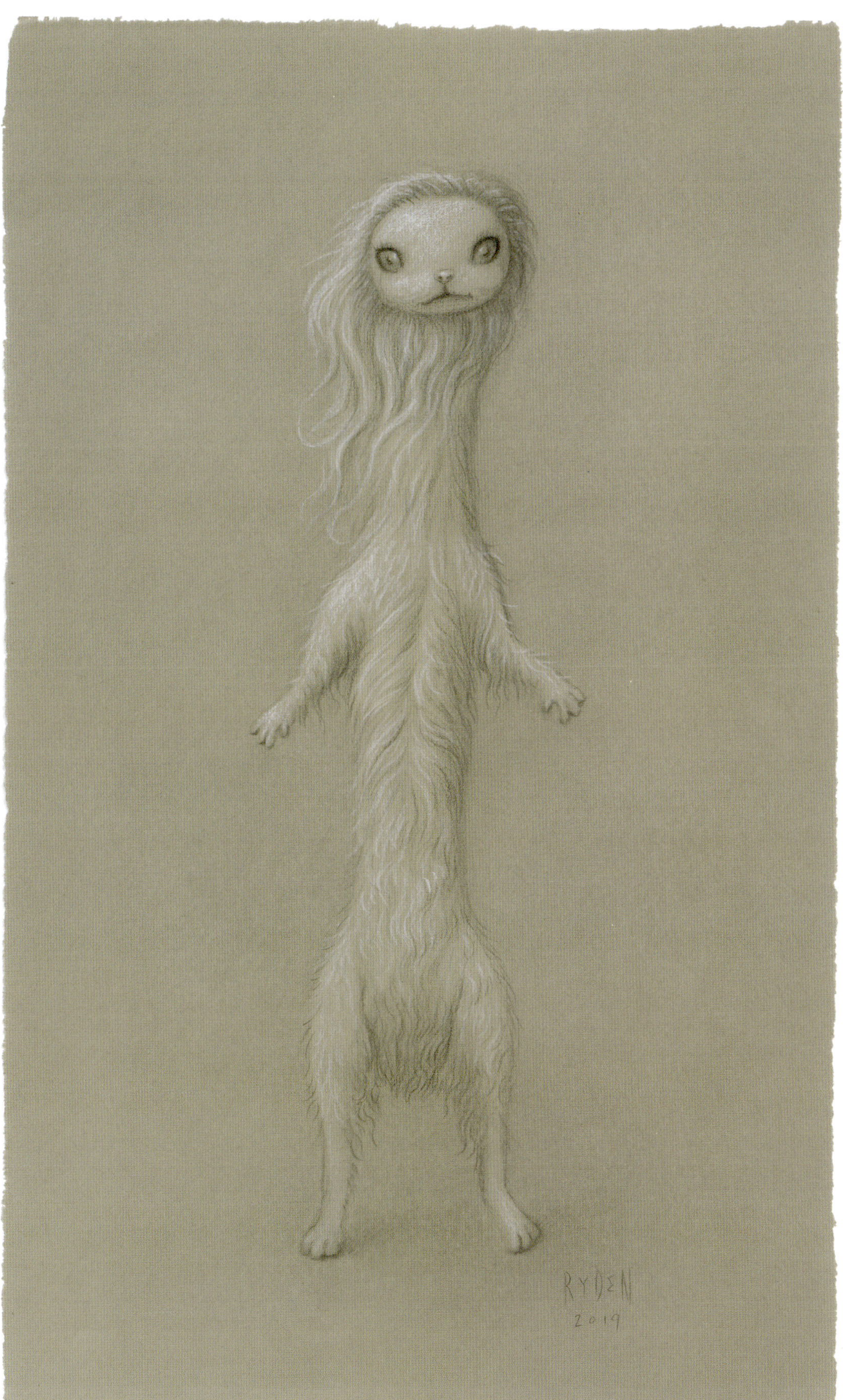

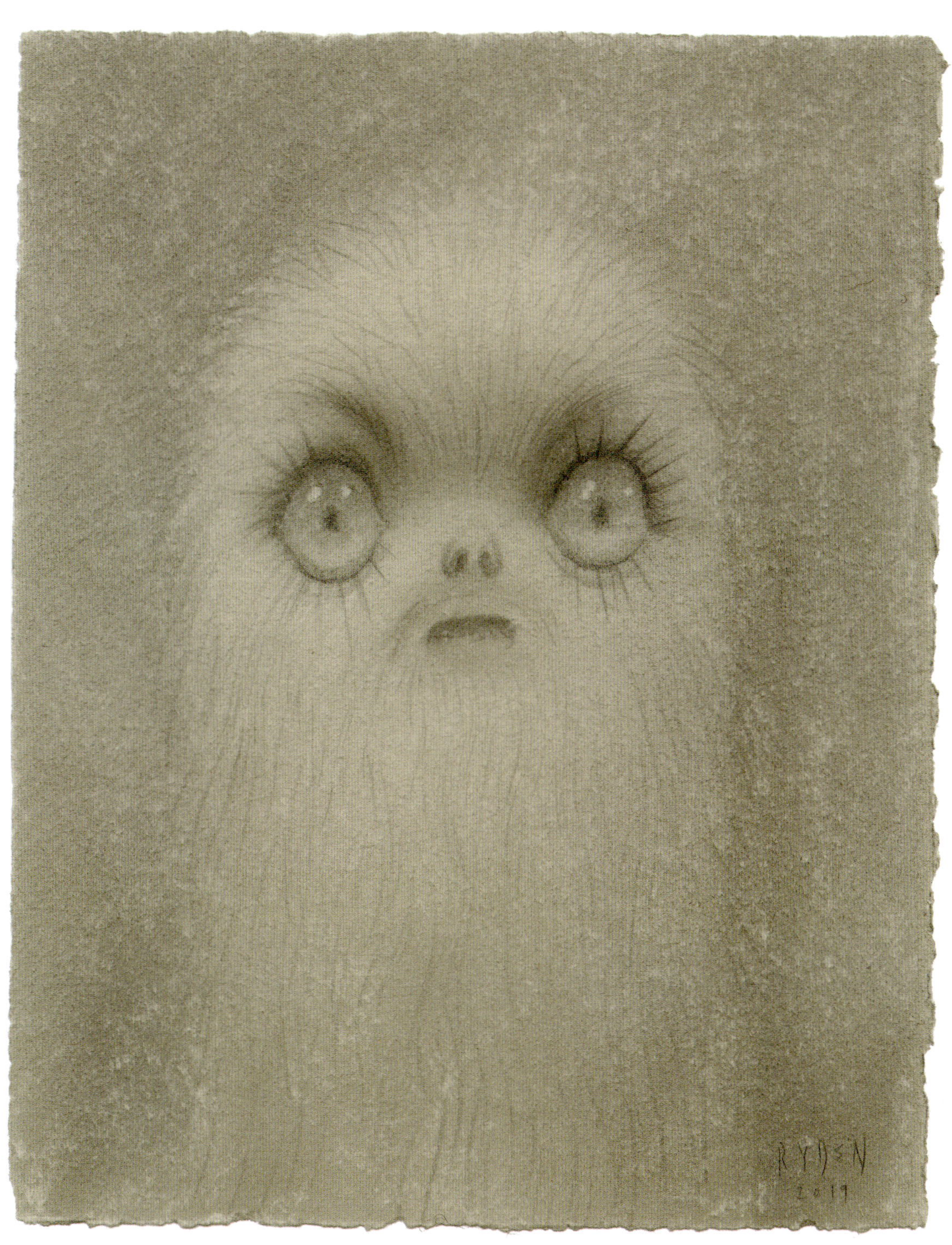

MESSENGER

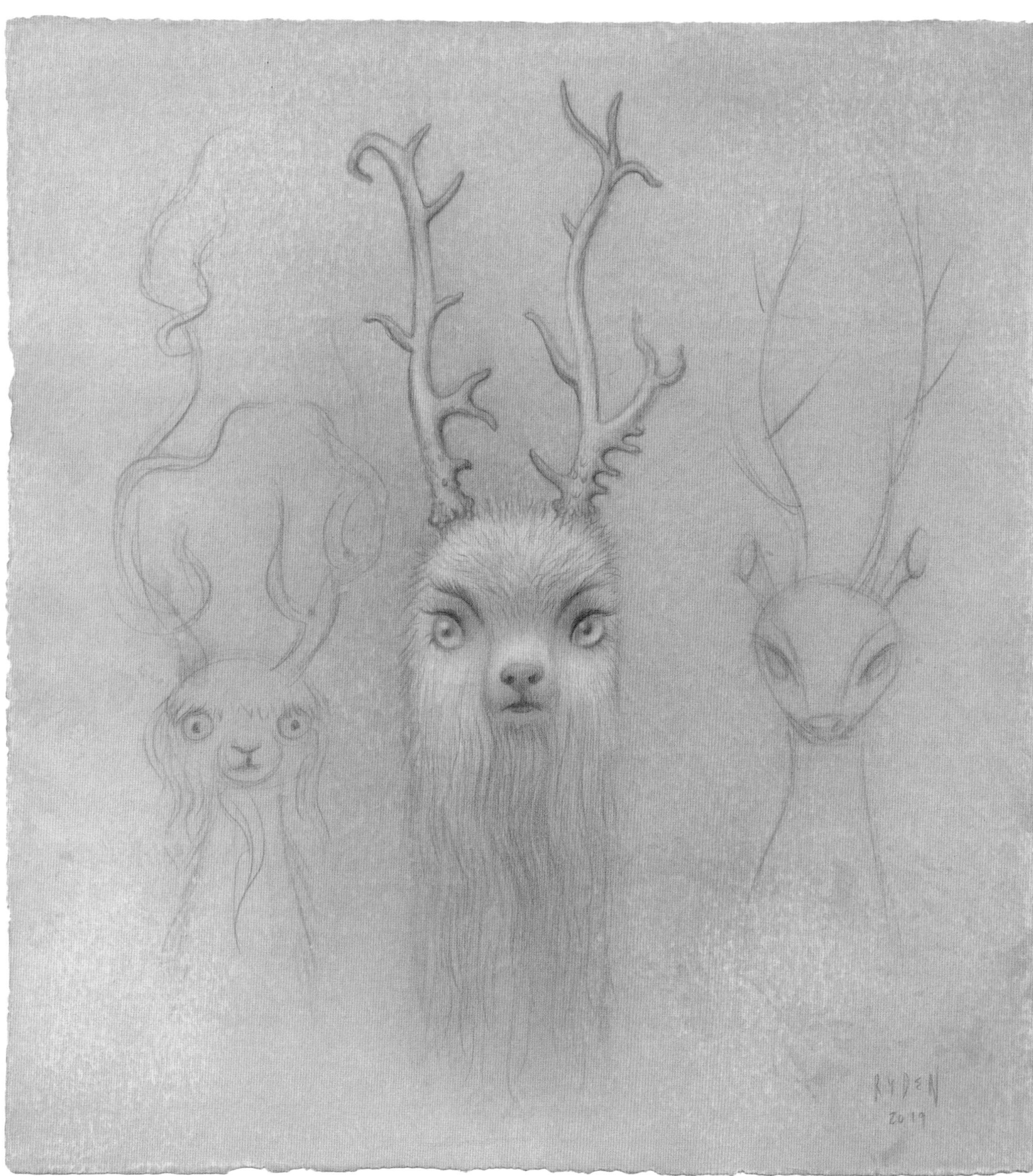

PRETTY YAK

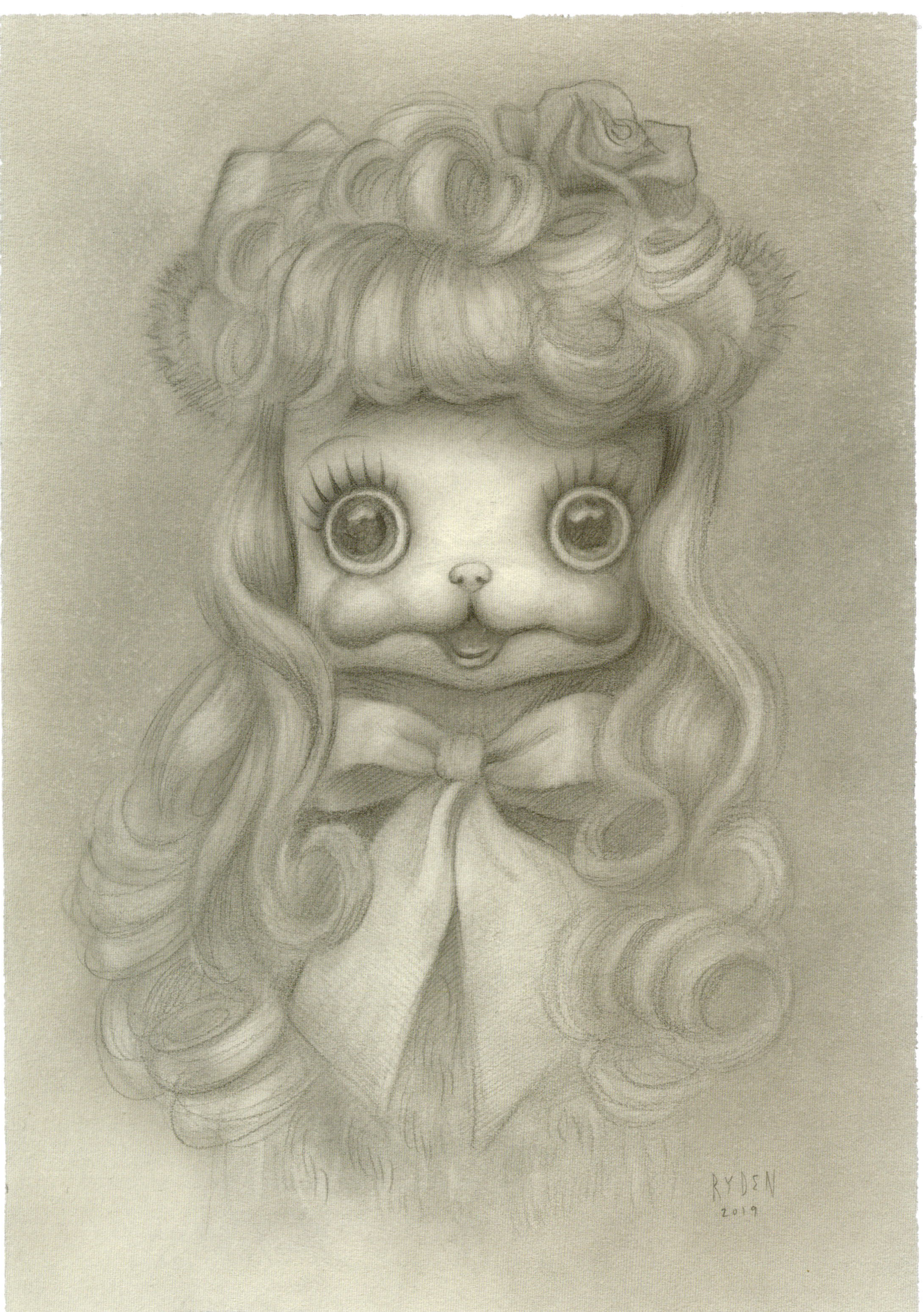
RYDEN
2019

GOD YAK

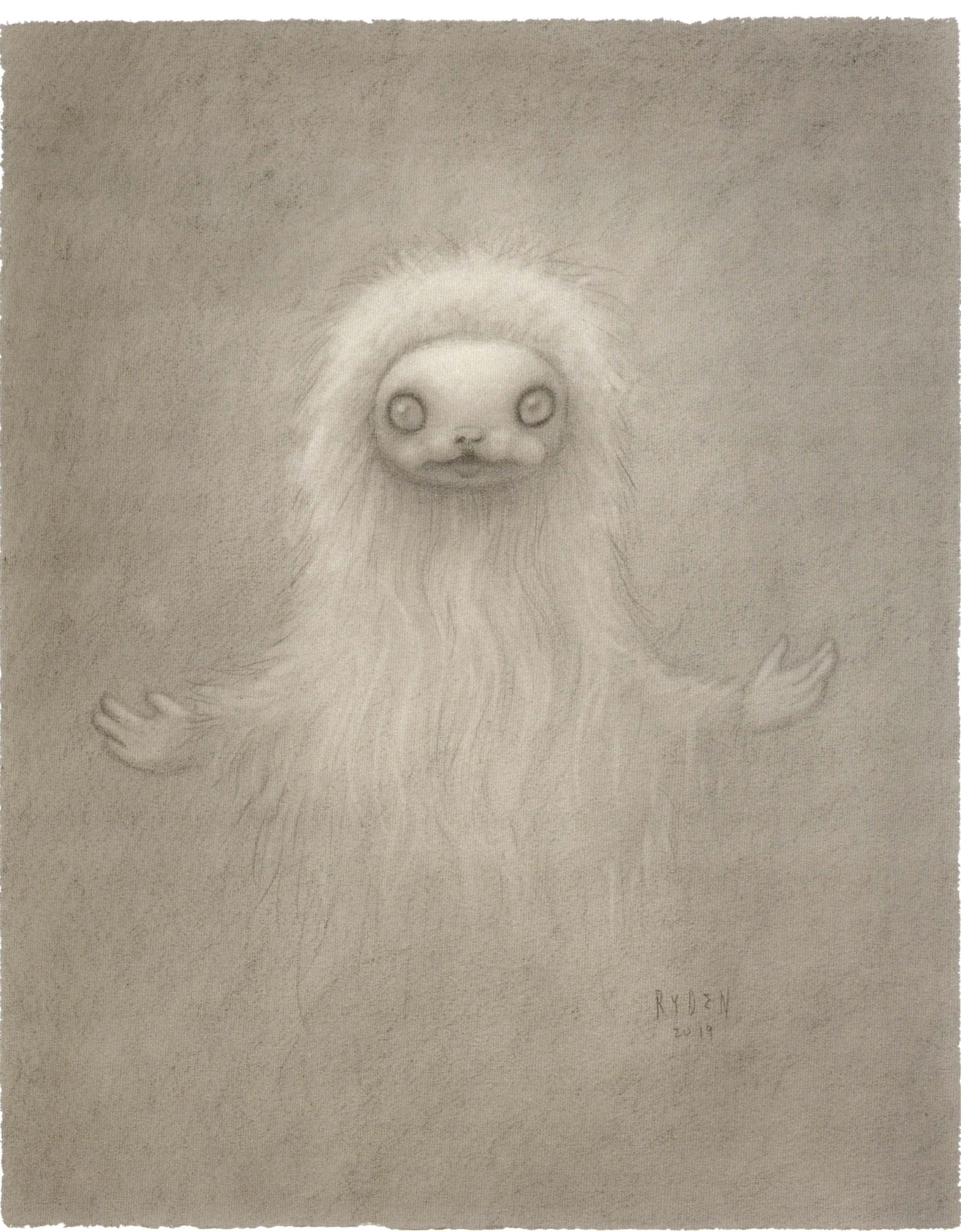
RYDEN
20 19

YAK WITH HORNS

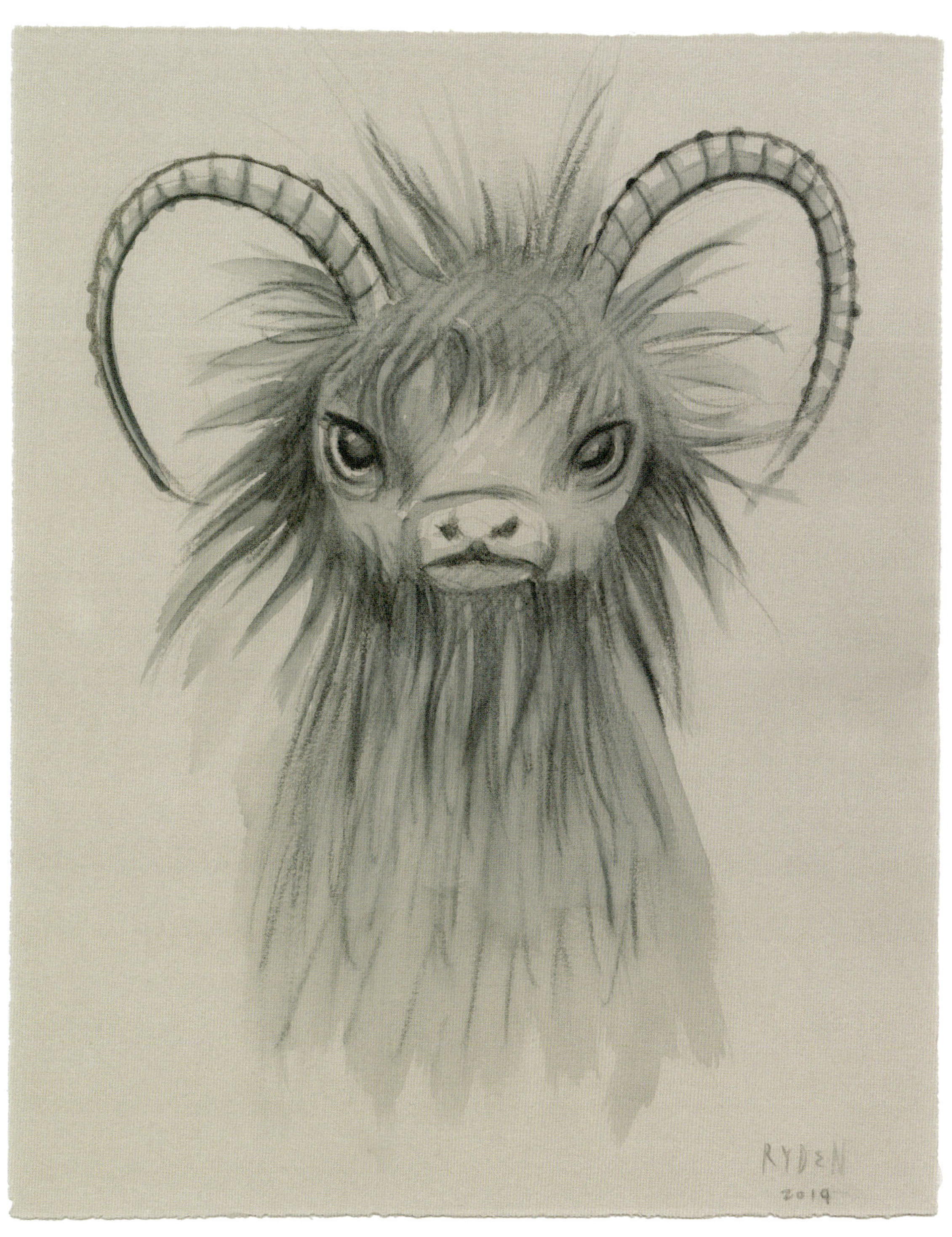
RYDEN
2019

HELLO YAK

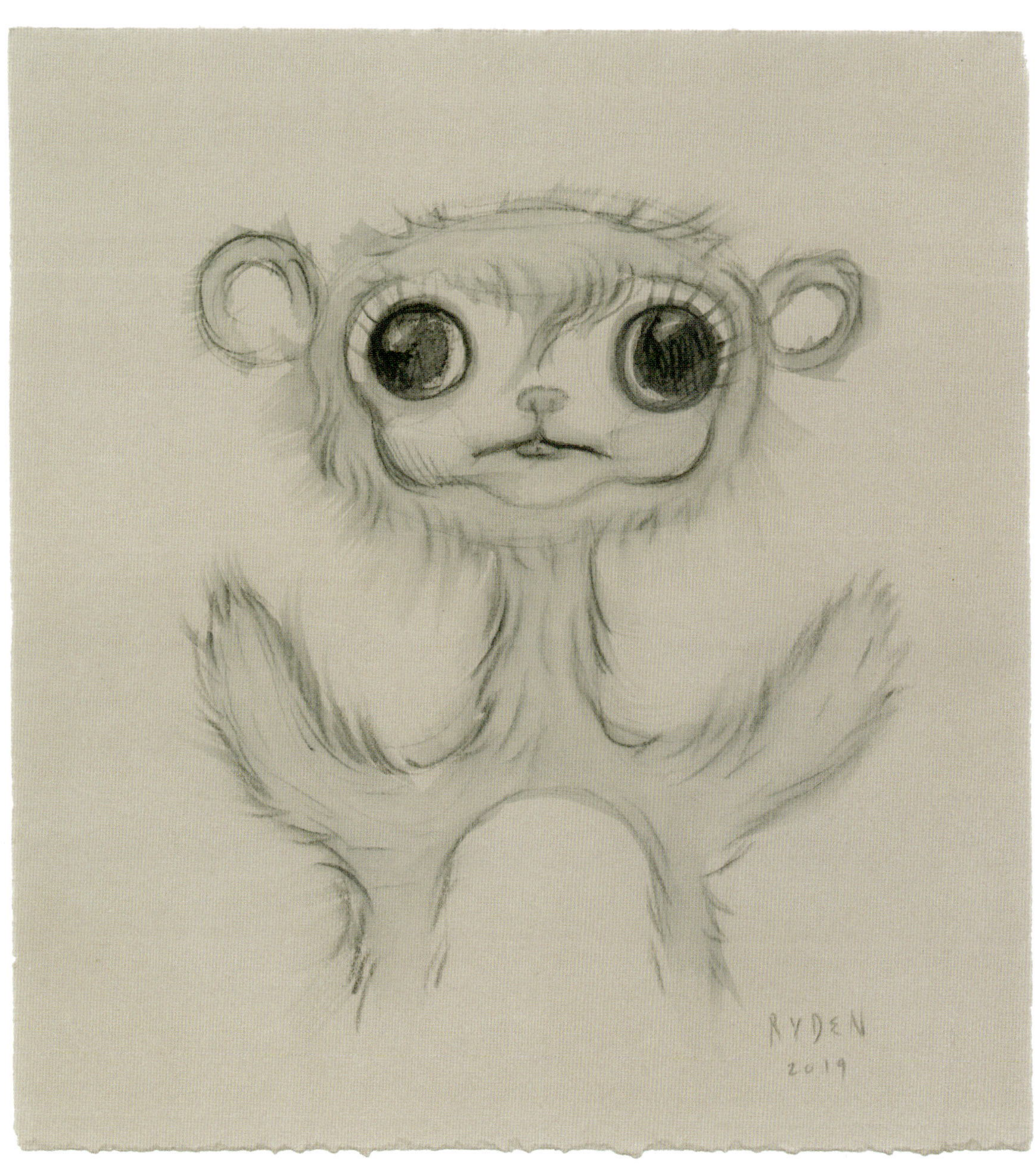

RYDEN
2019

SAM

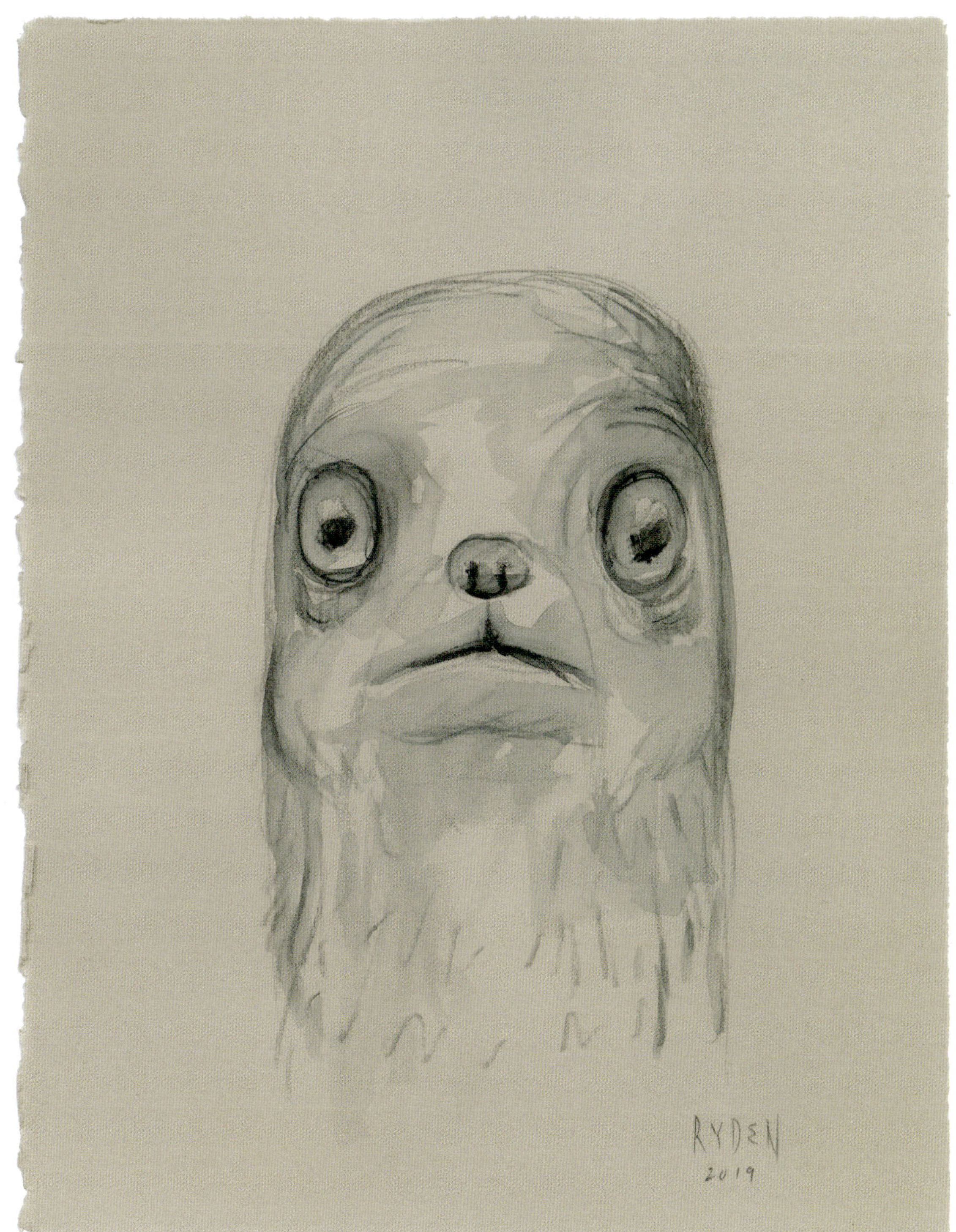

RYDEN
2019

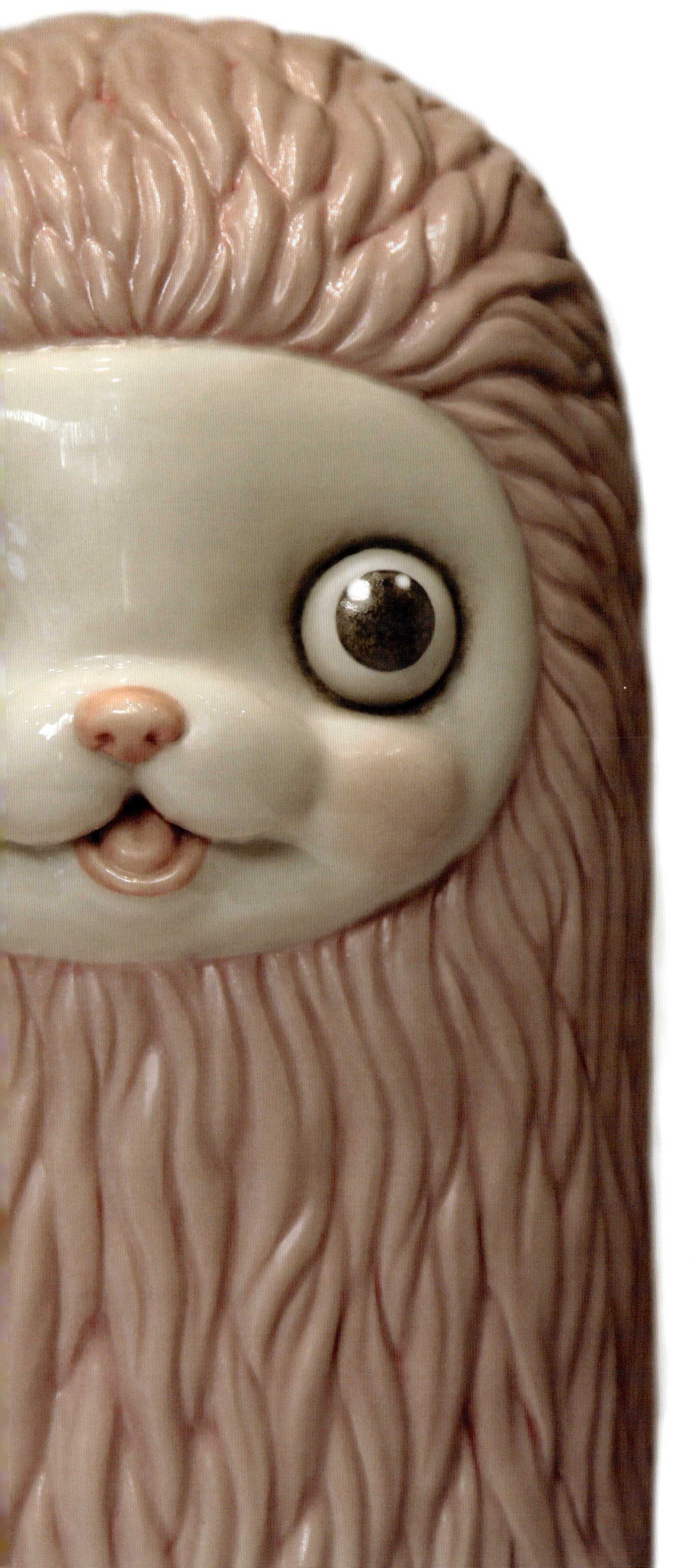

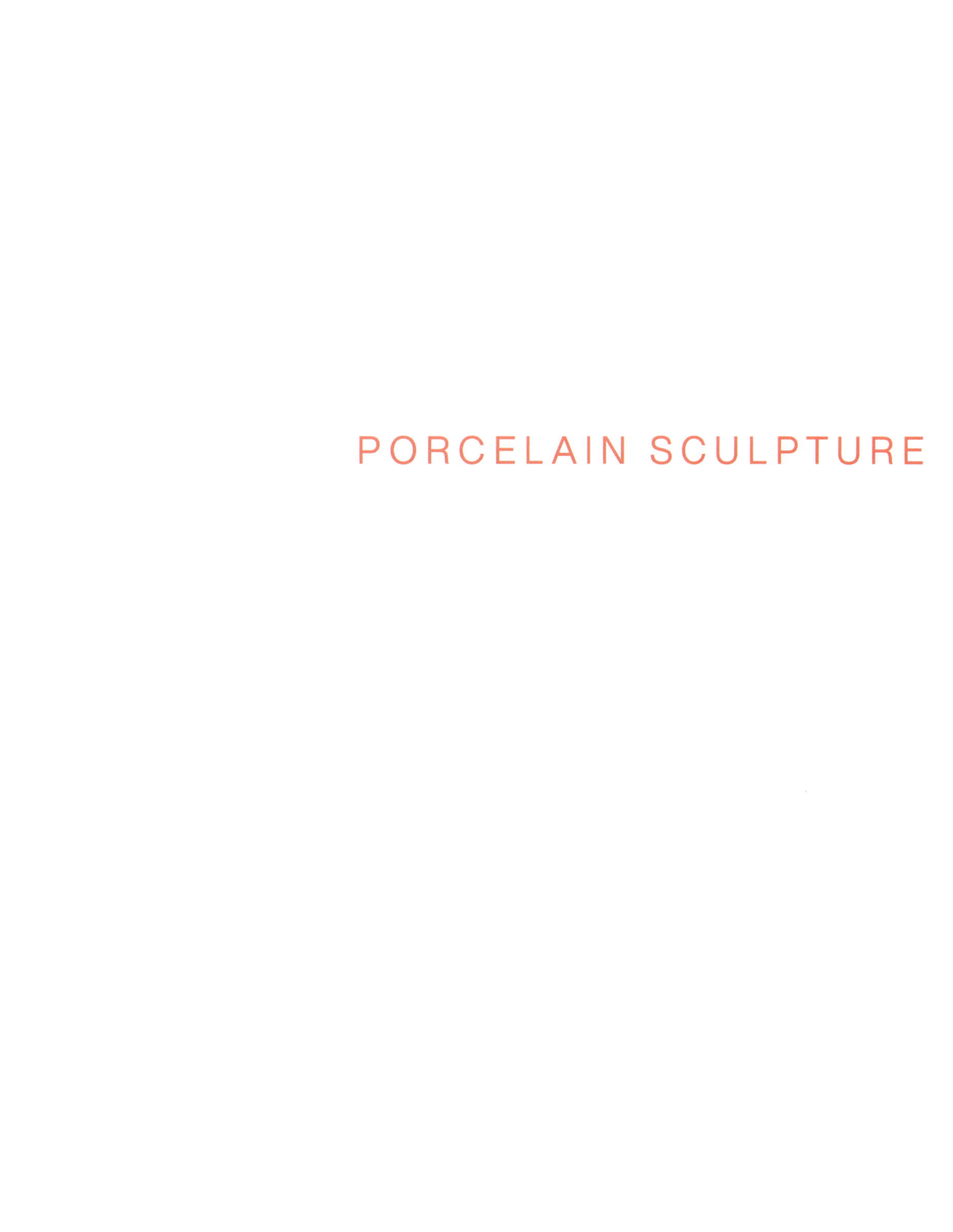

PORCELAIN SCULPTURE

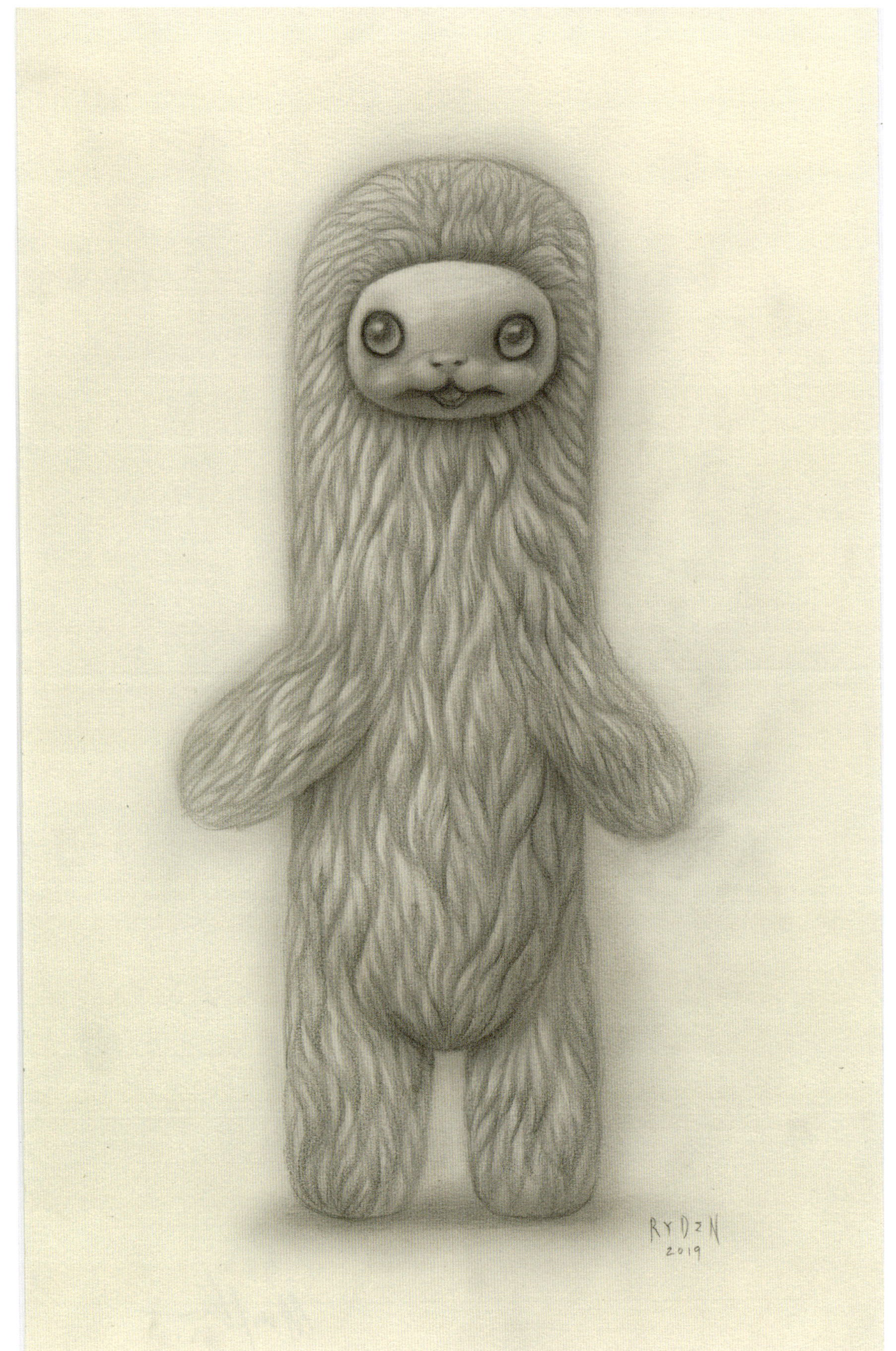

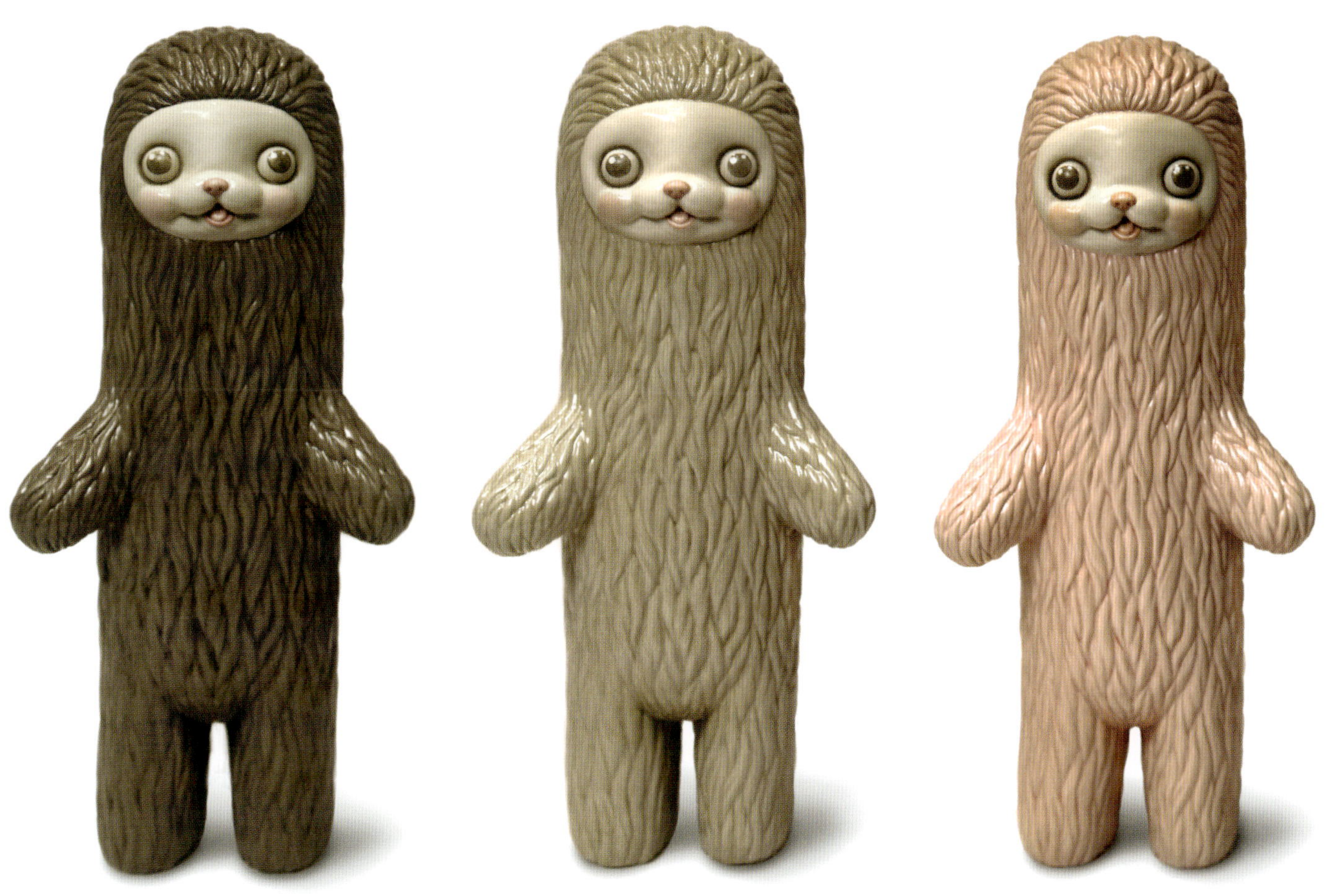

BOS

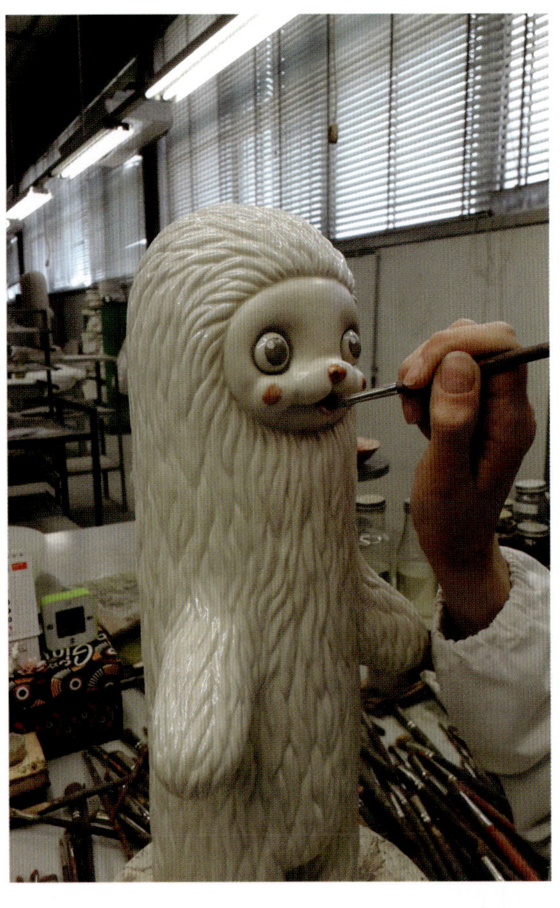
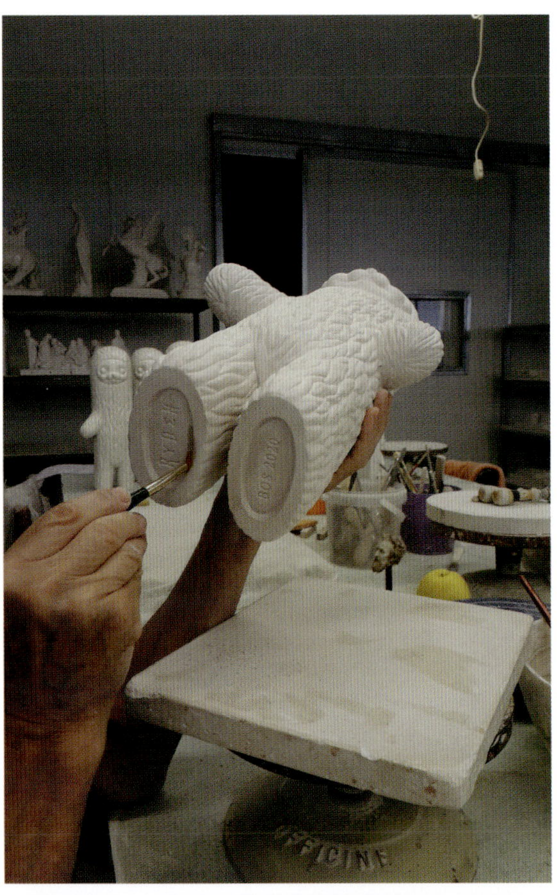
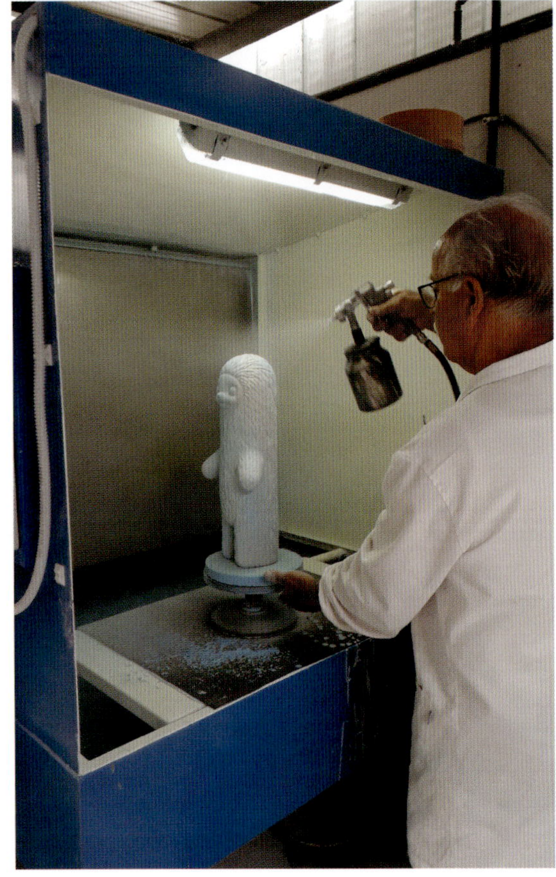
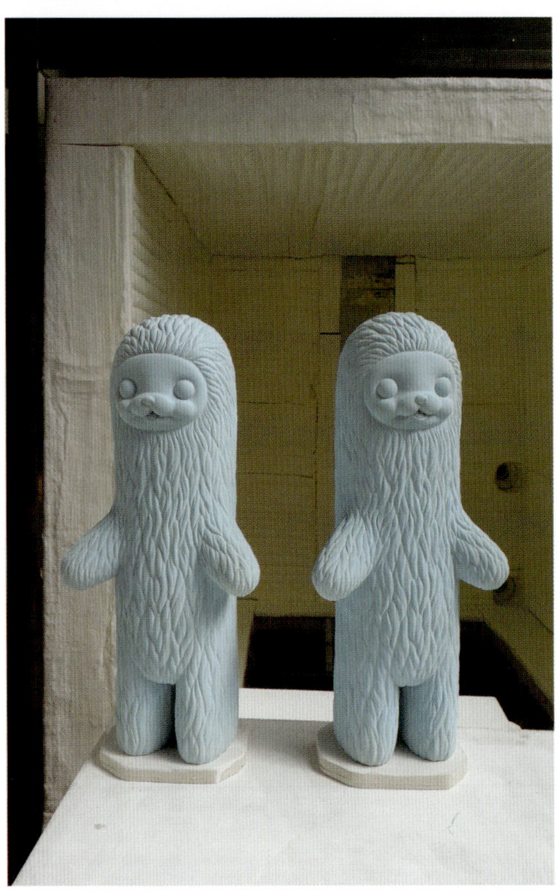

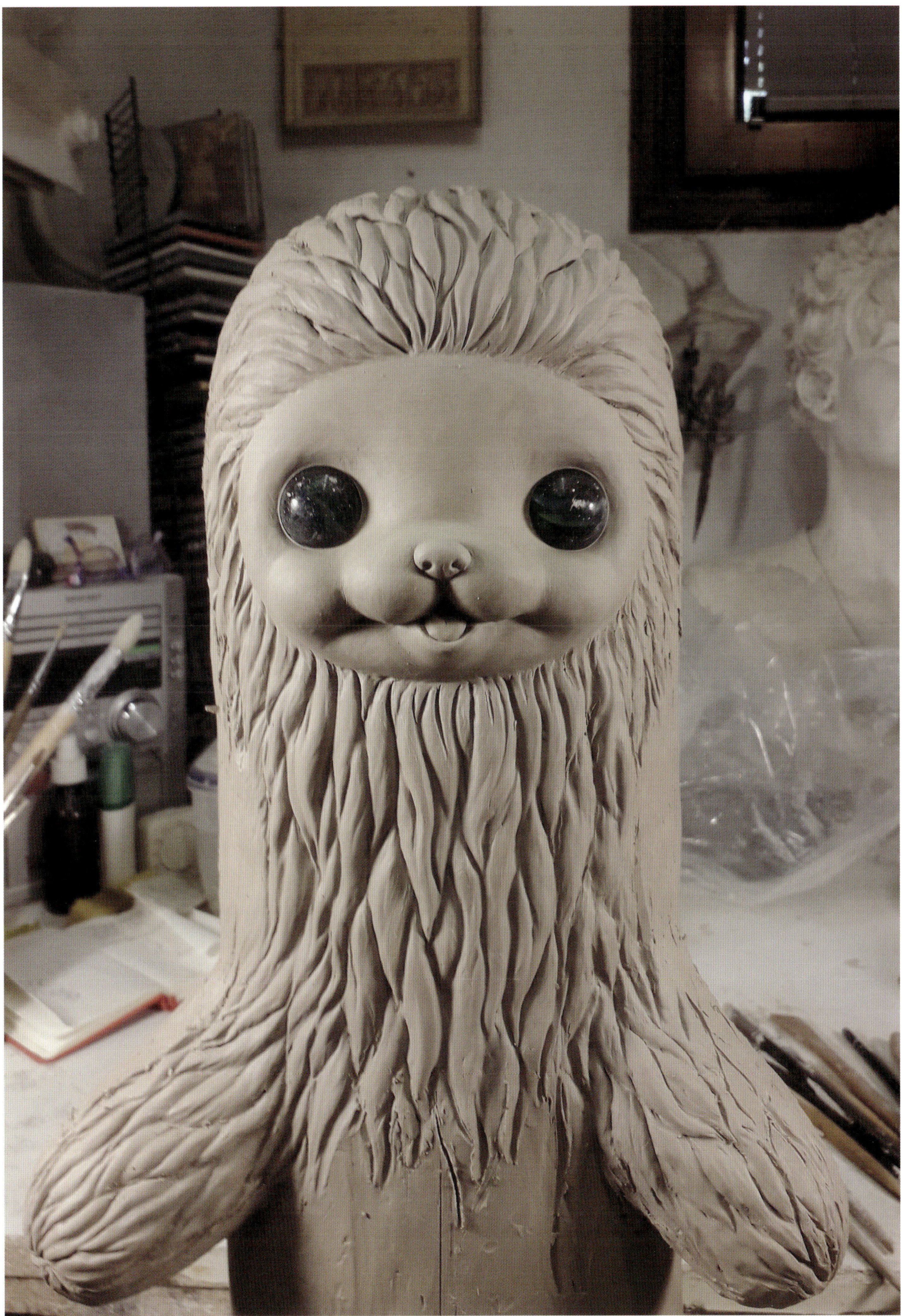

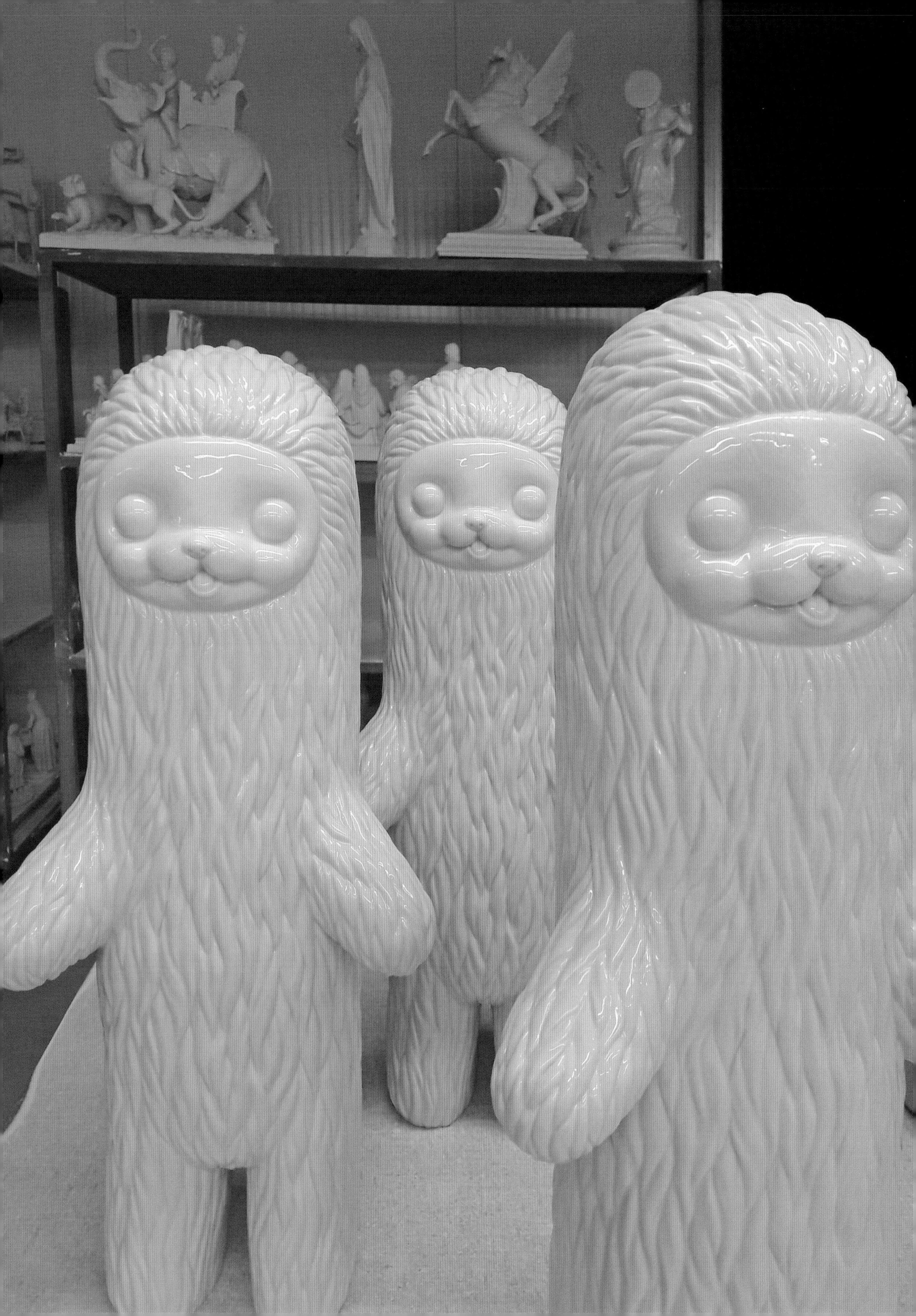

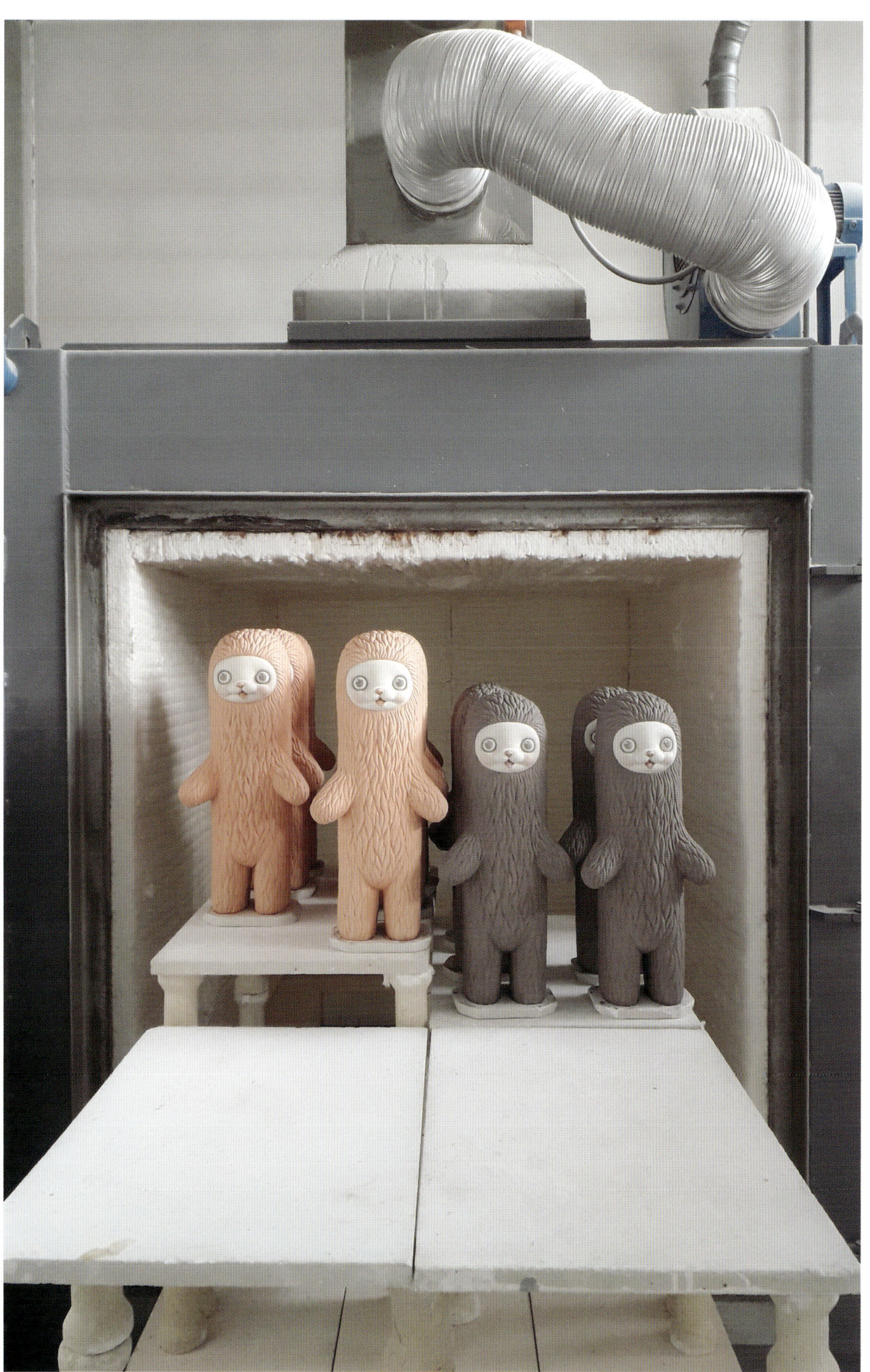

View of the exhibition *Mark Ryden: Anima Animals* at Perrotin Shanghai, 2020.
Courtesy of the artist and Perrotin.

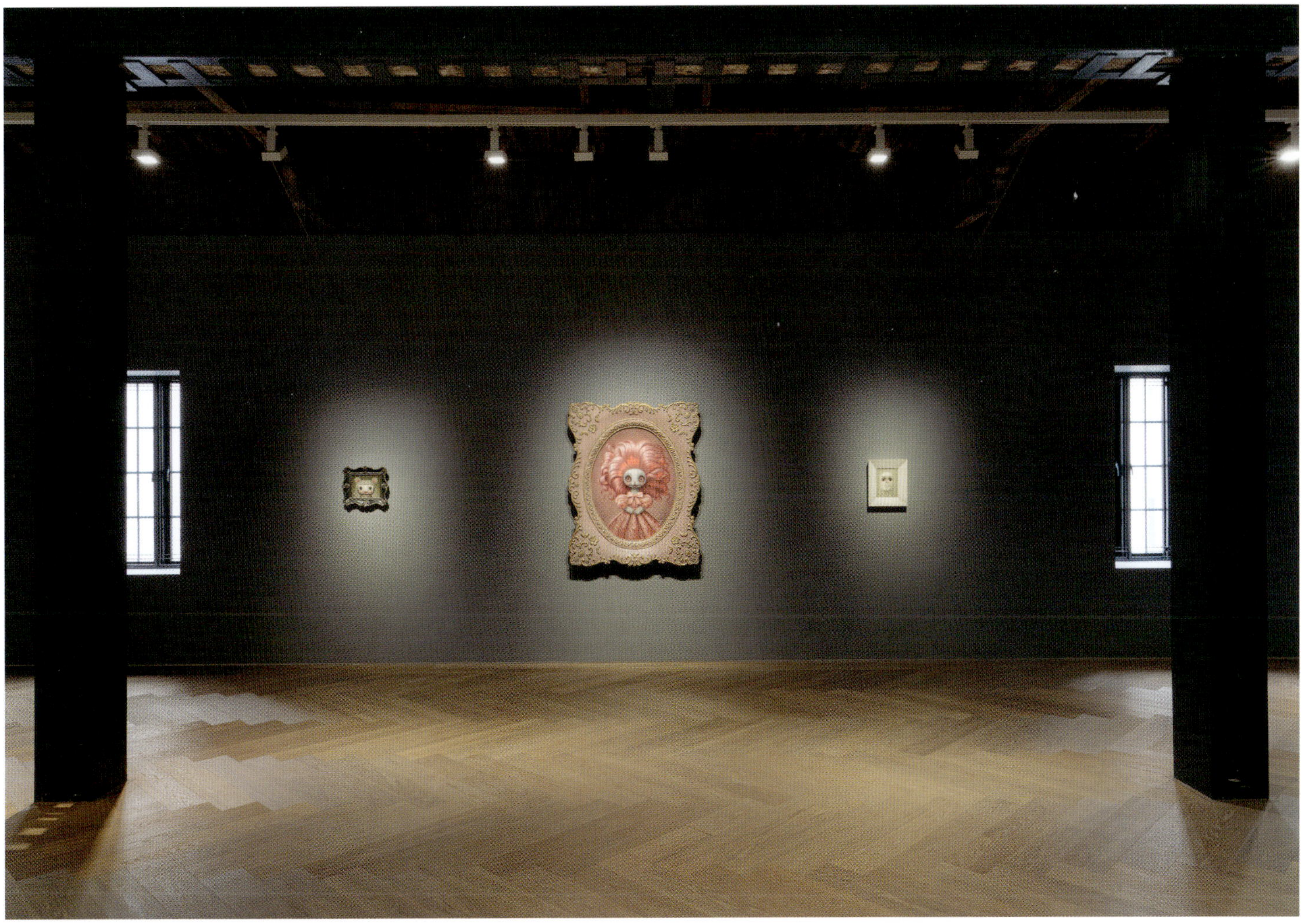

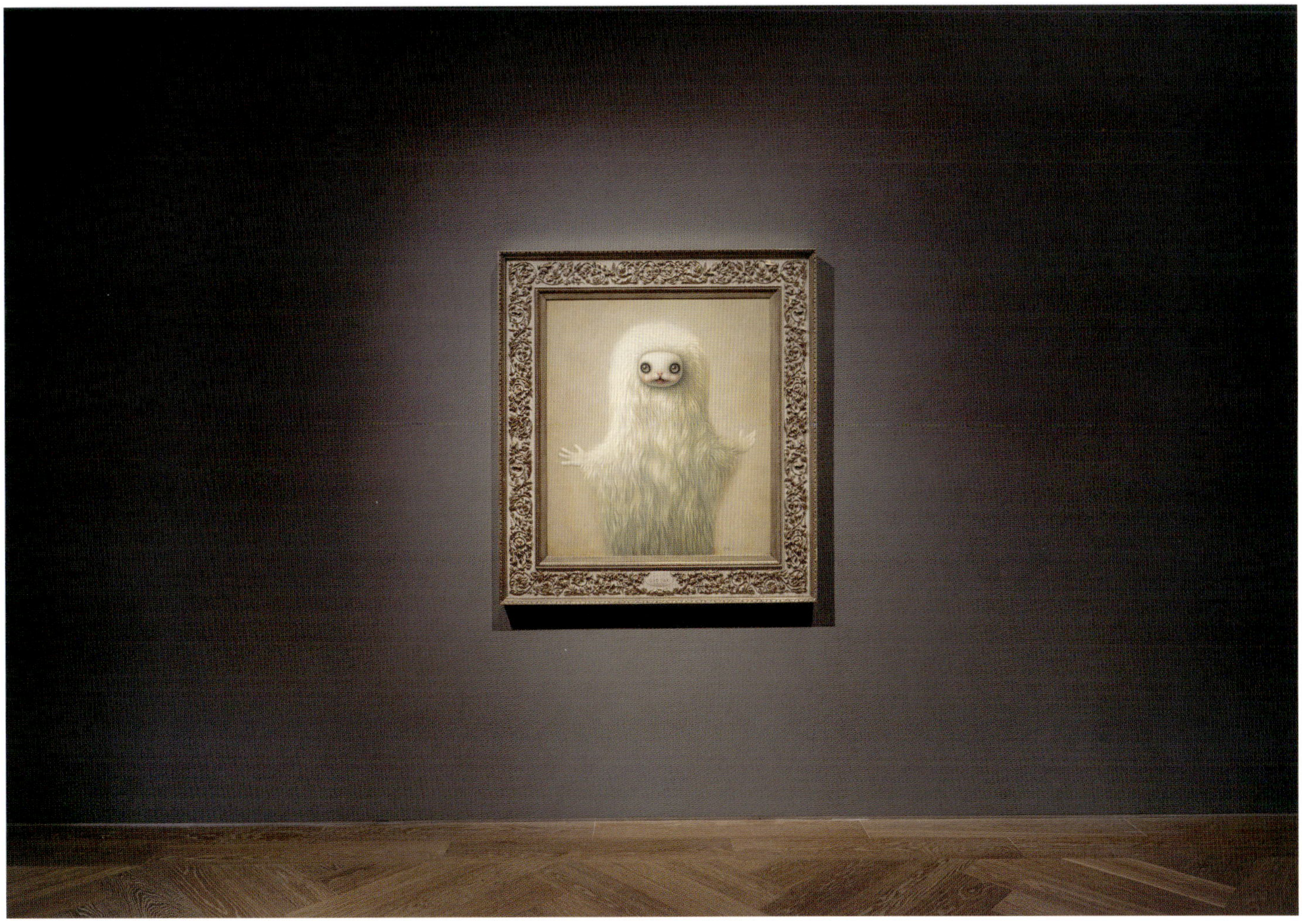

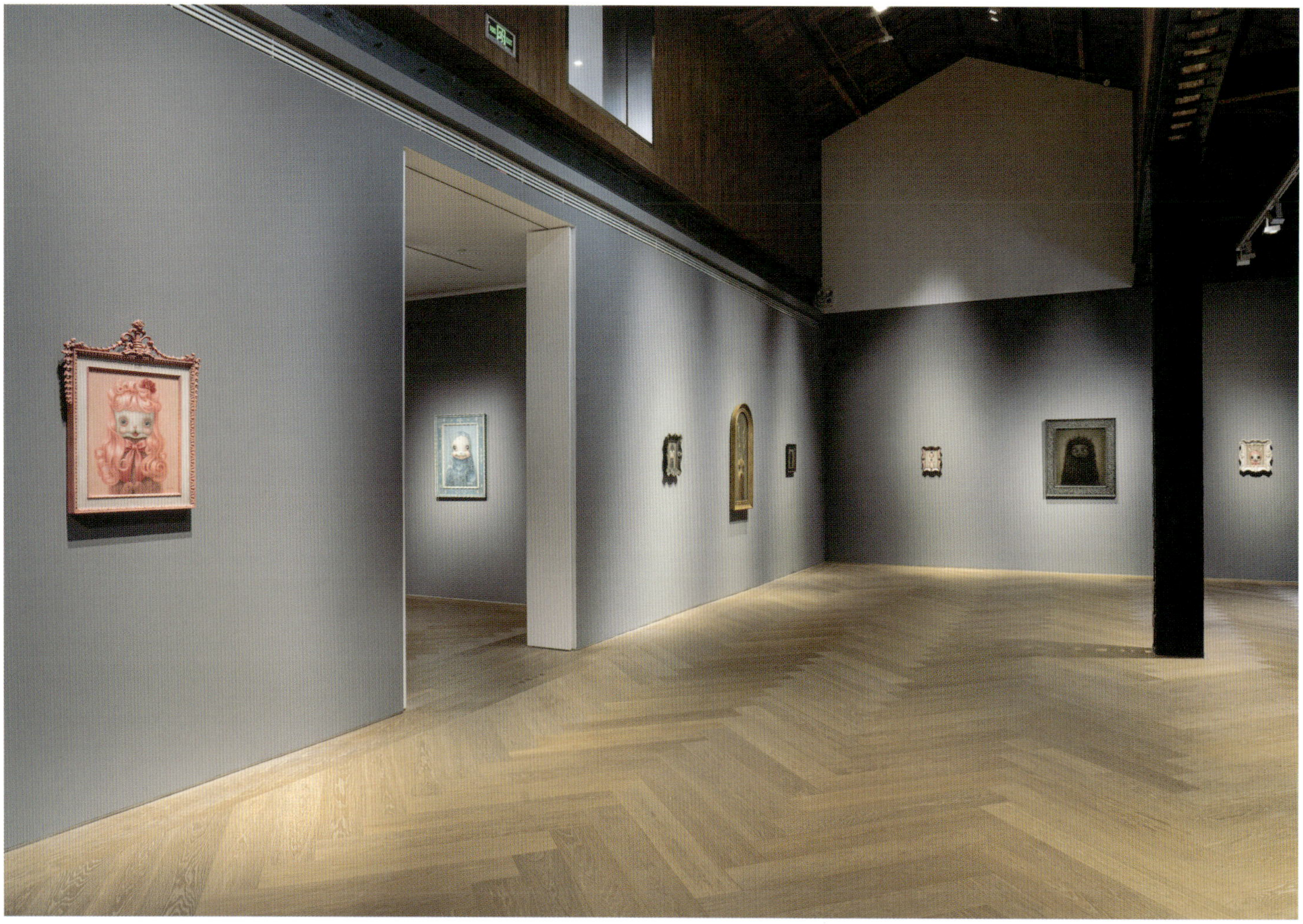

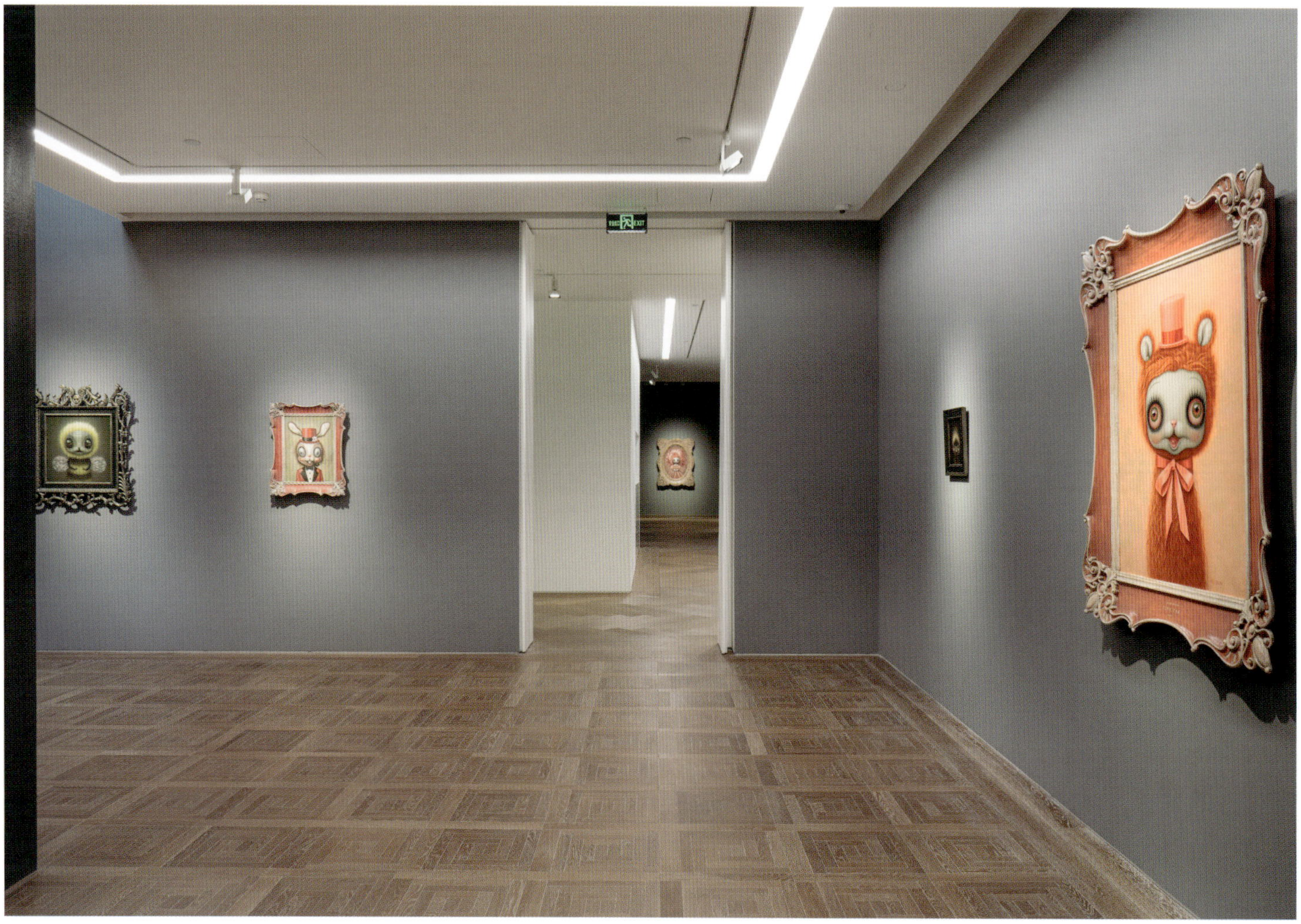

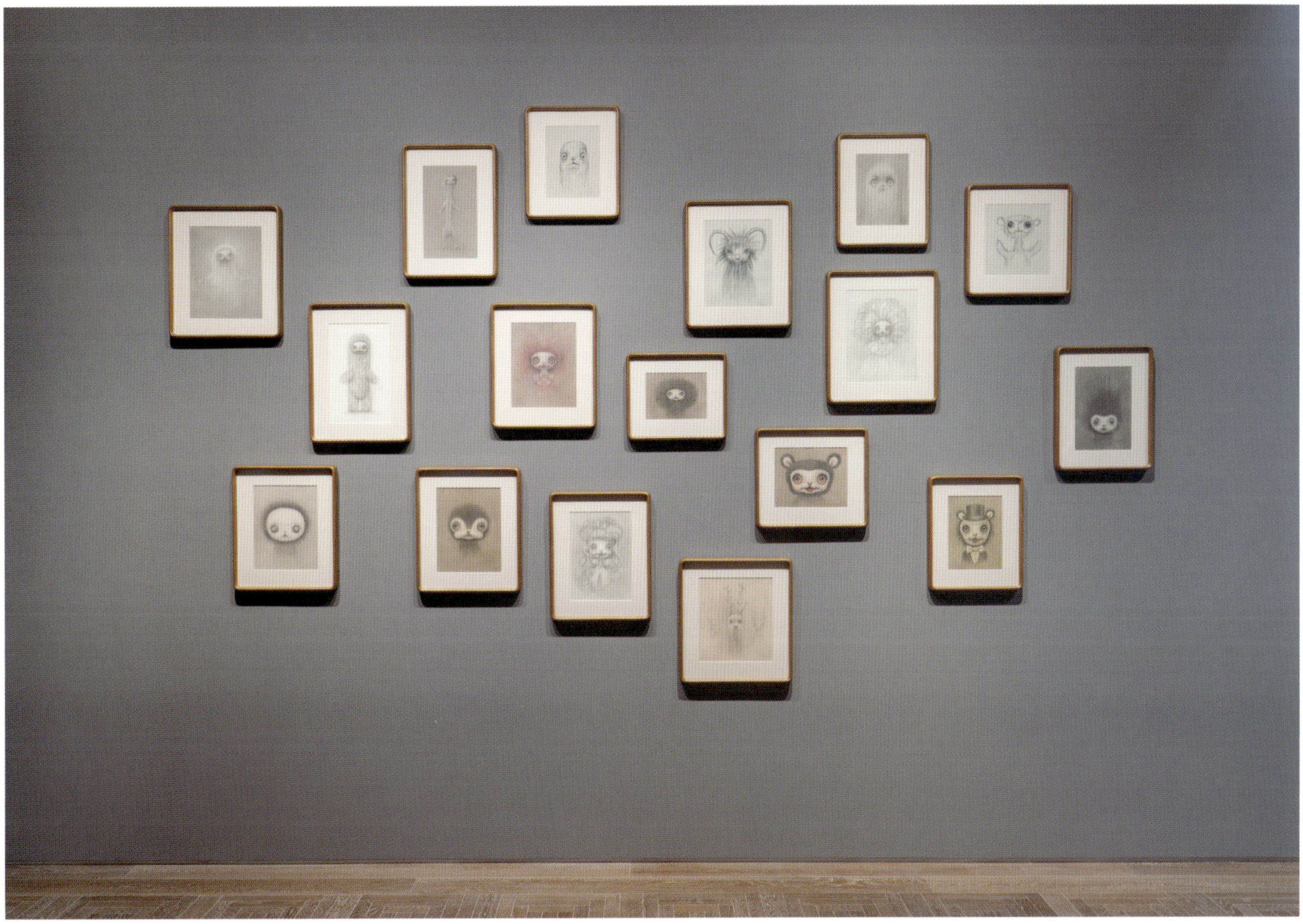

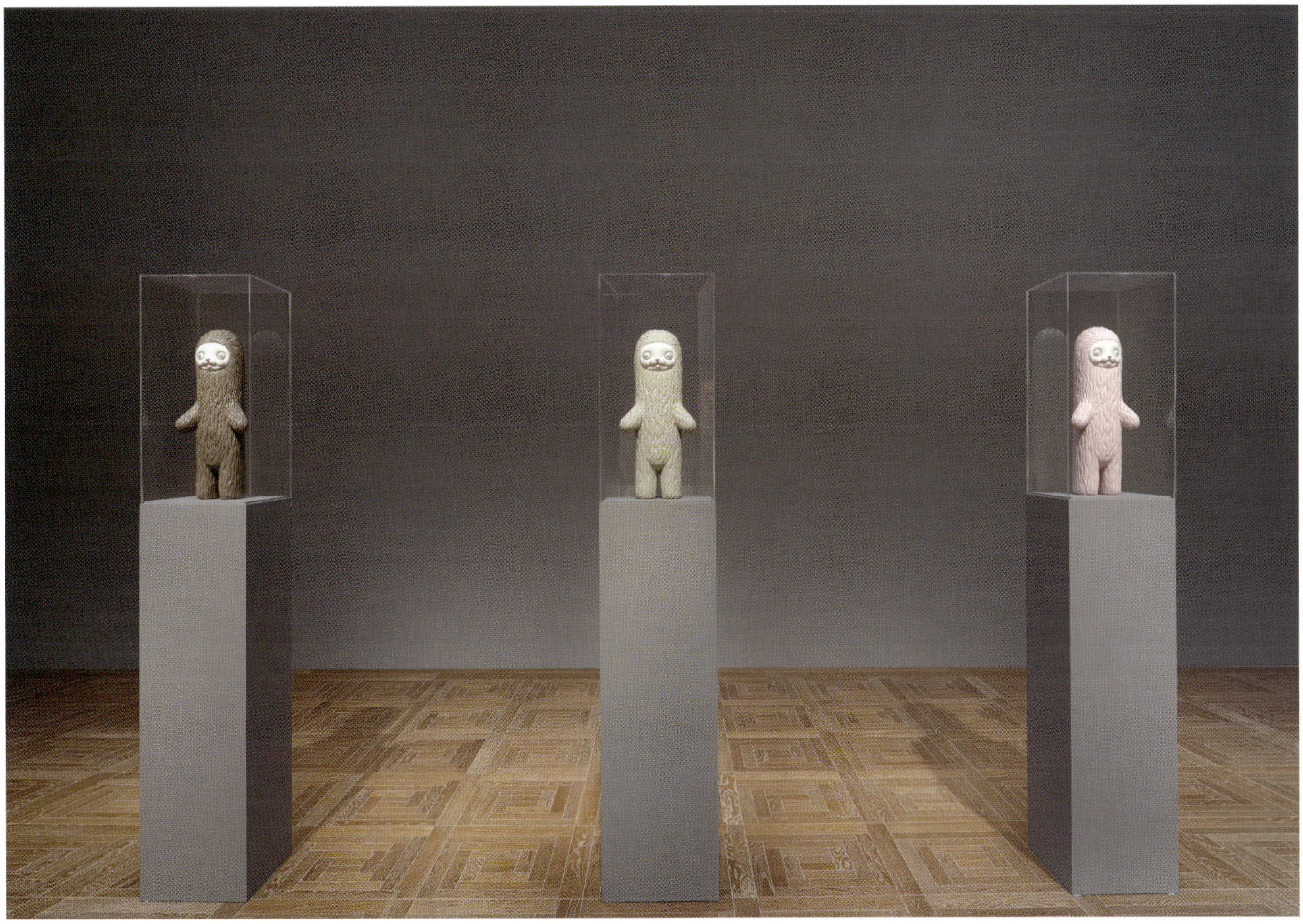

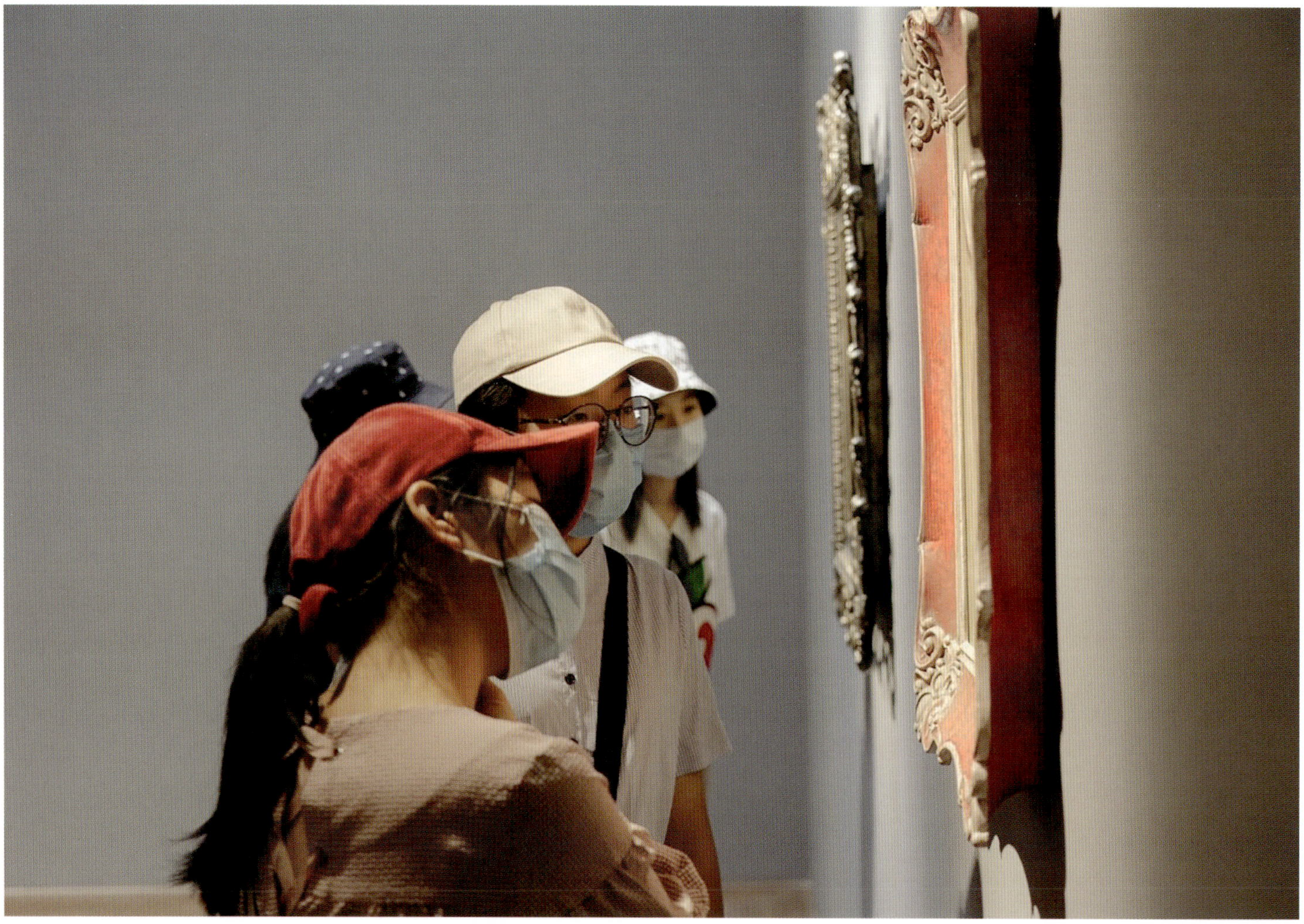

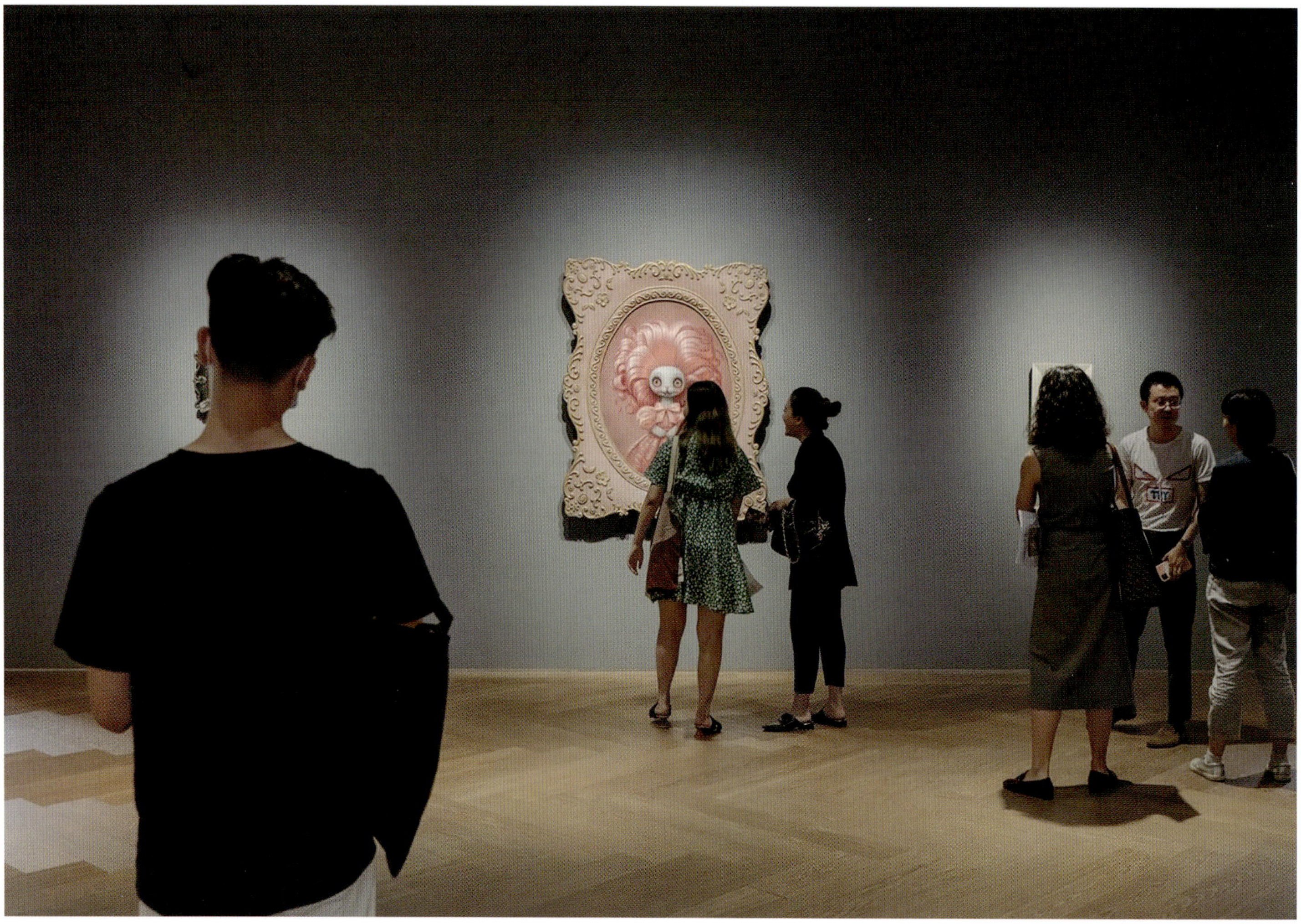

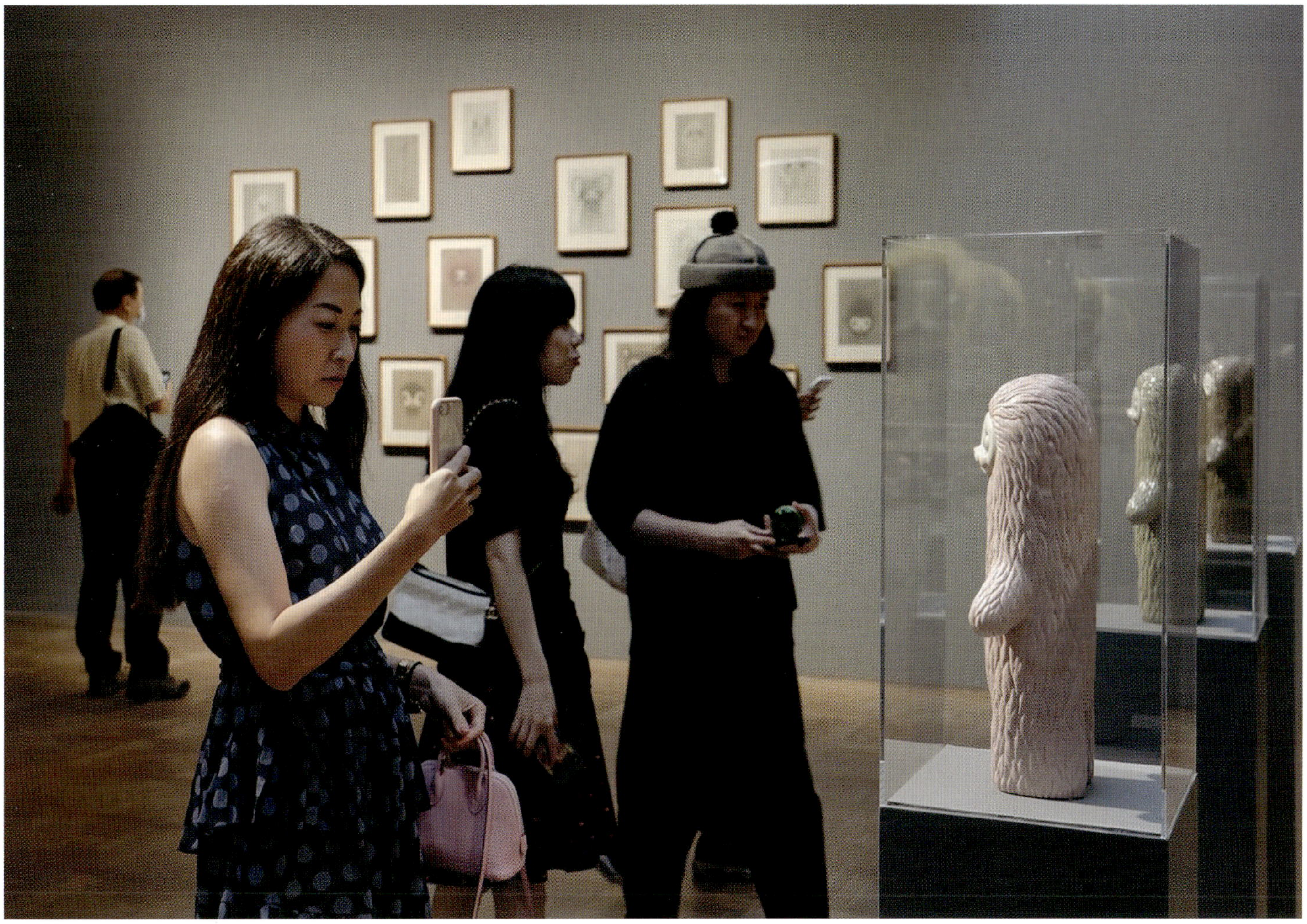

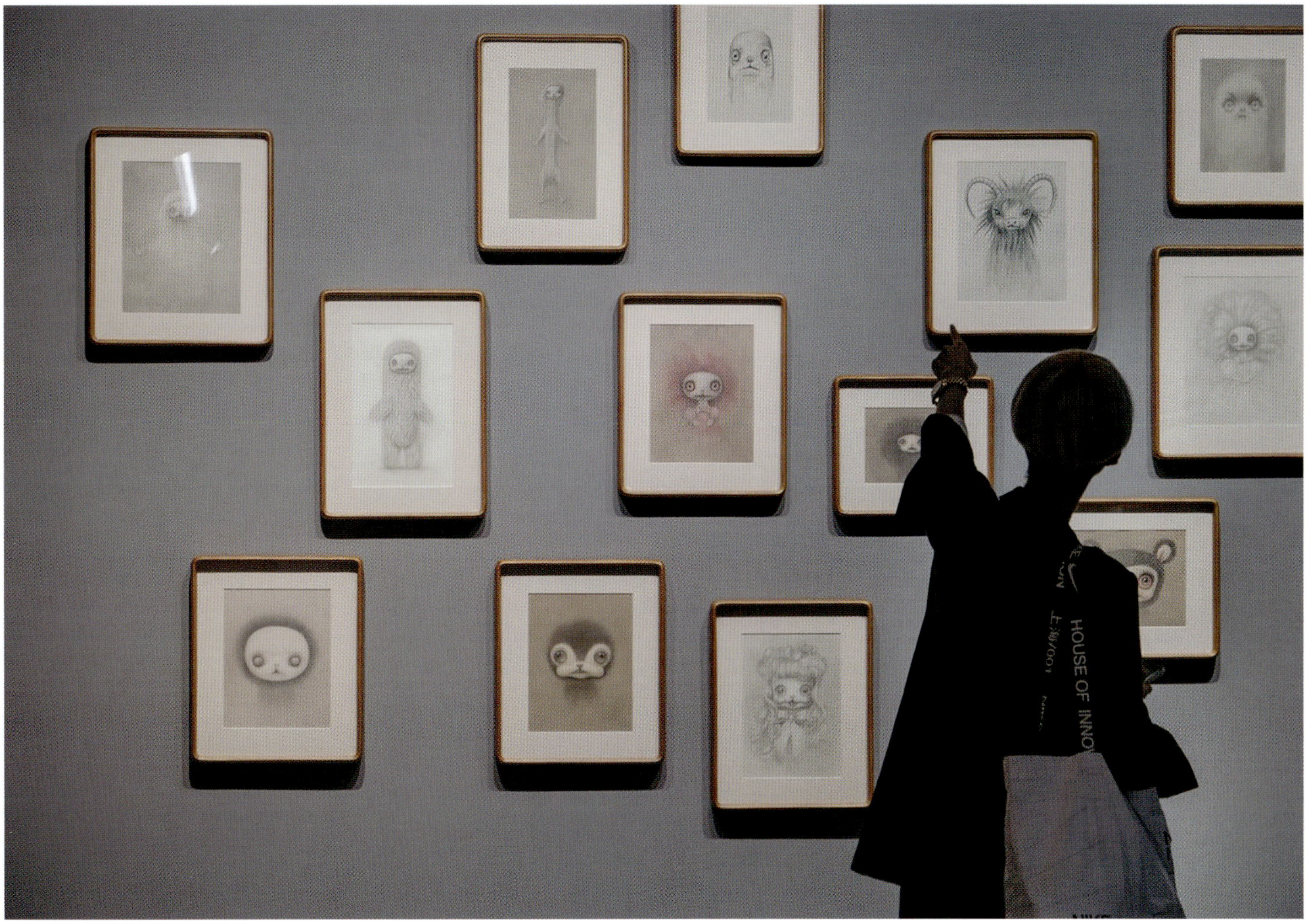

Born in Medford, Oregon, 1963.
Currently lives and works in Portland, Oregon.

Blending themes of pop culture with techniques reminiscent of the old masters, Mark Ryden has devised a singular style that blurs traditional boundaries. His work first garnered attention in the 1990s as he ushered in a new genre of painting, "Pop Surrealism," which developed the scope and spirit of the twentieth-century surrealism by embellishing its vocabulary with contemporary cultural references.

Ryden's work exquisitely renders a universe replete with fantastical characters amid enchanted landscapes that embody the artist's meticulously realized signature blend of archetype, kitsch, and narrative mysticism. Ryden's modern mythologies inseparably interweave twin senses of comfort and menace. "Most of my work engages with the relationship between the physical world and the spiritual world," he has said. His are scenes that exist in the ambiguous space between these two realms, in which nostalgia—and by extension memory, even death—are ever-present.

This time-honored, artistic craftsmanship elevates heavily sentimentalized elements of American tradition and antiquity, collected as though for a cabinet of wonders. The labor-intensive canvases deftly rework centuries of art history, combining the grandeur of Spanish and Italian religious painting with the decorative richness of Old Master compositions and the lush textures of French Neoclassicism. His ornately carved frames and meticulously glazed surfaces lend the paintings a baroque exuberance that adds gravity to their enigmatic themes.

Takashi Murakami has said: "Mark Ryden, Yoshitomo Nara, and I, among others, belong to a generation of artists who have been facing in the same general direction. What I mean by the 'same direction' is that as children, we were baptized in subculture and that experience remains intensely imprinted on each of our beings. When we subsequently began painting in our adolescent years, we also started to study art history while simultaneously developing our painting technique. Once we had full command of both of these, we succeeded in combining historical painting methods with subculture. That, in a nutshell, is our generation."

Ryden joined a rarified tradition of artists who have designed sets and costumes for the theater and ballet when he collaborated with American Ballet Theatre to create *Whipped Cream*, a reimagining of *Schlagobers*, a Richard Strauss ballet first performed at the Vienna State Opera in 1924. *Whipped Cream* had its New York debut at the Metropolitan Opera House in 2017. *The New Yorker* magazine called it "an extravaganza for the eyes and ears."

Mark Ryden received his BFA in 1987 from Art Center College of Design in Pasadena. His paintings have been exhibited in museums and galleries worldwide, including a career-spanning retrospective *Cámara de las maravillas* at The Centro de Arte Contemporáneo of Málaga, as well as an earlier retrospective *Wondertoonel* at the Frye Museum of Art in Seattle and Pasadena Museum of California Art. Mark Ryden currently lives and works in Portland, Oregon.

SOLO EXHIBITIONS

2020 *Anima Animals*, Perrotin Gallery and Kasmin Gallery,
Shanghai, China

2018 *Quintessence 132*, Hong Kong Cultural Center and PMQ, Hong Kong

2017 *The Art of Whipped Cream*, Paul Kasmin Gallery and Gallery Met
at the Metropolitan Opera House, New York, New York

2016 *Camara de las maravillas*, Centro de Arte Contemporáneo de Málaga,
Málaga, Spain

Diversaform, Hidari Zingaro Gallery, Tokyo, Japan

2015 *Dodecahedron*, Paul Kasmin Gallery, New York, New York

2014 *The Gay 90's West*, Michael Kohn Gallery, Los Angeles, California

2010 *The Gay 90's Olde Tyme Art Show*, Paul Kasmin Gallery, New York,
New York

2009 *The Snow Yak Show*, Tomio Koyama Gallery, Tokyo, Japan

2007 *The Tree Show*, Michael Kohn Gallery, Los Angeles, California

2005 *Wondertoonel*, Pasadena Museum of California Art, Pasadena,
California

2004 *Wondertoonel*, Frye Art Museum, Seattle, Washington

2003 *Blood*, Earl McGrath Gallery, Los Angeles, California

Insalata Mista, Mondo Bizzarro Gallery, Bologna, Italy

2002 *Bunnies and Bees*, Grand Central Art Center, Santa Ana, California

2001 *Bunnies and Bees*, Earl McGrath Gallery, New York, New York

Amalgamation, Outre Gallery, Melbourne, Australia

1998 *The Meat Show*, Mendenhall Gallery, Pasadena, California

GROUP EXHIBITIONS

2018 *Michael Jackson on the Wall*, National Portrait Gallery,
London, England, Jun 28 – Oct 1, 2018

Michael Jackson on the Wall, Paris Grand Palais,
Paris, France, Nov 23, 2018 – Feb 14, 2019

2016 *Turn the Page: the First Ten Years of Hi-Fructose*,
Virginia Museum Of Contemporary Art, Virginia Beach, Virginia

Juxtapoz x Superflat, Vancouver Art Gallery, Vancouver, Canada

Takashi Murakami's Superflat Collection, Yokohama Museum of Art,
Yokohama, Japan

2015 *HEY! modern art & pop culture / Act III*,
Musée de la Halle Saint Pierre, Paris, France

Fade to Black, Riverside Art Museum, Riverside, California

2014 *Lowbrow Insurgence: The Rise of Post-Pop Art*,
Harwood Museum of Art, Taos, New Mexico

2010 *The Artist's Museum, Los Angeles Artists 1980-2010*,
The Museum of Contemporary Art (MOCA), Los Angeles, California

Art Shack, Laguna Art Museum, Laguna Beach, California

2009 *Naked*, Paul Kasmin Gallery, New York, New York

Pictopia - Festival of New Character Worlds,
Haus der Kulturen der Welt, Berlin, Germany

2008 *Prints from the Cal State Fullerton University Collection II*,
Cal State Fullerton Main Art Gallery, Fullerton, California

In the Land of Retinal Delights, Laguna Art Museum,
Laguna Beach, California

2007 *Charity by Numbers*, Corey Helford Gallery, Culver City, California

El rey de la casa, Institut de Cultura de Barcelona, Spain

2006 *Drawn to Expression*, Art Center College of Design, Pasadena, California

2005 *Au Pays de Merveilles*, Galerie Magda Danysz, Paris, France

2004 *Innocence Found*, DFN Gallery, New York, New York

100 Artists See Satan, Grand Central Art Center, Santa Ana, California

Age of Aquarius, Copro-Nason Gallery, Culver City, California

Modern Love, M Modern Gallery, Palm Springs, California

From Your Valentine, Copro-Nason Gallery, Culver City, California

Juxtapoz 10th Anniversary Group Show, 111 Minna Gallery,
San Francisco, California

2003 *Dark Fairytales*, Roq La Rue Gallery, Seattle, Washington

Group Show, La Luz De Jesus Gallery, Los Angeles, California

Raising the Brow, Earl McGrath Gallery, Los Angeles, California

2002 *Hello*, PressPop Gallery, Tokyo, Japan

Gods and Monsters, Roq La Rue Gallery, Seattle, Washington

Group Show, La Luz De Jesus Gallery, Los Angeles, California

Draw, Roq La Rue Gallery, Seattle, Washington

Von Dutch an American Original, Northridge Art Galleries,
Northridge, California

2001 *Representing LA, Pictorial Currents in Southern CA Arts*,
Frye Art Museum, Seattle, Washington

Representing LA, Pictorial Currents in Southern CA Arts,
Laguna Art Museum, Laguna Beach, California

Group Show, La Luz De Jesus Gallery, Los Angeles, California

2000 *Margaret Keane and Keaneabilia*, Laguna Art Museum,
Laguna Beach, California

Luck of the Draw, La Luz De Jesus Gallery, Los Angeles, California

Retrospective, Mendenhall Gallery, Pasadena, California

Invitational III, La Luz De Jesus Gallery, Los Angeles, California

Up From the Underground, Hollywood Arts & Culture Center,
Hollywood, Florida

1999 *Group Show*, Copro-Nason Gallery, Culver City, California

Six Forms of Love and Despair, Merry Karnowsky Gallery,
Los Angeles, California

Tiki Group Show, Huntington Beach Arts Center,
Huntington Beach, California

Invitational II, La Luz De Jesus Gallery, Los Angeles, California

1998 *Kittens'n'Kads*, Merry Karnowsky Gallery, Los Angeles, California

Custom II, Acme Gallery, San Francisco, California

No Red Ribbons, Julie Rico Gallery, Santa Monica, California

Tribute to La Luz de Jesus, Track 16 Gallery, Los Angeles, California

Group Show, La Luz De Jesus Gallery, Los Angeles, California

1997 *Calivera Kustom*, Merry Karnowsky Gallery, Los Angeles, California

The Secret Society of Dog Art, Random Gallery, Los Angeles,
California

1996 *21st Century Tiki*, La Luz De Jesus Gallery, Los Angeles, California

1994 *Side Show*, Tamara Bane Gallery, Los Angeles, California

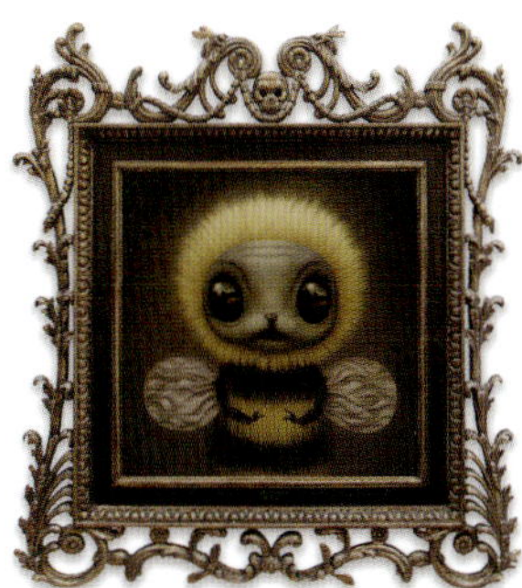

BEE (#144)

2019

Oil on panel and hand-carved wood frame

20 x 20 inches / 50.8 x 50.8 cm

36 x 34 x 2 ½ inches / 91.4 x 86.4 x 6.3 cm, framed

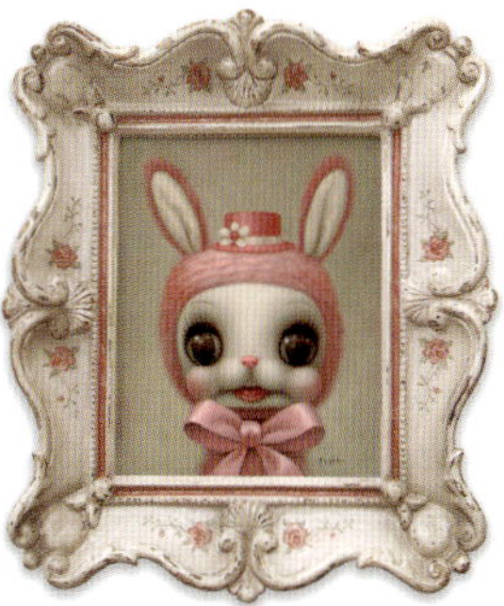

PINK BUNNY (#145)

2019

Oil on panel and hand-carved wood frame

10 x 8 inches / 25.4 x 20.3 cm

16 x 14 x 2 inches / 40.6 x 35.6 x 5.1 cm, framed

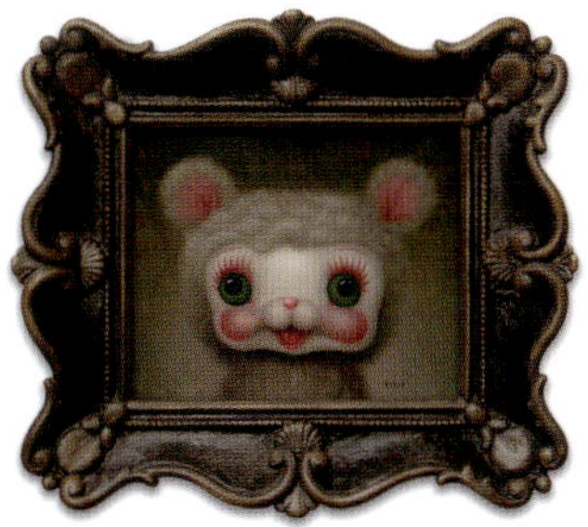

GREEN EYED YAK (#146)

2019

Oil on panel and hand-carved wood frame

8 x 10 inches / 20.3 x 25.4 cm

14 x 16 x 2 inches / 35.6 x 40.6 x 5.1 cm, framed

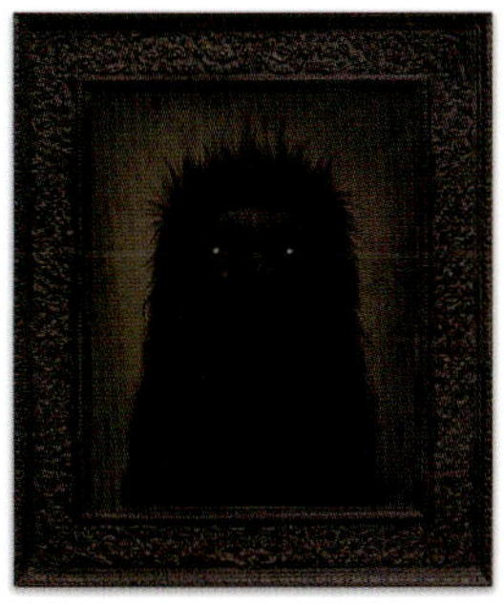

BLACK YAK (#147)

2019

Oil on canvas and hand-carved wood frame

30 x 24 inches / 76.2 x 61 cm

40 ½ x 34 ¼ x 2 inches / 102.9 x 86.9 x 5.1 cm, framed

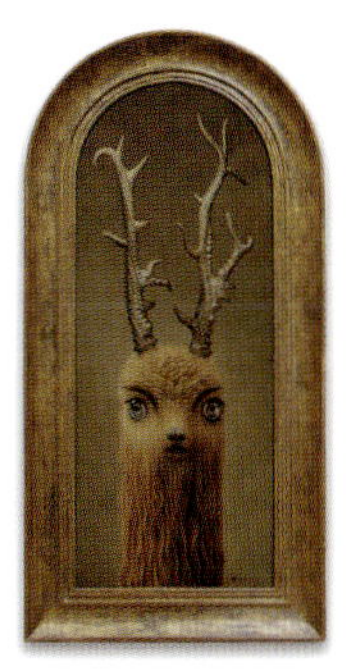

MESSENGER (#148)

2019

Oil on panel and hand-carved wood frame

40 x 16 inches / 101.6 x 40.6 cm

47 ½ x 23 ½ x 3 inches / 120.7 x 59.7 x 7.6 cm, framed

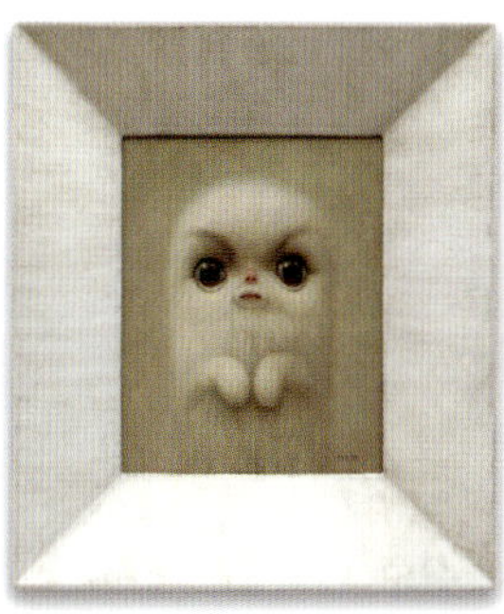

THE STOAT (#149)

2019

Oil on panel and hand-carved wood frame

10 x 8 inches / 25.4 x 20.3 cm

16 x 14 x 2 inches / 40.6 x 35.6 x 5.1 cm, framed

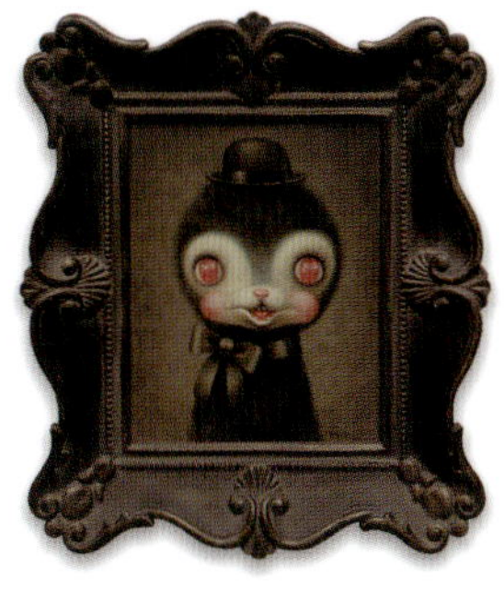

SHAG (#150)

2019

Oil on panel and hand-carved wood frame

10 x 8 inches / 25.4 x 20.3 cm

16 x 14 x 2 inches / 40.6 x 35.6 x 5.1 cm, framed

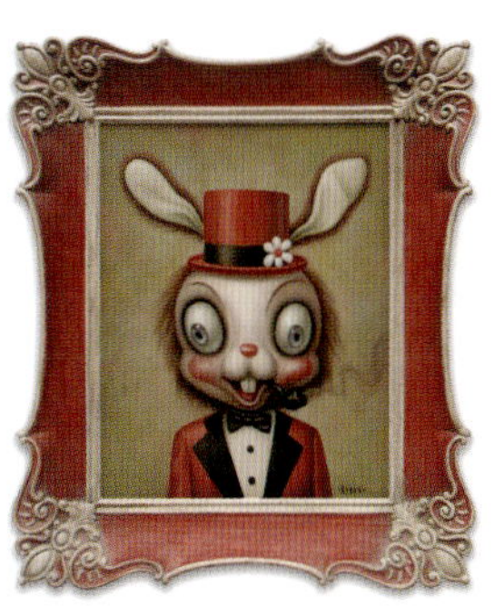

JACK RABBIT (#151)

2019

Oil on panel and hand-carved wood frame

20 x 16 inches / 50.8 x 40.6 cm

28 x 24 x 3 inches / 71.1 x 61 x 7.6 cm, framed

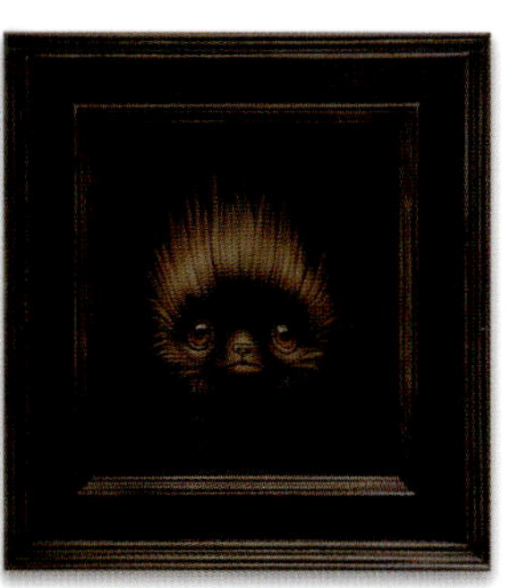

MAKKURO (#152)

2019

Oil on panel and hand-carved wood frame

10 x 9 inches / 25.4 x 22.9 cm

14 ¾ x 13 ¾ x 1 inches / 37.5 x 34.9 x 2.5 cm, framed

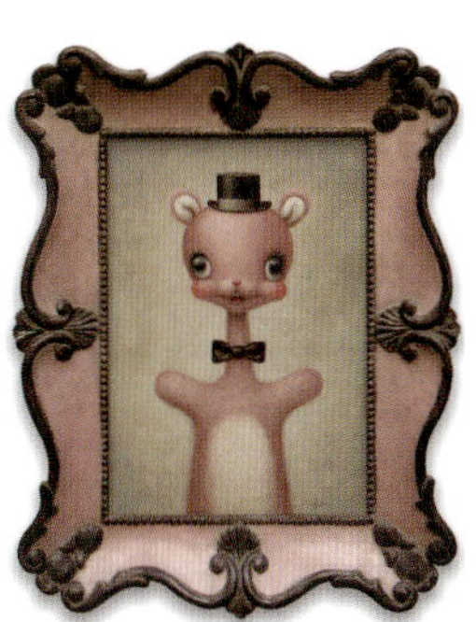

BLACK TIE YAK (#153)

2019

Oil on panel and hand-carved wood frame

10 x 7 1/2 inches / 25.4 x 19.1 cm

14 ¼ x 11 ¼ x 2 inches / 36.2 x 28.6 x 5.1 cm, framed

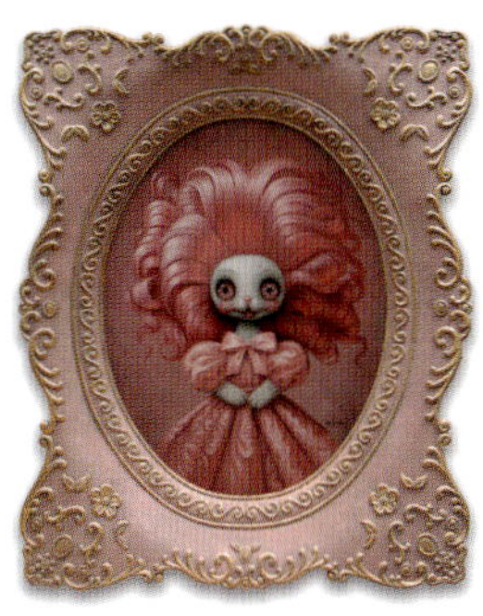

PINKIE (#154)

2020

Oil on panel and hand-carved wood frame

44 x 30 inches / 111.8 x 76.2 cm

50 x 44 x 4 inches / 127 x 111.8 x 10.2 cm, framed

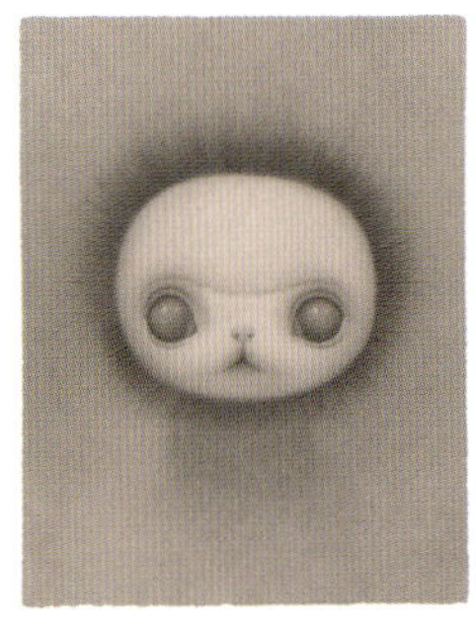
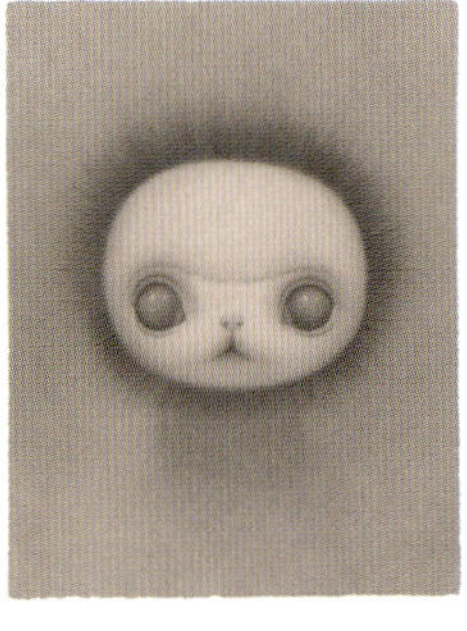

DIVOC (DRAWING)
2020
Mixed media on paper
12 x 9 ½ inches
30.5 x 24.1 cm

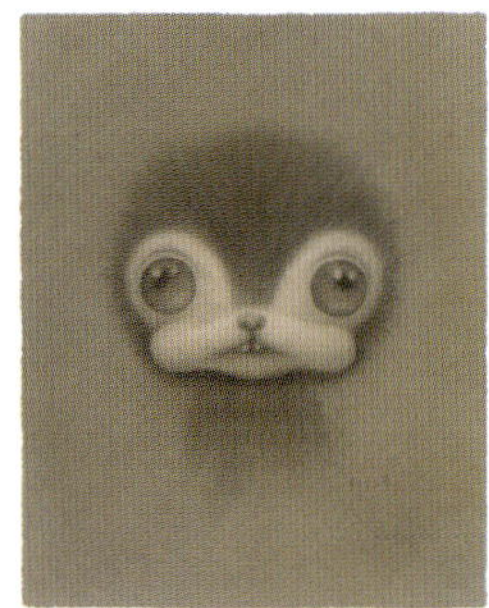

SHAG (DRAWING)
2020
Mixed media on paper
12 x 9 ½ inches
30.5 x 24.1 cm

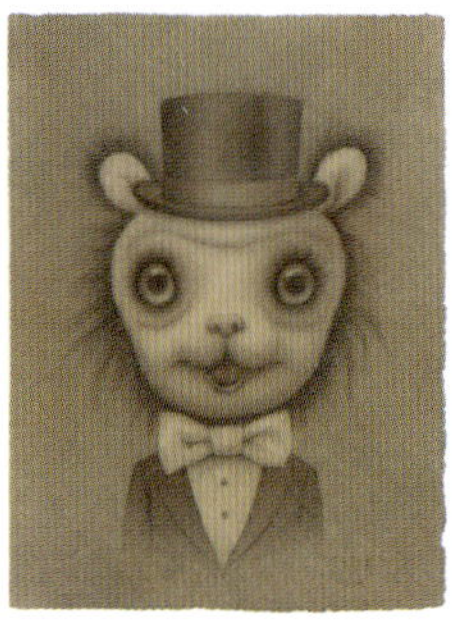

LOUIE (DRAWING)
2020
Mixed media on paper
10 ½ x 8 inches
26.7 x 20.3 cm

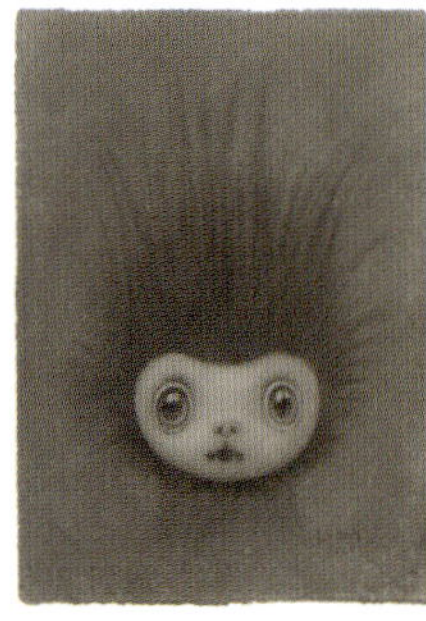

MAKKURO (DRAWING)
2020
Mixed media on paper
11 ¾ x 8 ½ inches
29.8 x 21.6 cm

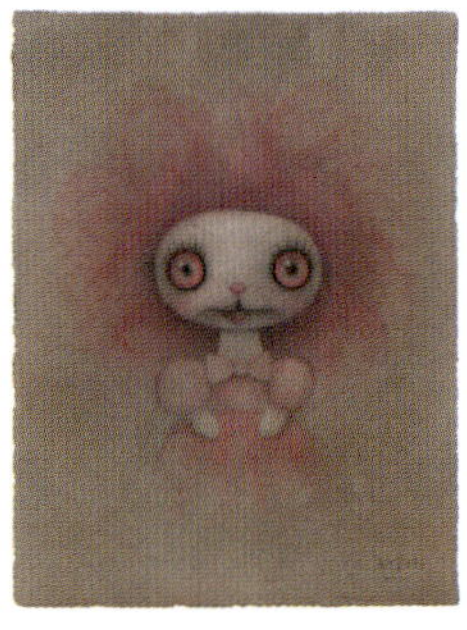

DIRTY GIRL (DRAWING)
2020
Mixed media on paper
12 x 9 ½ inches
30.5 x 24.1 cm

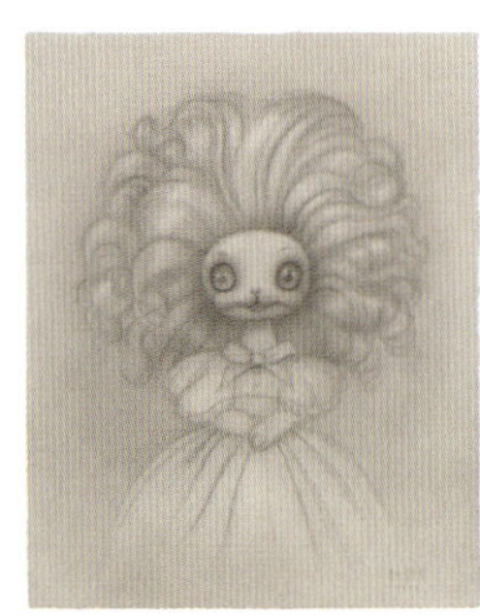

PINKIE (DRAWING)
2020
Graphite on paper
13 x 10 ½ inches
33 x 26.7 cm

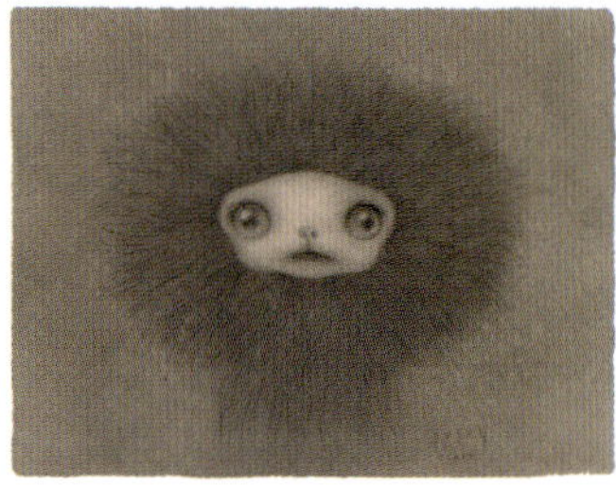

DOWRADU (DRAWING)
2020
Mixed media on paper
6 ¾ x 9 inches
17.1 x 22.9 cm

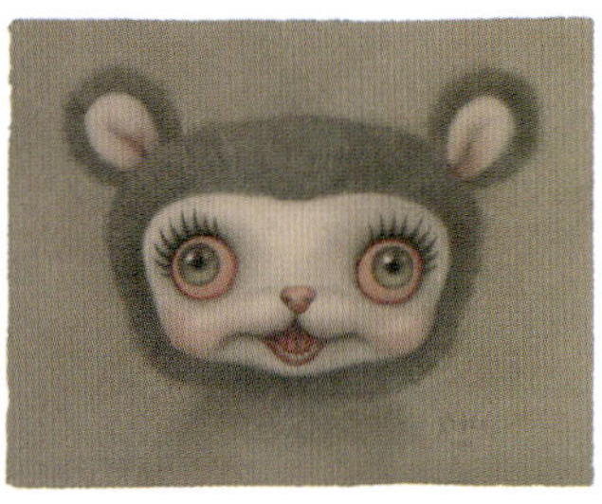

CLASSIC YAK (DRAWING)
2020
Mixed media on paper
8 ½ x 10 ¾ inches
21.6 x 27.3 cm

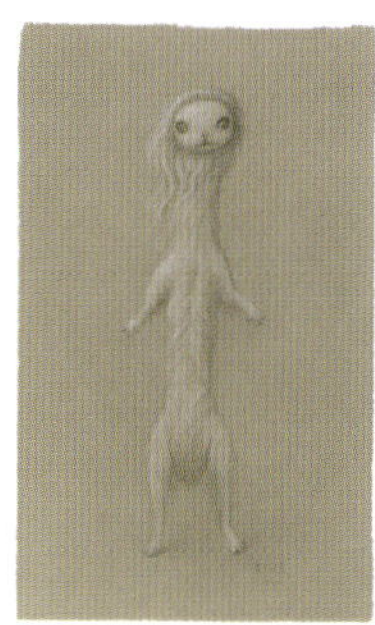

STANDING YAK (DRAWING)

2019

Pencil on paper

13 x 8 inches
33 x 20.3 cm

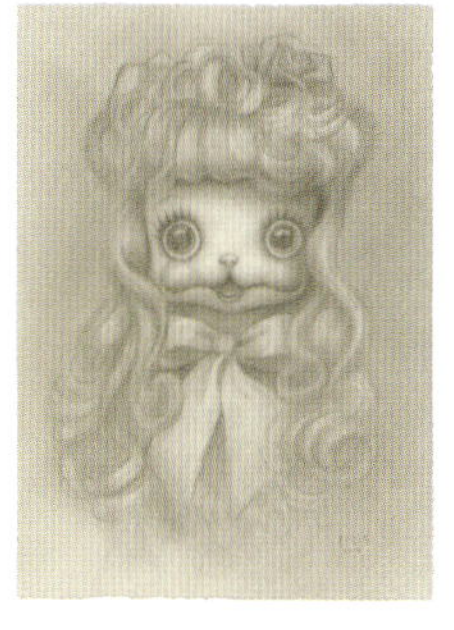

PRETTY YAK (DRAWING)

2019

Graphite on paper

12 ½ x 9 inches
31.8 x 22.9 cm

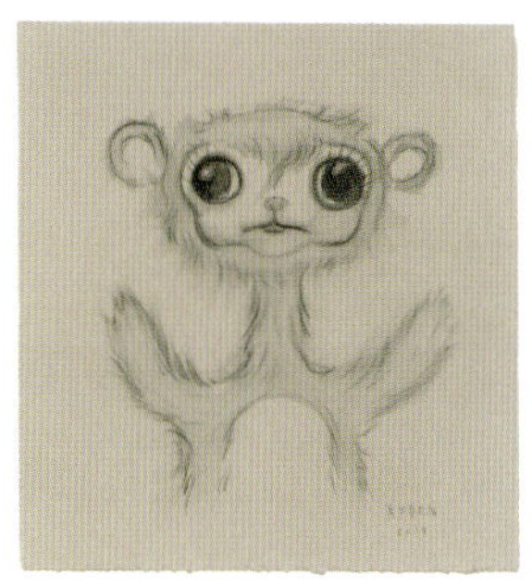

HELLO YAK (DRAWING)

2019

Mixed media on paper

10 x 9 ½ inches
25.4 x 24.1 cm

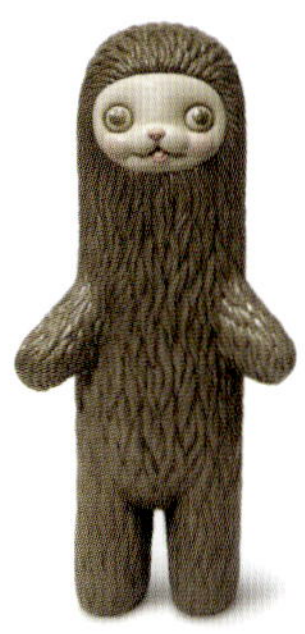

BISTRE BOS

2020

Porcelain edition of 10

17 ½ x 8 x 5 inches
44.5 x 20.3 x 12.7 cm

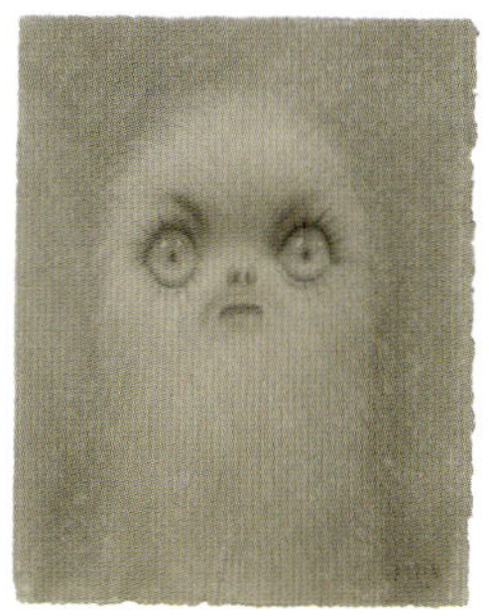

THE STOAT (DRAWING)

2019

Mixed media on paper

10 x 8 inches
25.4 x 20.3 cm

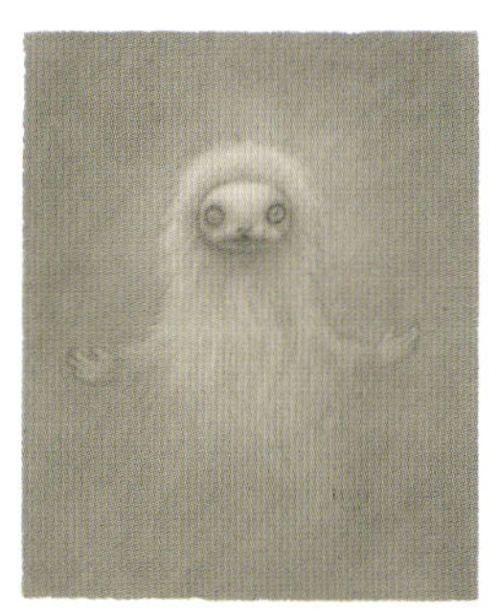

GOD YAK (DRAWING)

2019

Graphite on paper

13 x 10 ½ inches
33 x 26.7 cm

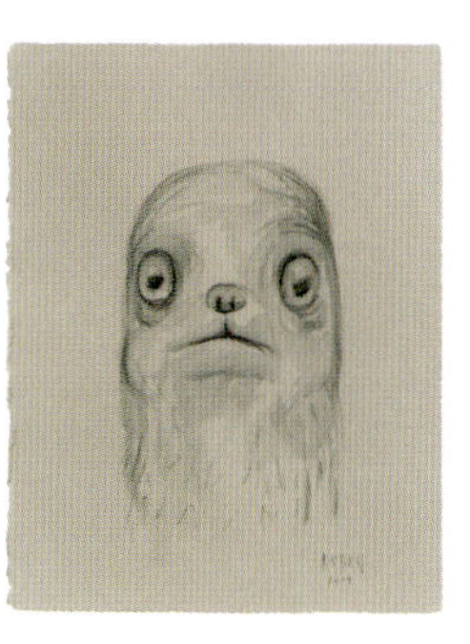

SAM (DRAWING)

2019

Mixed media on paper

10 ⅛ x 8 inches
25.7 x 20.3 cm

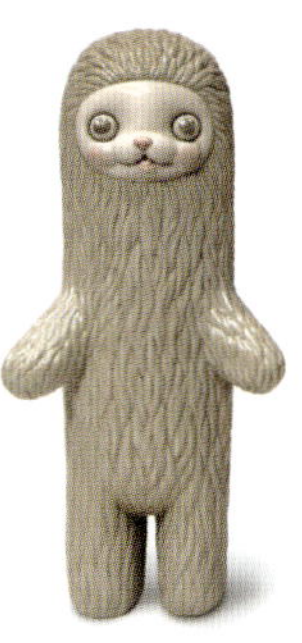

BUFF BOS

2020

Porcelain edition of 10

17 ½ x 8 x 5 inches
44.5 x 20.3 x 12.7 cm

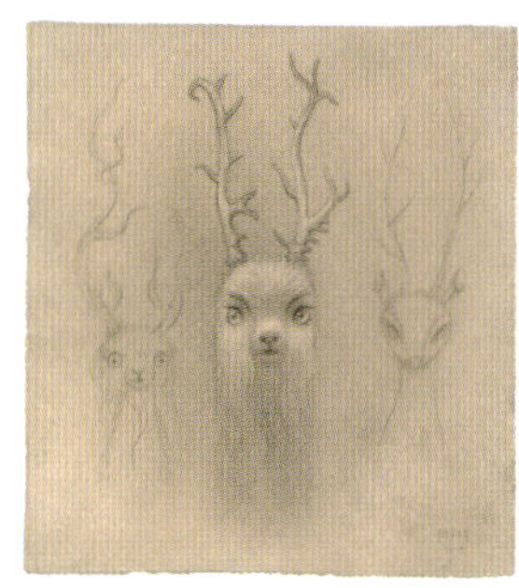

MESSENGER (DRAWING)

2019

Graphite on paper

12 x 11 inches
30.5 x 27.9 cm

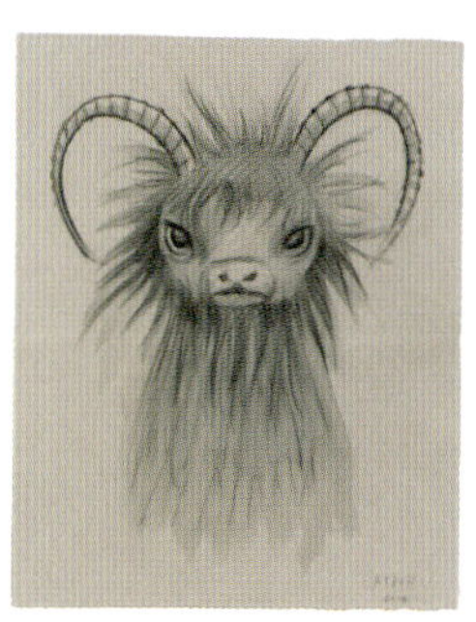

YAK WITH HORNS (DRAWING)

2019

Mixed media on paper

12 ¼ x 10 inches
31.1 x 25.4 cm

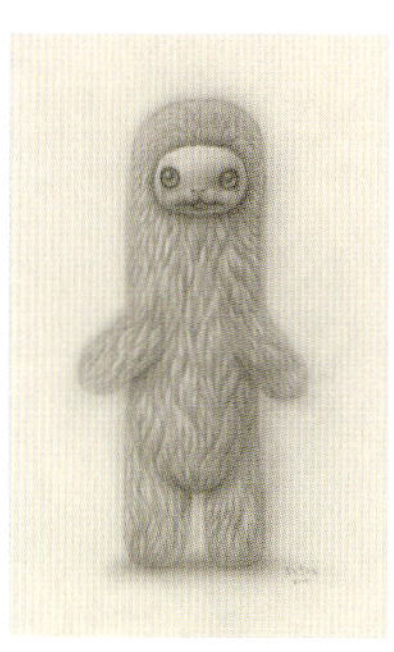

BOS (DRAWING)

2019

Graphite on paper

14 x 9 inches
35.6 x 22.9 cm

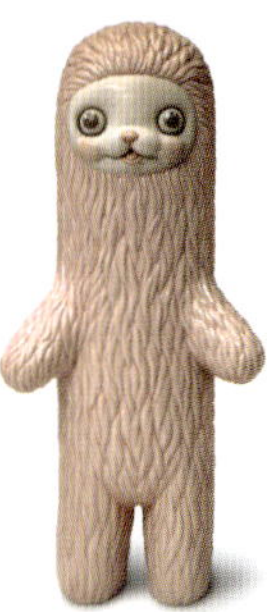

BLUSH BOS

2020

Porcelain edition of 10

17 ½ x 8 x 5 inches
44.5 x 20.3 x 12.7 cm

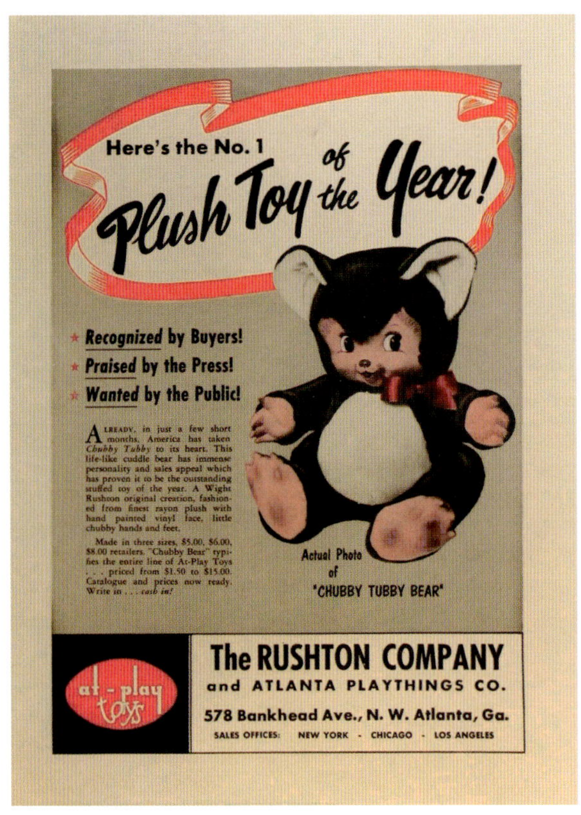

MARK RYDEN

ANIMA ANIMALS

ISBN: 978-2-37495-141-6

© 2020 Mark Ryden
www.markryden.com

Printed and bound in China
10 9 8 7 6 5 4

Text credits: respective authors
Photography credits: Christopher French (pp. 8–9, 11, 89),
Sebastiano Pellion (pp. 13), Mengqi Bao (pp. 133–137),
Cernunnos logo design: Mark Ryden
Book design: Benjamin Brard
Special thanks for framing services by Bernard Vandeuren

Published in 2020 by Cernunnos, an imprint of ABRAMS.
All rights reserved. No portion of this book may be
reproduced, stored in a retrieval system, or transmitted
in any form or by any means, mechanical, electronic,
photocopying, recording, or otherwise, without written
permission from the publisher.

Abrams books are available at special discounts when
purchased in quantity for premiums and promotions as
well as fundraising or educational use. Special editions
can also be created to specification. For details, contact
sales@abramsbooks.com or the address below.

Abrams® is a registered trademark of Harry N. Abrams, Inc.

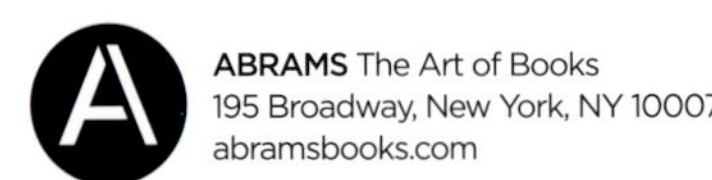

ABRAMS The Art of Books
195 Broadway, New York, NY 10007
abramsbooks.com

ABRAMS is represented in the UK and Europe by Abrams & Chronicle Books,
22-24 Ely Place, London EC1N 6TE and Média-Participations,
57 rue Gaston Tessier, 75166 Paris, France.
abramsandchronicle.co.uk and media-participations.com
info@abramsandchronicle.co.uk

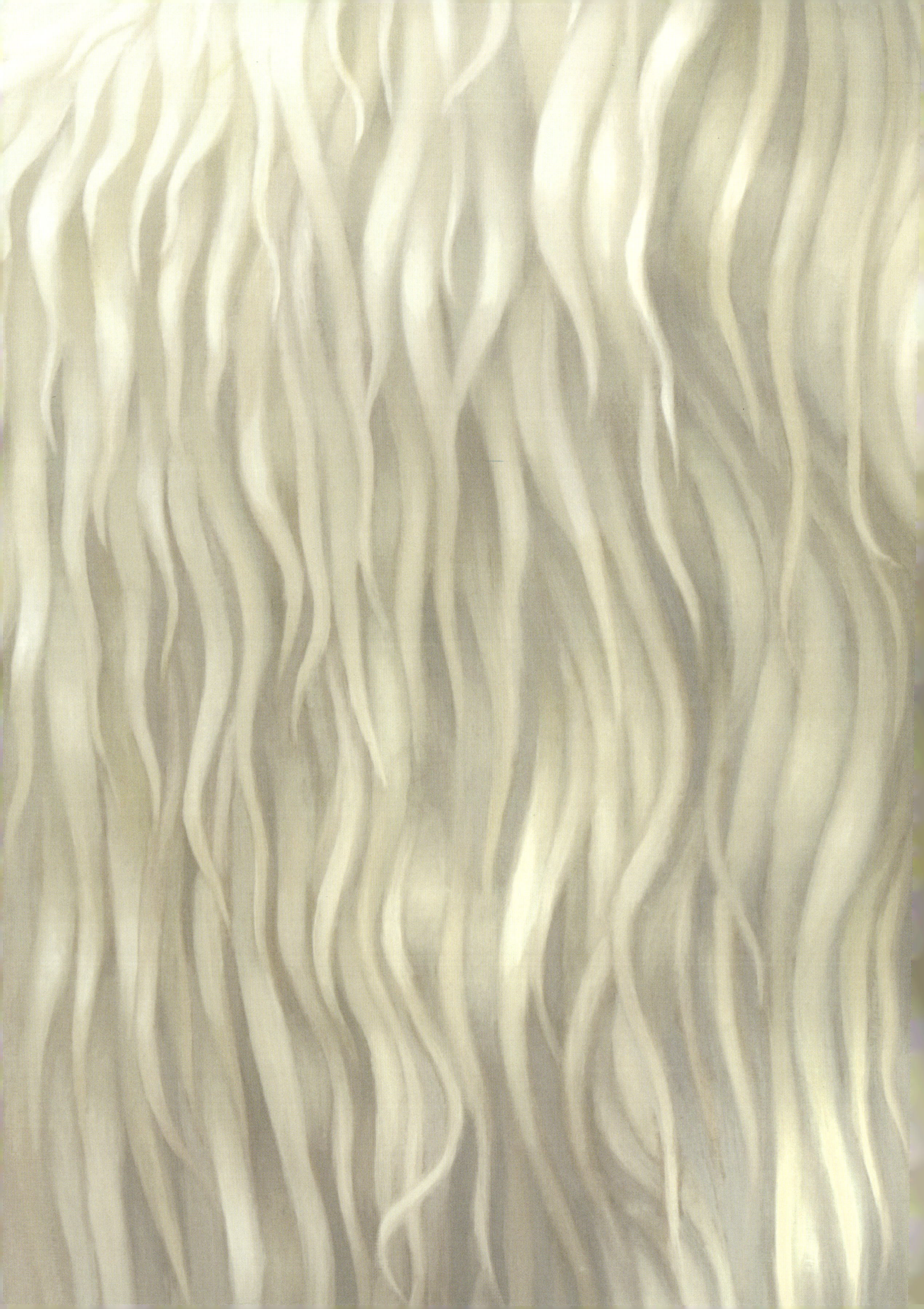